ASCENT

CENTER FOR TECHNICAL KNOWLEDGE

AF863863

Autodesk® Vault Basic 2025 Administrator Essentials

Learning Guide

Edition 1.0

Trademarks

Disclaimer

Published by
ASCENT Center for Technical Knowledge
630 Peter Jefferson Parkway, Suite 175
Charlottesville, VA 22911

866-527-2368

www.ascented.com

AS-VLT2501-BES1NU-SG // IS-VLT2501-BES1NU-SG

Contents

Preface v

In This Guide xi

Practice Files xiii

Chapter 1: Introduction to Autodesk Vault 1-1

1.1 **Autodesk Vault Overview** 1-2
Centralized Storage 1-3
Multi-User Support 1-4
Security 1-5
Version Management 1-6
File Relationships 1-7
File Properties 1-7
Integration with Applications 1-8

1.2 **Autodesk Data Management Server** 1-9
Autodesk Data Management Server Console 1-10

1.3 **Vault Clients** 1-11
Autodesk Vault Add-ins for Applications 1-13

1.4 **A Typical Workflow** 1-14

1.5 **Extending Vault Basic** 1-16

Chapter 2: Basic Vault Tasks 2-1

2.1 **Accessing the Vault** 2-2
Vault Clients 2-2
Using Autodesk Vault 2-2
Using Vault Add-Ins 2-4
Logging In to Autodesk Vault 2-6

2.2 **Autodesk Vault User Interface** 2-9
Vault Explorer UI 2-9

Practice 2a: Use the Vault Interface 2-12

Chapter 3: Autodesk Autoloader 3-1

3.1 Adding Inventor Models to a Vault 3-2
How Autodesk Inventor Files Are Organized 3-2
Autodesk Autoloader 3-5
Adding Inventor Files to a Vault 3-8

Practice 3a: Add Inventor Files to Vault Using Autoloader 3-12

Chapter 4: Organizing and Populating a Vault 4-1

4.1 How Autodesk Inventor Files Are Organized 4-2
About Project Files 4-2
About Model Files 4-6
About Library Files 4-8
About Content Center Files 4-11

4.2 Adding Existing Models to a Vault 4-13
Preparing Models 4-13
Uploading Models 4-17

Practice 4a: Add Existing Projects to a Vault 4-22

Chapter 5: Managing Vault 5-1

5.1 Setting Up Vault 5-2
Components of Autodesk Vault 5-2
Creating Vaults 5-4
Setting the Environment 5-6
Visualization Publishing Options 5-9

Practice 5a: Create and Set Up a Vault 5-15

5.2 Managing Users and Access 5-22
Creating Users and Groups 5-22

Practice 5b: Manage Users and Access 5-29

5.3 Managing File Properties 5-33
Renaming Properties 5-34
Changing Property States 5-35
Mapping Properties 5-36
Adding AutoCAD Attributes 5-42
Adding Other Properties 5-44
Re-Indexing Vault Databases 5-44

Practice 5c: Manage File Properties 5-47

5.4 Backing Up and Restoring Vaults 5-57
Backing Up a Vault 5-57
Restoring a Vault 5-62

Practice 5d: Back Up and Restore a Vault 5-64

5.5 Maintaining Vault 5-66
Viewing Vault Statistics 5-67
Vault Properties 5-68
Purging Versions 5-71
Tracking File Status 5-74
Indexing File Contents 5-77

Practice 5e: Perform Vault Maintenance 5-79

Preface

The *Autodesk® Vault Basic 2025: Administrator Essentials* guide introduces Autodesk Vault Basic 2025 to CAD administrators. Autodesk Vault Basic is the foundation module of the data management solution from Autodesk, enabling users to consolidate and organize all product information securely for easy reference, sharing, and reuse purposes.

This guide is intended for CAD administrators and focuses on administrative tasks. Hands-on exercises are included to reinforce how to administer Autodesk Vault Basic.

Important:

- Refer to the *Course and Classroom Setup* section for installing the practice files, setting up the database, and understanding the dependencies between course practices.

Topics Covered

- Introduction to Autodesk Vault features
- Basic Vault tasks
- Autoloader for Inventor
- Organizing and populating a vault
- Managing Vault

Prerequisites

- Access to the 2025 version of the software, to ensure compatibility with this guide. Future software updates that are released by Autodesk may include changes that are not reflected in this guide. The practices and files included with this guide might not be compatible with prior versions (e.g., 2024).
- It is highly recommended that you have a good working knowledge of Autodesk CAD programs and a working knowledge of one or more of the following products:
    - Microsoft® Office
    - Autodesk® Inventor®
    - AutoCAD®
    - AutoCAD® Mechanical
    - AutoCAD® Electrical
    - Autodesk® Civil 3D®
    - Microsoft Windows® 10

Course and Classroom Setup

Before you start the course, you must install Autodesk Vault Basic and the course datasets. The Autodesk Vault Professional software can also be installed and used; however, please note that the course was created using the Autodesk Vault Basic software and therefore the screenshots reflect the Autodesk Vault Basic interface.

Installing the Practice Files

To install the data files for the practices:

1. Download the Practice Files .zip file using the link on the *Practice Files* page in the guide.
2. Unzip the .zip file to the C: drive. The path for all the chapter folders should be *C:\Vault Basic Admin Training*.

After you install the data, this folder contains all the files required to complete each practice in this guide. If Autodesk Vault software has been previously used on the computer, restore default settings for the user interface.

Installing Autodesk Vault

You must install and run this courseware from individual computers. You cannot run the courseware from a shared server. Do not install the courseware on a computer that stores your working vault data.

Install both Autodesk Vault Basic Client and Autodesk Vault Basic Server on each computer. See the online Autodesk Vault Basic installation content for installation instructions at https://help.autodesk.com/.

Course Setup Information

By default, the data files for each practice are placed in the *C:\Vault Basic Admin Training* folder. Be aware that if you select a different installation location, you might need to manually edit some of the supplied project files to modify their library search paths. These folders contain parts, assemblies, drawing library files, and other files required by the practices.

The practices are designed to be used back-to-back from start to finish. It is recommended that you log in to Autodesk Vault at the beginning of each practice, and when finishing a practice, you should exit Autodesk Vault. The chapter folders contain subfolders holding documents for the chapter practices.

If you are using Autodesk Inventor in conjunction with Autodesk Vault, it must also be installed.

Classroom Environment

The courseware is intended for use in an instructor-led environment. If you plan to use the courseware on your own in a non-classroom environment, you must set up Autodesk Vault correctly. Before you set up your system, you should be aware of the following:

- Do not use a production vault for the practices. It is recommended that you set up a separate vault on a separate vault server.

- If you plan to repeat a practice, you must remove any files that were added to the vault when you previously completed the practice. It is recommended that you delete the entire vault and start again with a new vault.
- Do not attempt these practices on a production vault server until you are familiar with the procedures that are covered.

Setting Up the Database for the Practices

Before you start any practice, you need to perform the basic setup of the database for this course.

There are two methods of setting up the database. Please choose the method that works for your environment:

- **Method A: Create a Vault and Add a User** (works alongside other vaults and keeps current vault intact)
- **Method B: Restore the Database** (overwrites current vault set up)

Note that Method B will overwrite the current datasets and file stores in your current vault. Be sure to back up any necessary vaults that might be required at a later time.

Method A: Create a Vault and Add a User

Task 1 - Create a vault.

1. Select **Start>All Programs>Autodesk>Autodesk Data Management>Autodesk Data Management Server Console 2025**.
2. In the *Log In* dialog box:
   - For *User Name*, enter **Administrator**.
   - Leave *Password* blank.
   - Click **OK**.
   - The Autodesk Data Management Server Console displays.

3. Right-click on **Vaults** and click **Create**.

4. In the *Create Vault* dialog box, for *New Vault Name*, enter **Vault**. Click **OK**.

5. Click **OK**. The vault is added to the list of vaults (you might need to click on the + sign next to *Vaults* to see the list).

Task 2 - Add a user.

1. Select **Tools>Administration**.
2. In the *Global Settings* dialog box, on the *Security* tab, click **Manage Access...**.
3. In the *User and Group Management* dialog box, on the *Users* tab, click **New**.
4. In the *New User Profile* dialog box, enter the following information:
   - For *Display Name*, enter **vaultuser**.
   - For *First Name*, enter **Vault**.
   - For *Last Name*, enter **User**.
5. Click **Accounts** and select **Vault Account**. Leave the password blank. Click **OK**.
6. Click **Roles**.
   - In the *Add Roles* dialog box, select **Document Editor (Level 2)**.
   - Click **OK**.
7. Click **Vaults**.
   - Select **Vault** and click **OK**.
   - Ensure that the **Enable user** option is checked.
   - Click **OK** to close the *New User Profile* dialog box.
8. Select **File>Exit** to close the *User and Group Management* dialog box.
9. Click **Close** to close the *Global Settings* dialog box.
10. Select **File>Exit** to close the Autodesk Data Management Server Console.

Method B: Restore the Database

> *WARNING: The following procedure will overwrite the current datasets and file stores in your current vault. Be sure to back up any necessary vaults that might be required at a later time.*

1. Select **Start>All Programs>Autodesk>Autodesk Data Management>Autodesk Data Management Server Console 2025**.
2. In the *Log In* dialog box:
   - For *User Name*, enter **Administrator**.
   - Leave *Password* blank.
   - Click **OK**.
   - The Autodesk Data Management Server Console displays.
3. Select **Tools>Restore** (in Vault Basic). If using Vault Professional, select **Tools>Backup and Restore>Restore**, then click **Next**.
4. In the *Restore Vault* dialog box, in the *Select backup directory for restore:* field, navigate to the location on your local C: drive where the practice files were extracted and select the ***Method B-Vault Restore Backup*** folder, then set the following:
   - *Database data location:* **Default Restore Location**
   - *File Store location:* **Original Restore Location**
5. Click **OK**.
6. In the prompt that displays, click **Yes** (as shown below) **only if you are sure that you want to delete the current datasets**.

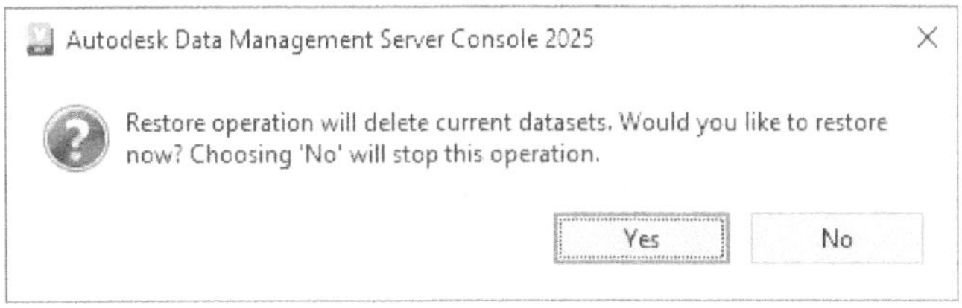

7. The *Restore Progress* dialog box displays the progress for restoring the database.
8. Click **Close** when complete.
9. In the Autodesk Data Management Server Console, select **File>Exit**.

In This Guide

The following highlights the key features of this guide.

Feature	Description
Practice Files	The Practice Files page includes a link to the practice files and instructions on how to download and install them. The practice files are required to complete the practices in this guide.
Chapters	A chapter consists of the following: Learning Objectives, Instructional Content, and Practices. • **Learning Objectives** define the skills you can acquire by learning the content provided in the chapter. • **Instructional Content**, which begins right after Learning Objectives, refers to the descriptive and procedural information related to various topics. Each main topic introduces a product feature, discusses various aspects of that feature, and provides step-by-step procedures on how to use that feature. Where relevant, examples, figures, helpful hints, and notes are provided. • **Practice** for a topic follows the instructional content. Practices enable you to use the software to perform a hands-on review of a topic. It is required that you download the practice files (using the link found on the Practice Files page) prior to starting the first practice.

Practice Files

To download the practice files for this guide, use the following steps:

1. Type the URL *exactly as shown below* into the address bar of your Internet browser to access the Course File Download page.

   Note: If you are using the ebook, you do not have to type the URL. Instead, you can access the page simply by clicking the URL below.

   https://www.ascented.com/getfile/id/boivinianusPF

2. On the Course File Download page, click the **DOWNLOAD NOW** button, as shown below, to download the .ZIP file that contains the practice files.

3. Once the download is complete, unzip the file and extract its contents.

   The recommended practice files folder location is:
   C:\Vault Basic Admin Training

   Note: It is recommended that you do not change the location of the practice files folder. Doing so may cause errors when completing the practices.

4. To set up the database, refer to the ***Setting Up the Database for the Practices*** section.

Stay Informed!

To receive information about upcoming events, promotional offers, and complimentary webcasts, visit:

www.ASCENTed.com/updates

Chapter 1

Introduction to Autodesk Vault

This chapter provides an overview of Autodesk® Vault features and functionality. You will learn how to use Autodesk Vault to manage engineering design data in a secure, centralized location.

Learning Objectives

- Describe the main features and functionality of Autodesk Vault.
- Describe the components of a vault server.
- List the clients you use to access a vault.
- Describe the workflow to edit a file stored in the vault.
- Describe how you can extend the capabilities of Autodesk Vault to include management of revisions, bills of materials, and the change process.

1.1 Autodesk Vault Overview

Autodesk Vault is a secure, centralized storage solution for your design data. It is a file management and version control system that you use to manage your project files. Vault offers security, version management, multi-user support, and integration with Autodesk applications.

An example of the Vault Basic Client, a stand-alone application that is used to perform common data management tasks, is shown in Figure 1–1.

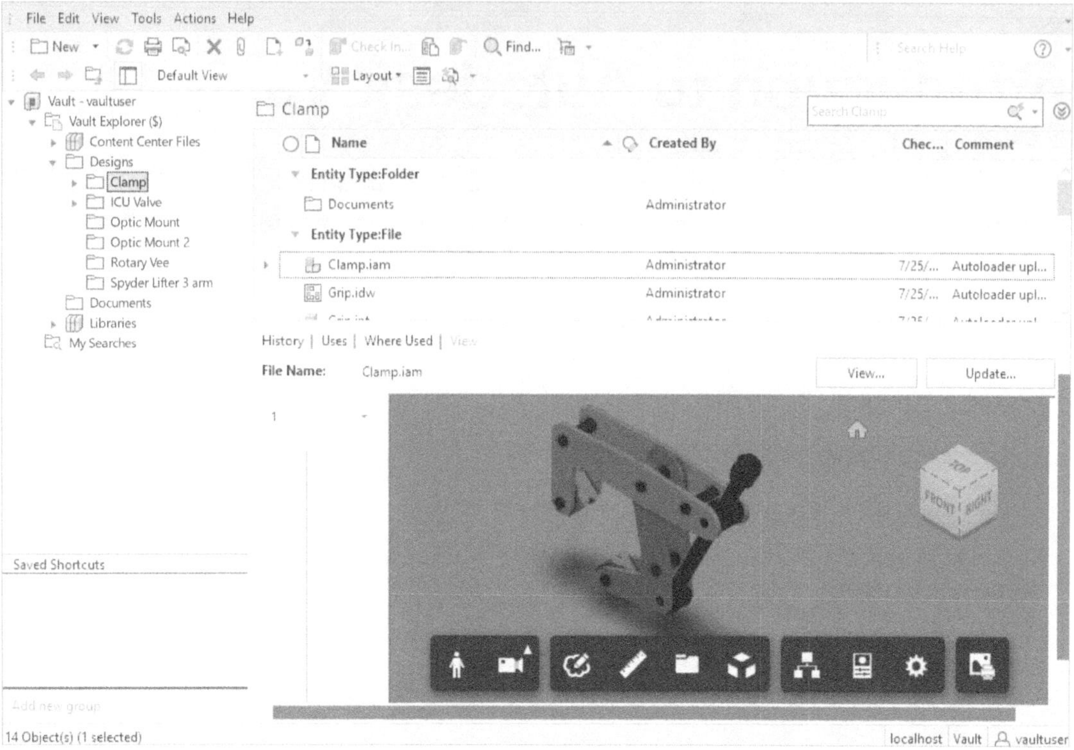

Figure 1–1

The versions of a design are displayed in the Autodesk Vault Client, as shown in Figure 1–2.

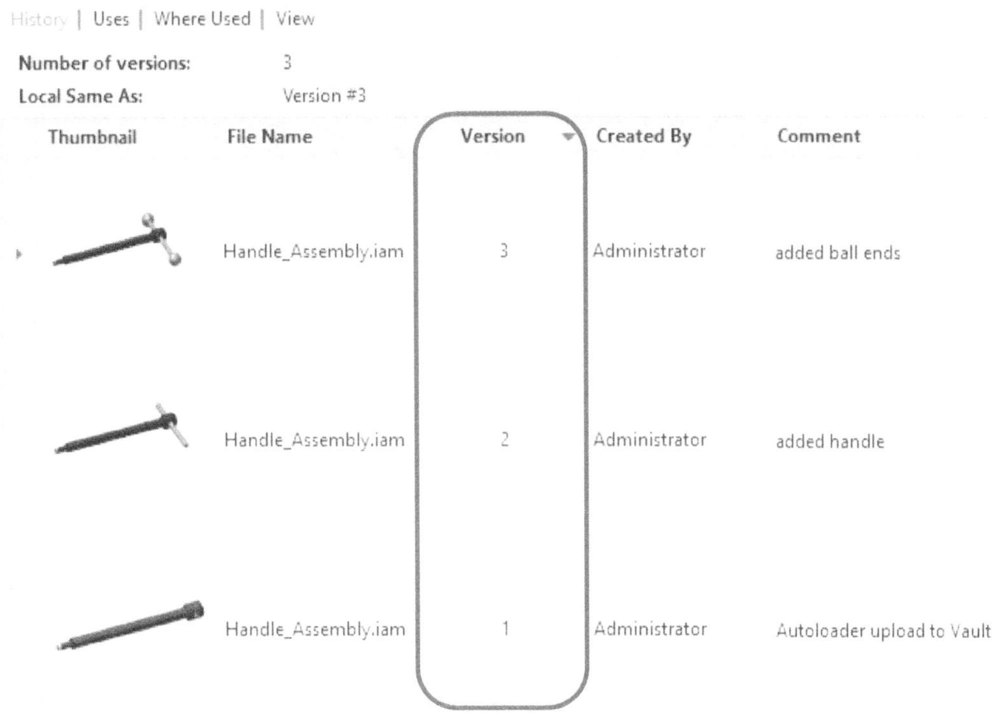

Figure 1–2

Centralized Storage

You can use Autodesk Vault to manage all your project files regardless of file format. This includes files from Autodesk Inventor, AutoCAD®-based products, Autodesk® 3ds Max®, Autodesk® Revit® products, Autodesk® Civil 3D®, FEA, CAM, Microsoft® Office, PDF files, and more. You can organize all your files and keep them in one central location for easy access by all members of the design team.

You organize files in the vault the same way that you organize files outside of the vault. You create folders and then add files to those folders, as shown in Figure 1–3.

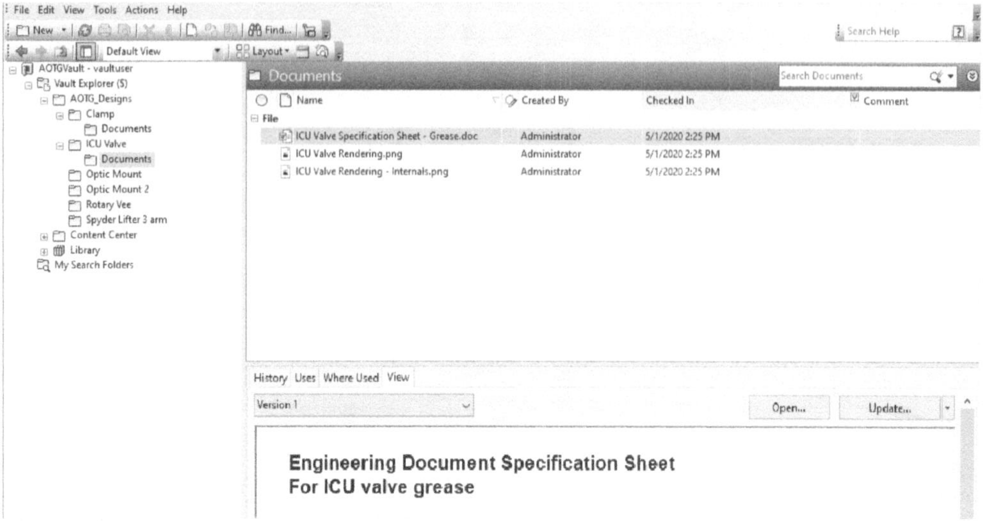

Figure 1–3

Multi-User Support

Autodesk Vault supports a single user on a single workstation, as shown in Figure 1–4, or multiple users with a shared server.

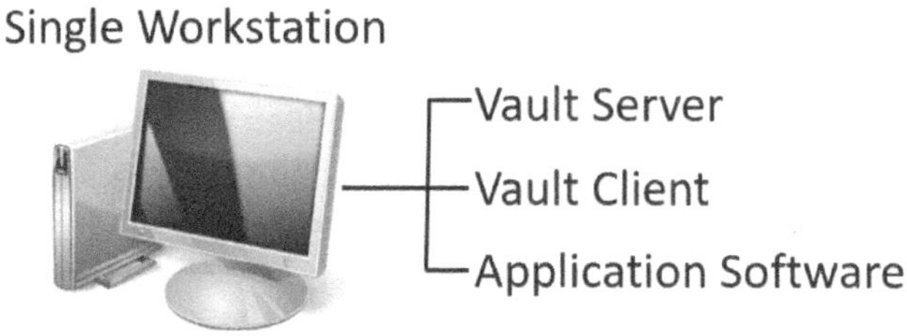

Figure 1–4

Several tools are available in Vault that assist design teams to work collaboratively, such as **Check Out** and **Check In**. **Check Out** prevents more than one user from editing a file at one time, and **Check In** enables all members of the design team to view and access the latest designs. Feedback via status icons and properties keeps all members of the design team informed of the status of files.

Security

Autodesk Vault provides an extra level of security over the standard file system. As shown in Figure 1–5, all users must log in to access design data. Autodesk Vault tracks each user's activities so that you can determine who modified a file. Because you cannot easily delete files, and because all file versions are retained, past versions are never misplaced or overwritten.

The following authentication options are available:

- **Autodesk ID:** Uses Autodesk ID credentials.
- **Vault Account:** Requires a Vault-specific user name with a password.
- **Windows Account:** Uses Windows Active Directory credentials, which are entered for you.
- **Content Center library read only user:** A user name and password are not required since you do not need to log in to the vault. You obtain read-only access to the Content Center libraries in the vault.

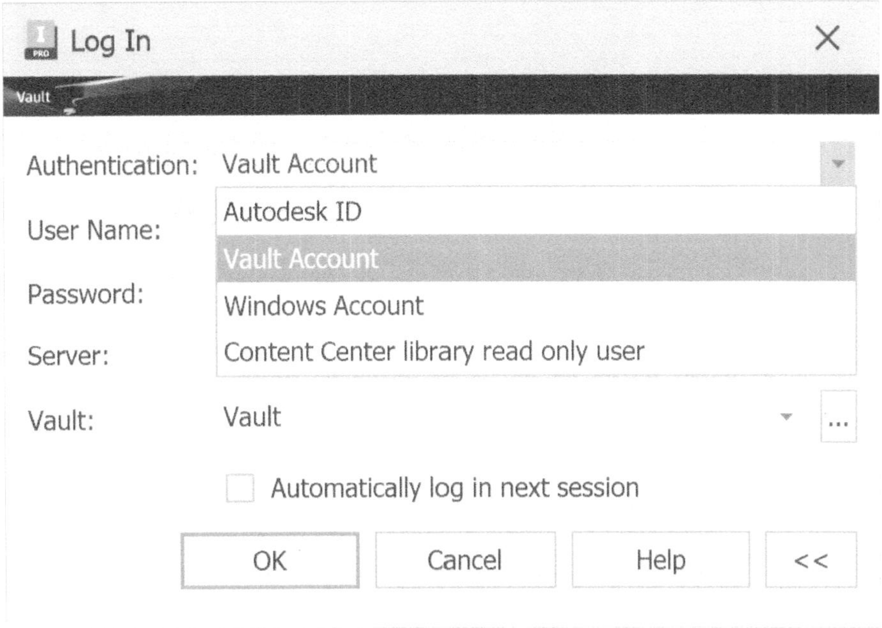

Figure 1–5

Version Management

Autodesk Vault stores every version of a file and its dependencies. You can view any previous version and its associated files or roll back the design to a previous version. An example displaying three versions of an Autodesk Inventor assembly is shown in Figure 1–6.

Figure 1–6

File Relationships

Autodesk Vault understands the relationships between files and maintains those relationships for you. If you rename or move files in the vault, the required parent files are updated so the correct relationship is maintained.

You can view file relationships to determine how a change might impact other designs. For example, before you edit a file, you can determine which designs use the file so that you understand the scope of your changes. The *Where Used* information indicates which designs use an Autodesk Inventor part file, as shown in Figure 1–7.

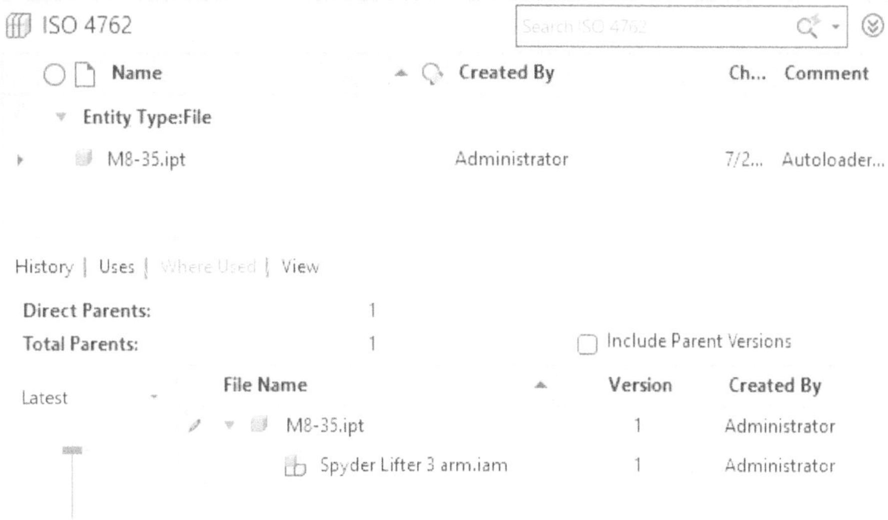

Figure 1–7

File Properties

When you add a file to Autodesk Vault, the file's properties are extracted and saved in the database. Additional properties are added to the database, including your user name, the version number, the date, and comments. Using Vault Client, you can view file properties and search for files based on their properties.

The **Find** tool (shown in Figure 1–8) can be used to find a file based on its properties.

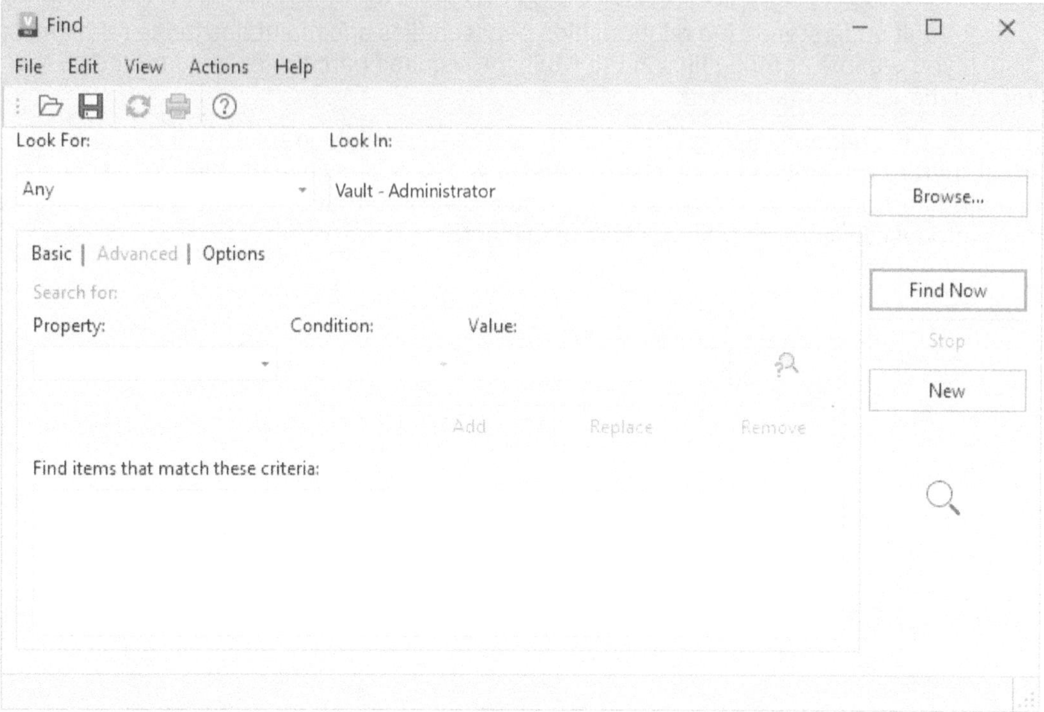

Figure 1–8

Integration with Applications

Autodesk Vault is integrated into Autodesk Inventor, AutoCAD, AutoCAD Mechanical, AutoCAD Electrical, Autodesk Civil 3D, Autodesk 3ds Max, Microsoft Office, and more. The integration, called an *add-in*, provides commands within the application that you can use to perform most Vault tasks without leaving the application.

Autodesk Vault makes it easy to keep other members of the design team up to date by automatically publishing visualization files, such as DWF™ and DWFx, each time a file changes. You can publish to a shared folder outside the vault. Project Sync is available in Vault Professional.

1.2 Autodesk Data Management Server

The vault server consists of a computer and the software required to manage the vault itself and the transactions between the vault and the vault clients. The server can be located on a single workstation to support a single user or it can be located on a shared workstation or server, which is best practice, to support multiple users.

The vault server includes a secure database that stores file properties and file relationships so you can quickly search across all your designs or determine where files are used. The server also includes a secure file store where the versions of your design files are stored. You create, manage, and maintain vaults and Content Center libraries with the Autodesk Data Management Server (ADMS) software.

In a typical multi-user installation, as shown in Figure 1–9, the Vault server software is installed on a server that is accessible by all workstations throughout a network. The Vault Client and the Vault add-ins (for specific applications) are installed on each client workstation.

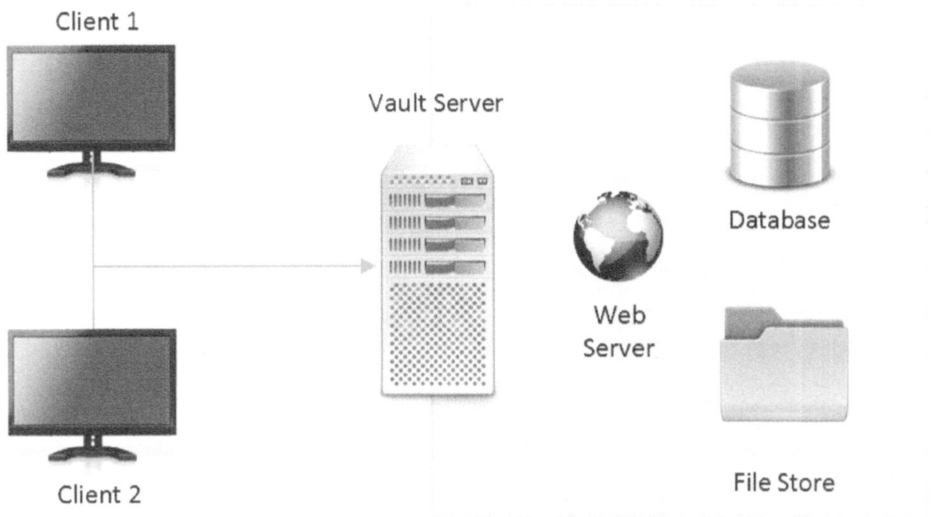

Figure 1–9

In a single-user, single-workstation environment, the server and clients can be installed on a single workstation.

Autodesk Data Management Server Console

The Autodesk Data Management Server (ADMS) Console is installed during the Vault Server installation and is one component that runs on the server. You use the ADMS Console to perform maintenance and management tasks on vaults, such as:

- Creating and deleting vaults
- Backing up and restoring vaults
- Moving vault databases and file stores
- Purging unneeded versions of files
- Defragmenting vault databases

The ADMS application is shown in Figure 1–10.

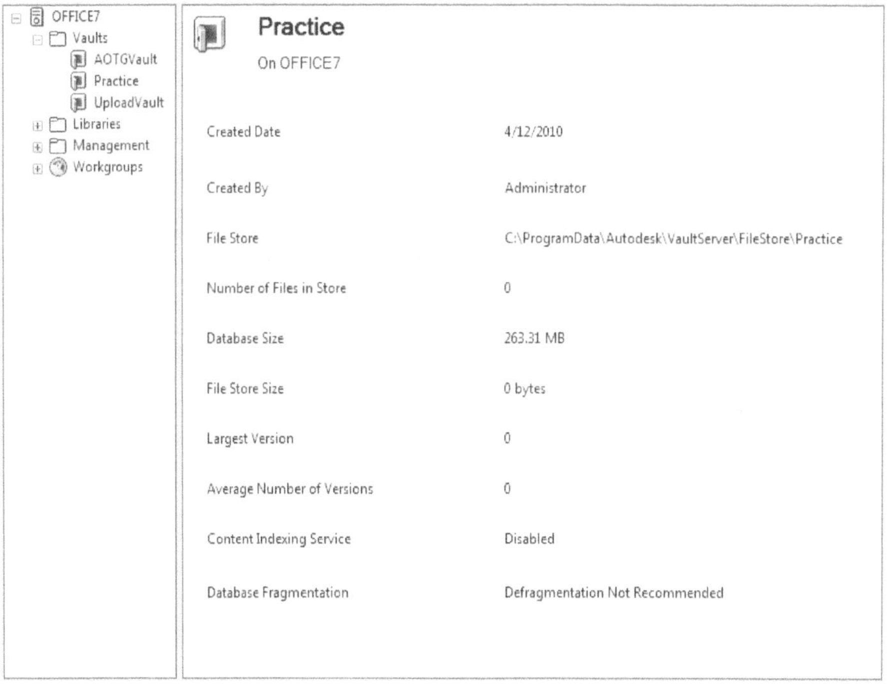

Figure 1–10

1.3 Vault Clients

A vault client is any stand-alone application or integrated add-in that connects to the vault server to access files and perform vault operations. You access files in the Vault using vault clients that run on your workstation. You use a stand-alone client, called Vault Client (or Vault Thick Client or Vault Explorer), to perform common tasks on all files and folders in a vault. In each application that you run, such as Inventor, you use the built-in client, known as an add-in, to seamlessly work with the files associated with that application.

Stand-alone clients also include Vault Thin Client and Vault Office Client. Vault Thin Client is a web browser that is used to release vault files and is usually used by personnel outside of the engineering department, such as a shop manager. Vault Office Client is similar to Vault Client but it provides only non-CAD file and folder data management options and is usually used by project managers.

Autodesk Vault Client is used to perform vault tasks such as:

- Viewing files and properties
- Determining the status of a file
- Finding designs based on file properties
- Viewing the history of designs
- Viewing file relationships to determine where a file is used
- Moving and renaming files
- Copying an existing design as a start point for a new design
- Creating folders in a vault
- Checking out files and opening them (in the corresponding application)

The Autodesk Vault Basic Client application is shown in Figure 1–11.

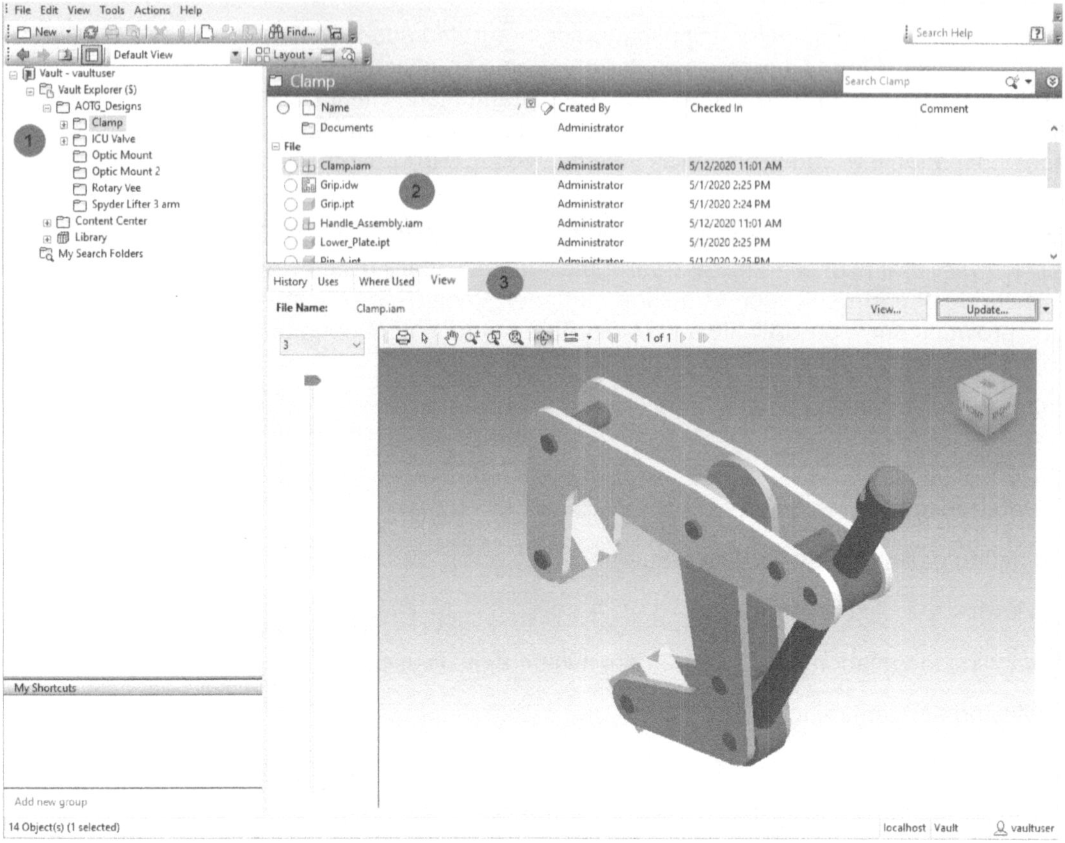

Figure 1–11

①	The folder structure indicates how files are organized in the vault. You organize files in the vault using the same techniques that you use to organize files on a local drive.
②	The file pane lists the contents of the selected folder. Details for each file are shown such as the current status, the latest version number, who checked out the file, and comments. You can customize the file pane to show any of the properties that are stored in the vault.
③	The tabs provide access to detailed information on the selected file, file history, and relationships to other files. The *View* tab displays the associated visualization file.

Autodesk Vault Add-ins for Applications

The add-ins that you use are integrated into your application. Vault add-ins are available for most Autodesk products and for Microsoft Office applications. Using commands built in to each application, you can perform common editing-related vault tasks, such as:

- Determining the status of files
- Adding files to a vault
- Checking out files and opening them in their associated application
- Getting files from the vault
- Checking files in and out of the vault

For example, in Inventor, you can access common Vault commands from either the ribbon or a toolbar, as shown in Figure 1–12.

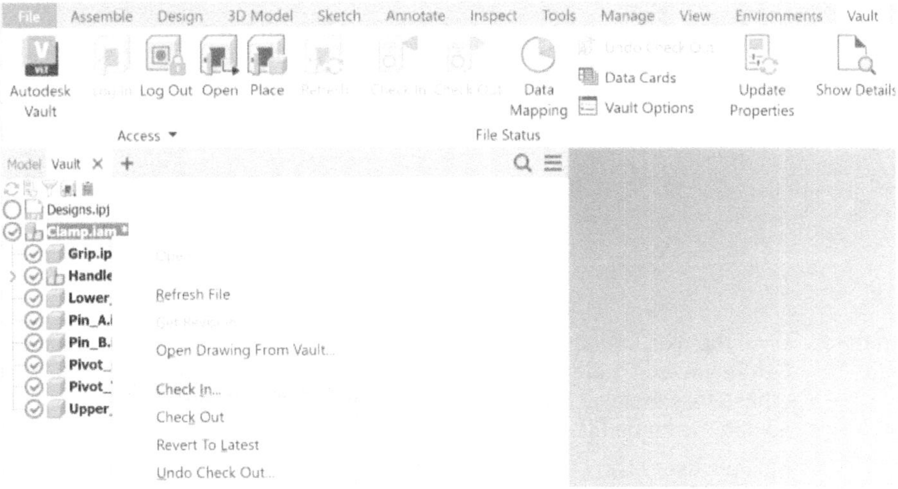

Figure 1–12

1.4 A Typical Workflow

The following steps describe a typical workflow for editing a file from the vault.

Step	Description
Get a copy of the file from the vault	The first step is to get a copy of the file from the vault onto your local computer. The vault contains the master copy of all the files so that all users have access to the latest versions. When you are editing files, you always work on copies of the files on your local computer. The local copy of the file is copied to the working folder on your workstation, as shown in Figure 1–13. 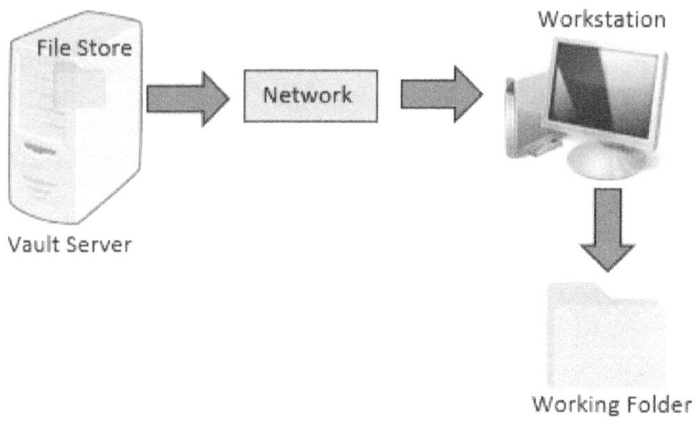 **Figure 1–13**
Check out the files to edit	Once the files are on your computer, you work on them as you normally would. Before you edit a file, however, you must check it out of the vault. This informs all other users that you have the file reserved for editing and prevents them from editing the same file. Multiple users can have copies of the same files on their computers but a file can be checked out to just one user at a time. While the file is checked out, other members of the design team can still get read-only copies of files from the vault for viewing or for reference in their designs or can check out another file in the same model for editing.

Step	Description
Check in the completed files	Once you finish editing a file, you check it back in to the vault. When other users check the status of the files, they will be informed that you have finished editing the file and they can refresh their local copies of the model files to get the latest version from the vault. When you check in a file, the local copy of the file is copied back to the Vault server, as shown in Figure 1–14. The previous version is not overwritten— the file and its dependencies are saved so you can recall the previous version of the model at any time.

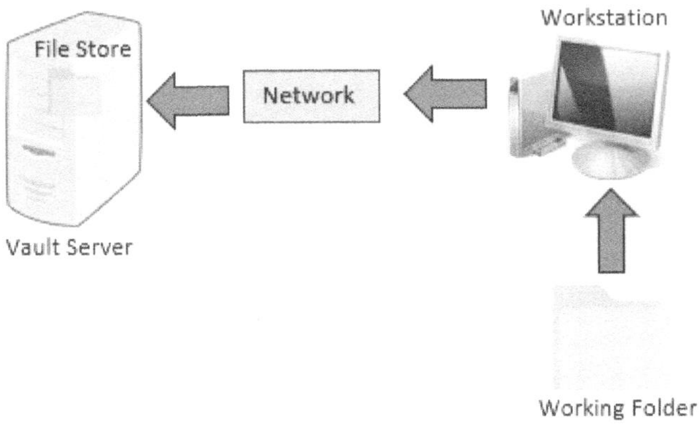

Figure 1–14

Key Points

- You do not work on files in the vault. You work on files on your local computer that you have copied from the vault.
- You must check a file back in to the vault in order to update the copy in the vault.

1.5 Extending Vault Basic

As your needs grow, you can extend Autodesk Vault Basic by purchasing Autodesk Vault Professional. Each application builds on Vault by adding capabilities to manage revisions, bills of materials, and the engineering change process. Autodesk Vault Basic forms the basis for all of these applications and continues to provide secure storage, version management, property management, and collaboration capabilities.

Chapter

2

Basic Vault Tasks

In this chapter, you will learn how to log in to Autodesk® Vault and navigate the Autodesk Vault user interface.

Learning Objectives

- Log in to Autodesk Vault.
- Describe elements of the Autodesk Vault user interface.
- Use Autodesk Vault to view and manage files in the vault.
- Use an application's Vault add-in to access files in the vault directly from the application software.

2.1 Accessing the Vault

In order to work with and manage files placed in the vault, you first must be able to access them. This section details the methods of accessing files in the vault.

One of the important benefits of working with Autodesk Vault is security. Your files are protected, and only authorized users can access them.

Vault Clients

There are two main types of clients for Autodesk Vault:

Client	Definition
Autodesk Vault	Autodesk Vault is a stand-alone application for viewing files in the vault.
Vault Add-ins	Vault add-ins are modules that integrate Vault functionality into software applications. They enable you to log in and out of the vault, check files in and out of the vault, use shortcuts and saved searches to files in the vault, and manage file versions. There are many add-ins for Autodesk design software such as Autodesk® Inventor®, AutoCAD®, AutoCAD® Mechanical, AutoCAD® Electrical, Autodesk® Civil 3D®, Autodesk® Alias®, etc. There is also an add-in for Microsoft® Office applications.

Using Autodesk Vault

Autodesk Vault is a stand-alone application for viewing and managing the files in the vault. When you open a vault, the Navigation pane on the left side displays the folder hierarchy of the vault, as shown in Figure 2–1.

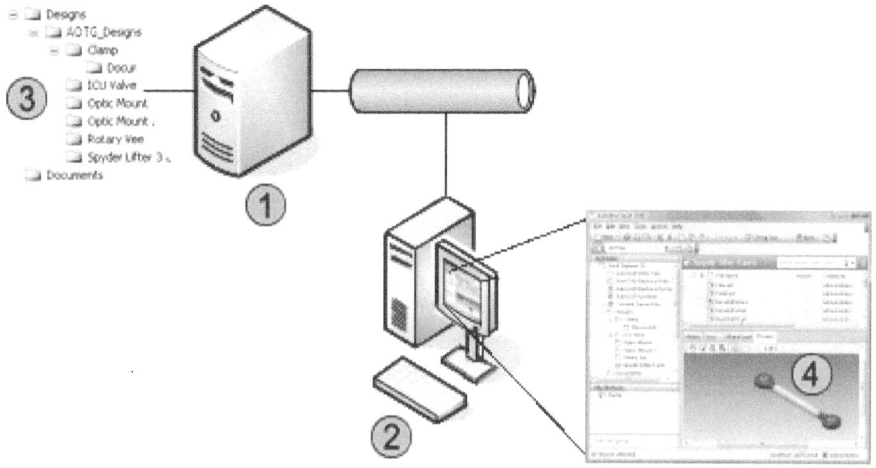

Figure 2–1

1	Autodesk Data Management Server containing the vault
2	Workstation with Vault
3	Folder hierarchy in the vault
4	Vault showing the folder hierarchy in the vault

Figure 2–2 displays an example of a vault. The contents of a folder are shown in the Main pane to the right. Below the Main pane is the Preview pane, which displays versions of files selected in the main table. You can also use the Preview pane to determine parent-child relationships and to preview the files.

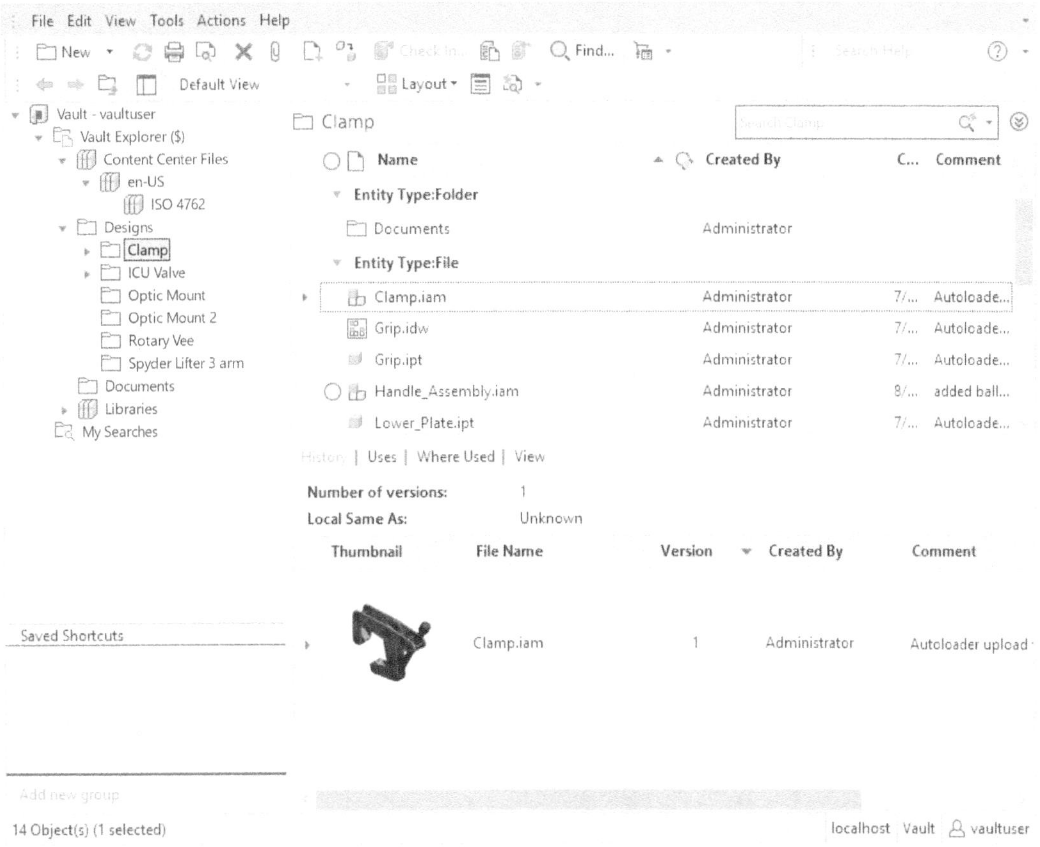

Figure 2–2

Uses of Autodesk Vault

You can use Autodesk Vault to do the following:

- View a vault folder hierarchy and create and remove folders
- View files in a folder and their properties
- Search for files
- Preview files, their versions, and their relationships
- Create and use shortcuts to searches, files, and folders
- Add non-CAD files to the vault
- Check files in and out of the vault
- Copy a design
- Perform administrative tasks, such as creating new users and assigning roles (administrative access required)

Using Vault Add-Ins

By default, you cannot add design files, such as Inventor or AutoCAD files, directly to Autodesk Vault or drag and drop them into Autodesk Vault. You must use the Vault add-in for the application to open and check files in and out of the vault, thereby maintaining all file relationships. This option can be disabled in Autodesk Vault, but it is highly recommended that you leave this restriction in place.

A Vault add-in is installed with an application and gives you access to vault files directly in the application. For CAD applications such as Autodesk Inventor and AutoCAD, the Vault Add-In also helps maintain the relationships between files as they are checked in and out of the vault.

Vault Add-In for Autodesk Inventor

When you are working in Autodesk Inventor, you have direct access to Vault and the files that it contains. To access Vault from the ribbon in Autodesk Inventor, in the *Vault* tab>*Access* panel, click **Log In**, as shown in Figure 2–3.

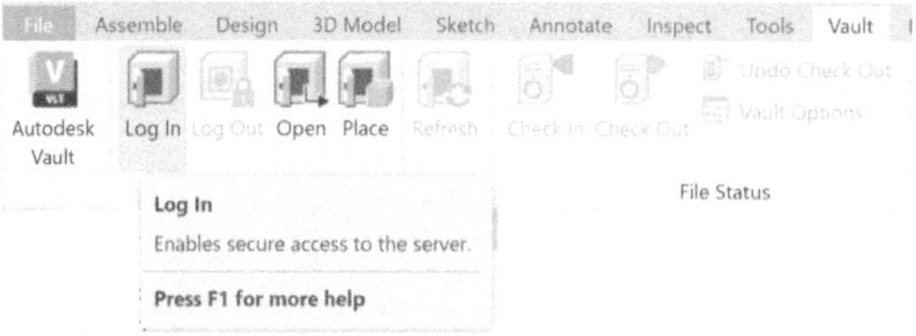

Figure 2–3

Once you are logged in, you access the vault using the Vault browser, as shown in Figure 2–4.

Note: *If you do not see the vault browser, select the Vault tab in the Model browser.*

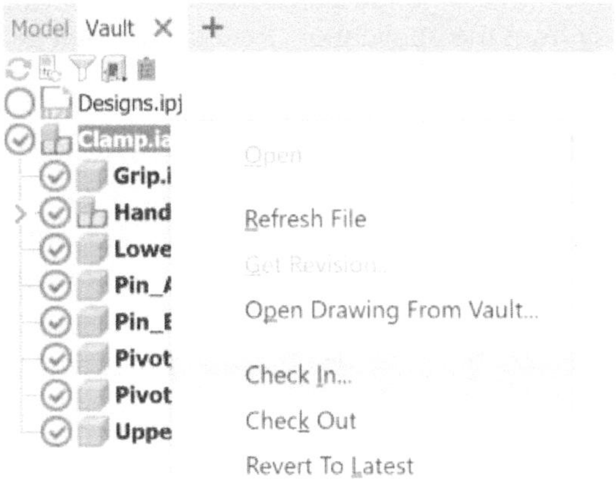

Figure 2–4

Vault Add-In for AutoCAD

When you are working in AutoCAD, you have direct access to Vault and the files that it contains. To access Vault from AutoCAD, in the *Vault* tab>*Access* panel, click **Log In**, as shown in Figure 2–5.

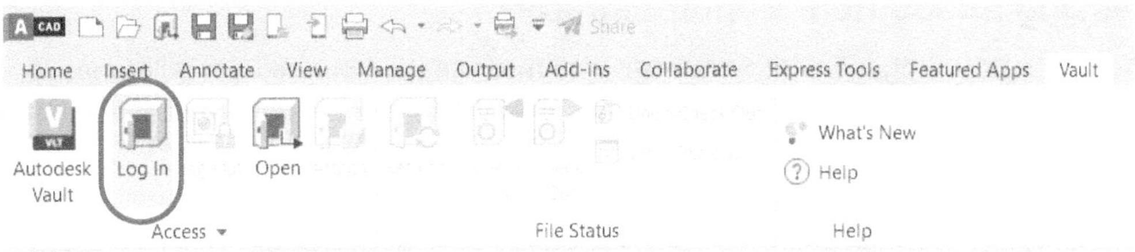

Figure 2–5

The Vault Add-In for Microsoft Office

In Microsoft Word, you can log in to the vault from the *Autodesk Vault* tab, as shown in Figure 2–6.

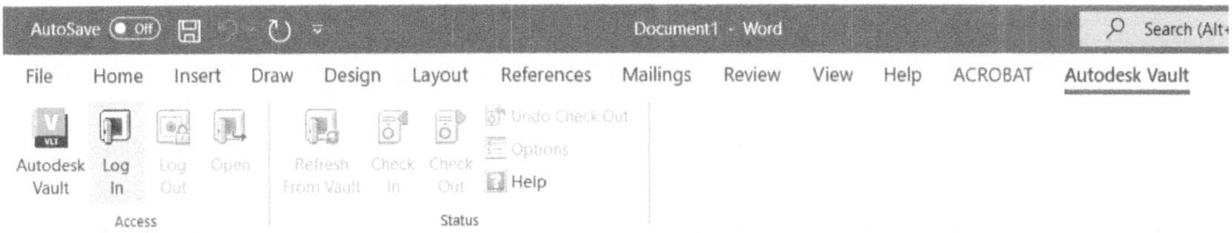

Figure 2–6

You then open a file from the vault, check the file out, edit it, and check it back in.

Vault Add-Ins for AutoCAD Mechanical, AutoCAD Electrical, Autodesk Civil 3D, and Others

When you are working in one of the other add-on software, you have access to Vault and the files that it contains directly from the application. Accessing Vault is similar to accessing it from AutoCAD and Inventor.

Logging In to Autodesk Vault

Autodesk Vault requires users to log in to access the vault data. This is part of the security features of Autodesk Vault. By creating user accounts and setting up user roles, administrators can control access to the vault.

When you log in to a vault, you are given access based on your assigned role in the vault.

Guidelines for Accessing the Vault

- **Use a unique user name and password:** If multiple users are to access the same vault, then each user should be assigned their own user name and password. Ask your Vault administrator for your log in information.
- **Use one vault:** It is recommended you have only one vault for all your designs. You can have additional vaults for training and special purposes, but your production data should reside in one vault.

Accessing the Content Center Libraries

The Autodesk Data Management Server can also manage the Content Center libraries for Autodesk Inventor. Installing Content Center libraries in ADMS is done to save space on the user workstation and if you have custom content libraries that are shared between users. The Content Center libraries are not installed by default during the server installation. Instead they can be selected as an option to install.

If you only want to access the Content Center libraries in the vault, you can select **Content Center library read only user** when logging in to Vault from Inventor. You do not need to log in to the vault and you obtain read-only access to the Content Center libraries.

If your content libraries were installed as desktop content and not with ADMS, you do not need to log in to the vault to access the Content Center, as shown in Figure 2–7.

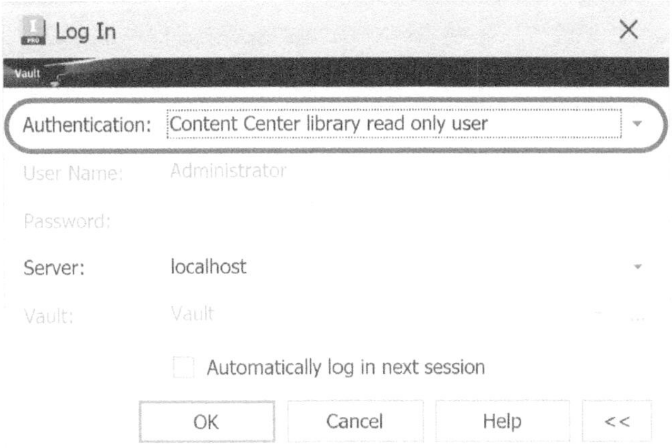

Figure 2–7

Access Separate Servers for the Content Center and Vault

The Autodesk Data Management Server enables you to use one server for both content and vault data, or you can use separate servers, so your Content Center data can be installed on your computer while the vault data is accessed from a different computer. You can set this up in Autodesk Inventor in the *Connection Options* dialog box.

To access the *Connection Options* dialog box, select **Application Icon>Vault Server> Connection Options**.

How To: Log In to Vault

The following steps describe how to log in to a vault.

1. Click **Log In**.

   Note: *Logging in to the Vault is the same from any client. The steps to log in can vary from one application to another, but the Log In dialog box and the following steps are the same for all clients.*

2. In the *Log In* dialog box, enter a user name and a password.
3. For *Server*, enter the server name or leave as the default localhost if the server is installed on the same computer as the client.

4. For *Vault*, enter the name of the vault you want to access, as shown in Figure 2–8.

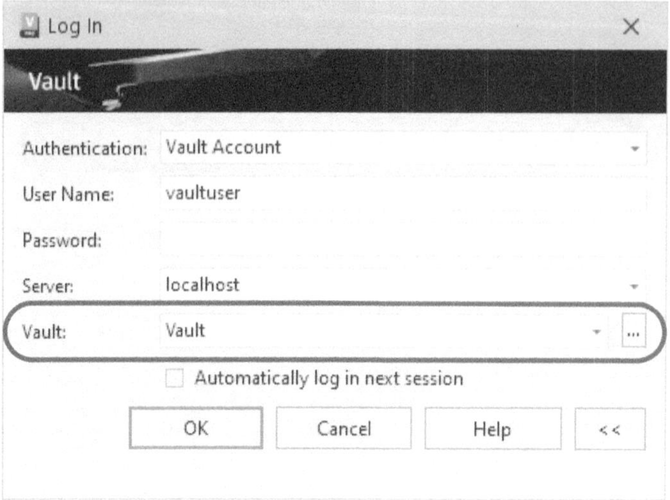

Figure 2–8

Note: *If you cannot remember the name of the vault, click [...] to the right of the Vault drop-down list. The vault (or vaults) available on the server will be listed.*

2.2 Autodesk Vault User Interface

This section describes the elements of the Vault user interface (shown in Figure 2–9).

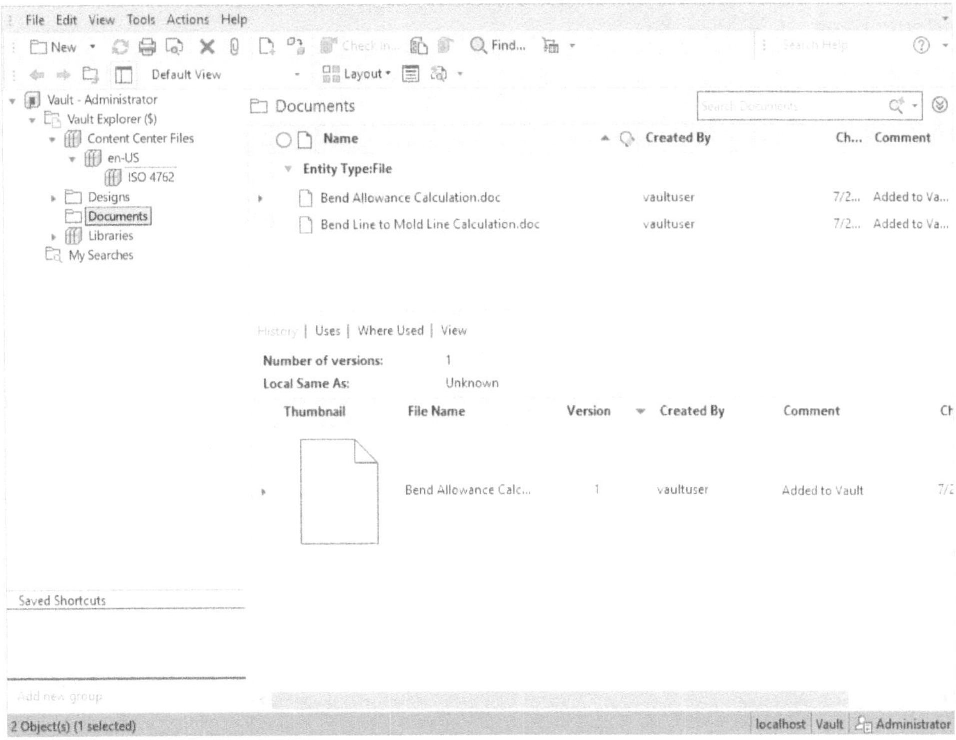

Figure 2–9

You can use Autodesk Vault for viewing and managing files in the vault, creating and removing folders, managing file history, and more.

Vault Explorer UI

Vault provides a way to access the Vault files and folder structure. The organization of the Vault user interface makes it easy to use.

Elements of the Vault User Interface

The Vault user interface (shown in Figure 2–10) contains the following:

- Navigation pane
- Shortcuts pane
- Main pane
- Preview pane

Figure 2–10

The navigation and shortcuts panes show data in a tree format, while the main and preview panes show data organized in a column format.

In the main and preview panes, each column represents a field. You can resize, rearrange, or group these columns. You can easily sort the contents of any column from ascending to descending order. By customizing the panes to display what you need, you can quickly view important information without extensive searching. An example Vault Basic user interface is shown in Figure 2–11.

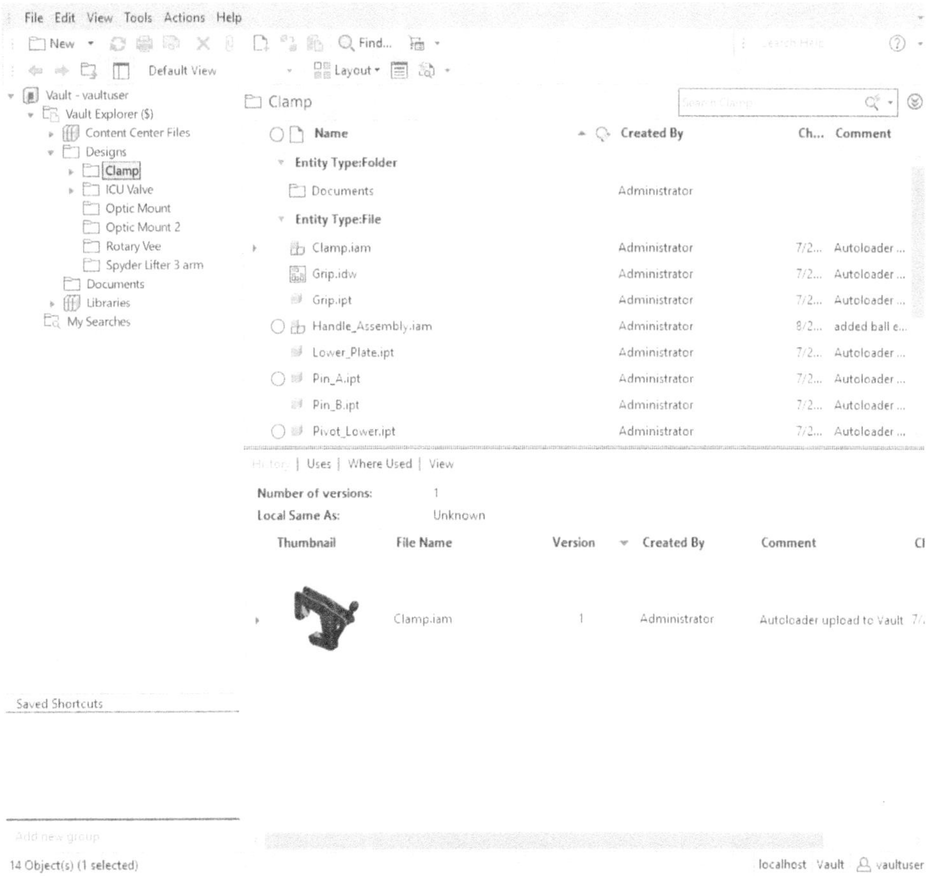

Figure 2–11

The navigation pane displays the folder hierarchy of the vault and the saved searches. The saved searches are unique to each user and are saved in the user's profile in Windows, rather than in the vault.

The shortcuts pane contains shortcuts that you use to quickly navigate to folders and files in the vault. These shortcuts are unique to each user and are saved on each user's workstation, rather than in the vault.

- You can toggle off all panes except the main pane from the **View** menu.
- You can access Vault commands from the menus, toolbars, or shortcut menus.

Practice 2a
Use the Vault Interface

Practice Objectives

- Log in to Vault.
- Create a new folder in the vault.
- Add files to the vault.

In this practice, you will log in to Vault, create a new folder, and add two files, as shown in Figure 2–12.

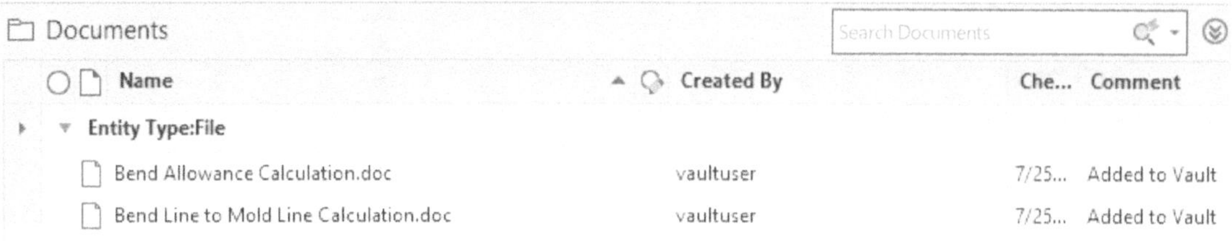

Figure 2–12

*Note: If you did not create a vault named **Vault** and a user named **vaultuser** during the database set up, refer to **Setting Up the Database for the Practices** in the **Preface** and follow the instructions in **Method A: Create a Vault and Add a User** to create the vault first and then the user.*

1. Start Autodesk Vault Client. Log in using the following information:
   - For *User Name*, enter **vaultuser**.
   - For *Password*, leave the box empty.
   - For *Vault*, select **Vault**. If required, click the three dots button to select **Vault** from the *Vaults* dialog box.
2. Review the vault structure in the navigation pane. The current vault is empty, as shown in Figure 2–13.

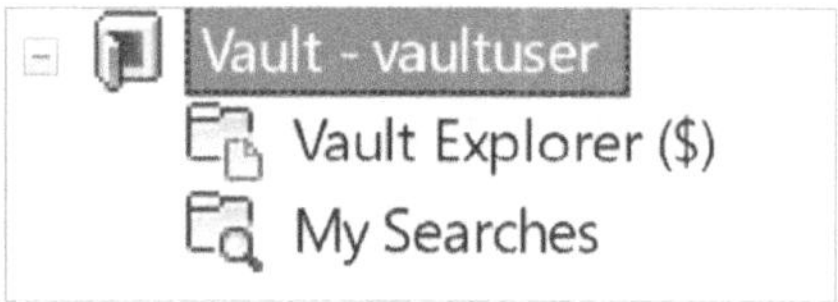

Figure 2–13

3. In the navigation pane, right-click on the vault root folder **Vault Explorer ($)**. Click **Details**.

4. In the *Details for '$'* dialog box, click **Change**. Navigate to *C:\Vault Basic Admin Training\VaultWorkingFolder*. Click **Select Folder**. The working folder is updated, as shown in Figure 2–14.

Figure 2–14

5. Click **OK** to close the *Details* dialog box.
6. In the navigation pane, right-click on **Vault Explorer ($)**. Do the following:
   - Click **New Folder**.
   - For *Folder*, enter **Documents**.
   - Click **OK**.
7. In the navigation pane, right-click on the **Documents** folder. Do the following:
   - Click **Add Files**.
   - Navigate to *C:\Vault Basic Admin Training\Chapter2\Documents*.
   - Select **Bend Allowance Calculation.doc** and **Bend Line to Mold Line Calculation.doc** (use <Ctrl> to select both files), as shown in Figure 2–15.
   - Click **Open**.

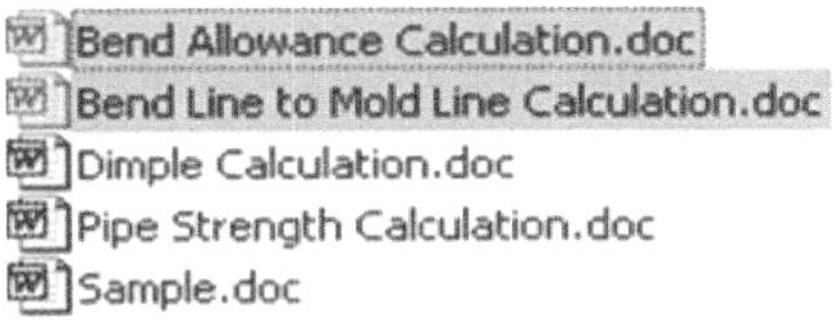

Figure 2–15

8. In the *Add Files - Multiple Files* dialog box, under *Enter comments to include with this version*, enter **Added to Vault**, as shown in Figure 2–16. Click **OK**.

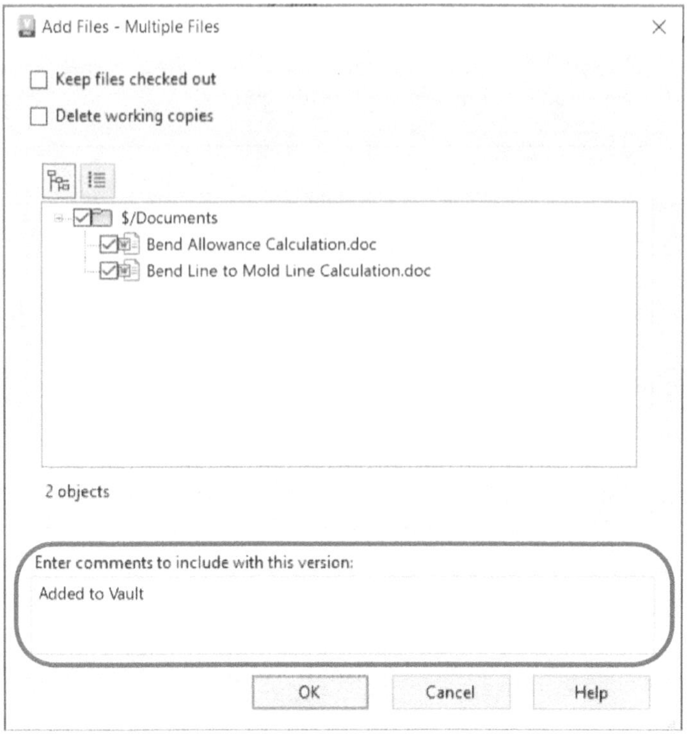

Figure 2–16

9. In the navigation pane, click **Documents**. The two Word files are displayed in the main pane, as shown in Figure 2–17.

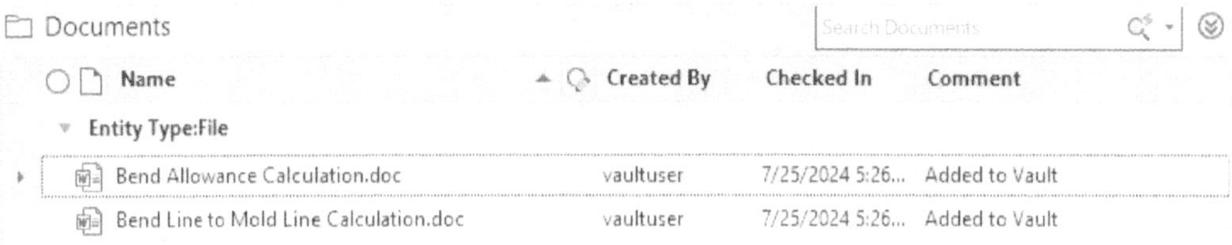

Figure 2–17

10. In the main pane, click **Bend Allowance Calculation.doc**. Note the file details displayed in the preview pane, as shown in Figure 2–18.

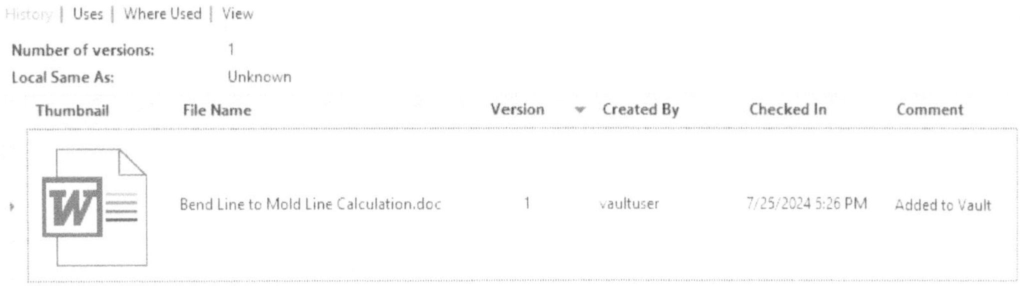

Figure 2–18

End of practice

Chapter 3

Autodesk Autoloader

In this chapter, you learn how to use Autodesk® Autoloader to add Autodesk® Inventor® design files to a vault.

Learning Objectives

- Use Autodesk Autoloader to add Autodesk Inventor files to a vault.
- Describe how Autodesk Inventor files are organized.
- Organize designs before loading them into the vault and control the creation of visualization files for files loaded to the vault.
- Add existing projects to the vault using Autodesk Autoloader.

3.1 Adding Inventor Models to a Vault

When you start working with Autodesk Vault, the first step is often to add one or more existing projects to the vault. In this section, you learn how to add existing projects using Autodesk Autoloader.

How Autodesk Inventor Files Are Organized

Autodesk Inventor models can contain a large number of files. Models can include parts that are unique to the design, and standard parts such as fasteners, bearings, or hydraulic components that are shared by many designs. These files must be organized so they can be added to and retrieved from the vault and shared with other designs.

Before you add files to a vault, you should have a basic understanding of how Autodesk Inventor files are organized in the vault and how Autodesk Inventor uses project files to locate, move, and rename design files.

About Inventor Project Files

In Autodesk Inventor, a project file must be active before you can work with other files. Project files include several settings that Inventor uses to find model files. When Inventor opens an assembly, it looks for the subassemblies and parts that make up the assembly in the locations specified in the project file.

In the project file (*Type = Vault*) example shown in Figure 3–1, the *Workspace*, *Libraries*, and *Content Center Files* folders specify where Inventor searches for files. Note that all of the paths are relative to the location of the project file.

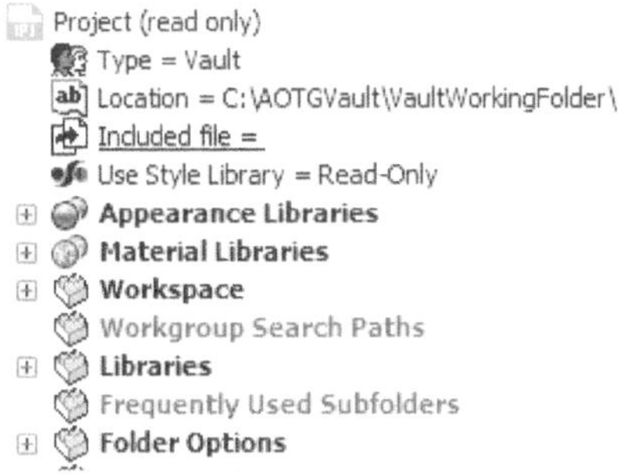

Figure 3–1

Organize your vault so you use one project file no matter how many designs you have in the vault. The project file is stored in the vault and you must ensure that you have the latest copy in your local working folder. A default *Autodesk Inventor Project File for Vault Options* can be set by your administrator in Vault in the *Working Folder Options* dialog box, as shown in Figure 3–2 (**Tools>Administration>Vault Settings** and click **Define** in the *Working Folder* section).

> ***Note:*** *This project is only for Vault-related tasks, such as file rename or file move. It does not enforce a project file for Inventor users and does not set a particular project to be active in Inventor. Additional information about setting Vault project files is covered in the next chapter.*

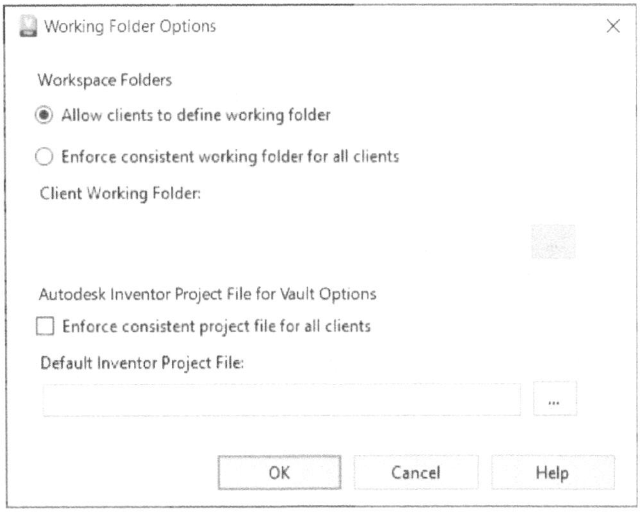

Figure 3–2

How the Vault Is Organized

There are a number of ways to organize Autodesk Inventor files in the vault. Before you add these files to the vault, you must learn how the files are organized so that you add files to the correct locations.

For best results with Autodesk Vault, a single Vault project file is stored in the root of the vault, one level above the model and library folders. Your designs are stored in subfolders below one of the folders. Vault stores Content Center parts under one library folder. Another folder contains folders for other library parts, as shown in Figure 3–3.

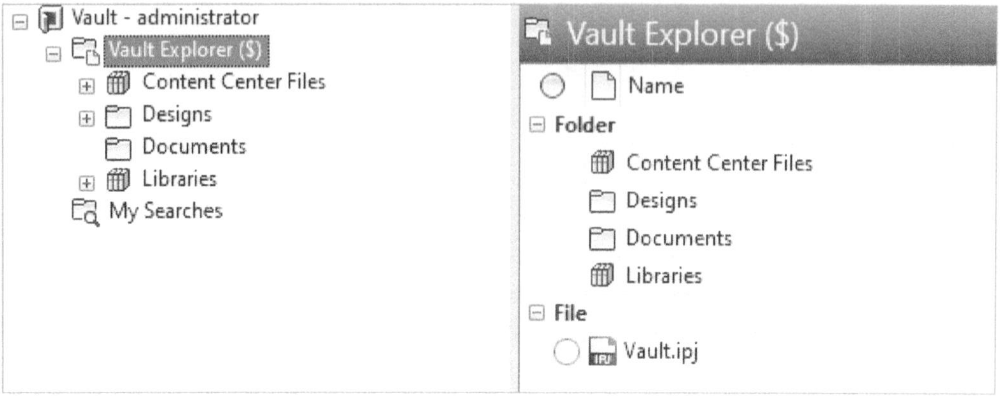

Figure 3–3

Vault stores each design in a separate folder below the top-level *Designs* folder. Subfolders help you to organize the model's files, as shown in Figure 3–4. You can organize the folders by product, customer, or other methods that meet your design requirements.

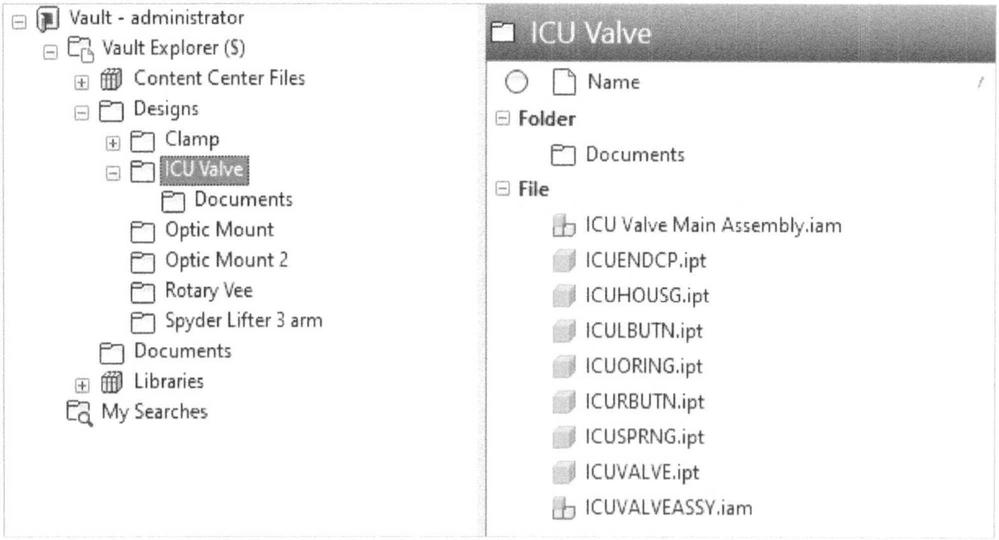

Figure 3–4

When you work on files, Vault automatically creates local folders to match the structure in the vault. Figure 3–5 displays the local working folder after two designs were downloaded from the vault. The structure and the relative location of files are identical to the vault.

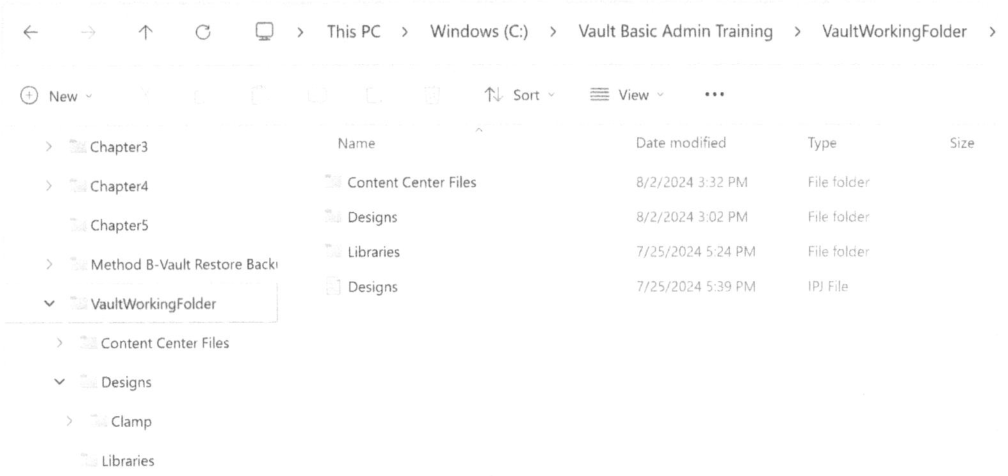

Figure 3–5

Autodesk Autoloader

Autodesk Inventor files typically contain relationships to other files. For example, an assembly file has references to its parts and subassemblies, and a drawing file has references to the models documented on its sheets.

To maintain the references when you add the files to a vault, you must add Autodesk Inventor files to the vault using one of the following:

- The Autodesk Vault for Inventor add-in (from inside Autodesk Inventor)
- Autodesk Autoloader (a stand-alone application)

About Autodesk Autoloader

Autodesk Autoloader is a stand-alone application that you use to prepare and upload files from existing Inventor designs to the vault. Autoloader works with all project types, including single-user and Vault.

Autoloader helps you to prepare your models for uploading and verifies that files are ready to upload. Autoloader works with one project file at a time and uses the workspace, workgroup, library, and Content Center files paths from the project file to locate the files to upload. Any files that fail to resolve are reported so you can fix the problem before Autoloader collects all of the files and uploads them to the vault.

If you use Autoloader to upload files to an empty vault, Autoloader creates the required folders for you in the vault. Autoloader also creates a single project file that contains all of the correct paths so you can immediately start to work on your models with Autodesk Inventor.

Autodesk Autoloader also includes non-Inventor files found in the folders in the selected project file. These files are not attached to Autodesk Inventor files, but you can use Vault Explorer to attach them to other files after they are uploaded to the vault.

Hint: Multiple Project Files

Autodesk Autoloader selects the active project file to resolve file references in the selected Inventor documents. You can activate the required project file before starting Autoloader, or you can select a different project file in Autoloader after selecting the folder to upload to the vault.

About Visualization Files and Vault

Visualization files display CAD files in Autodesk Vault. Autodesk Autoloader can optionally create the files from all of the Inventor files it loads into the vault. The creation of visualization files for large datasets can take considerable time. You can toggle off the creation of these files as you add the files to the vault and then use the Task Scheduler to create them for all or some of the files in the vault. You can also use **Update** to create or update the visualization file on demand.

Vault stores the visualization files in the vault and uses them to display the CAD file on the *View* tab, as shown in Figure 3–6. A visualization file can be either a .DWF or .DWFx file.

Vault stores a visualization file in the same folder as its associated CAD file, but the visualization file is hidden by default.

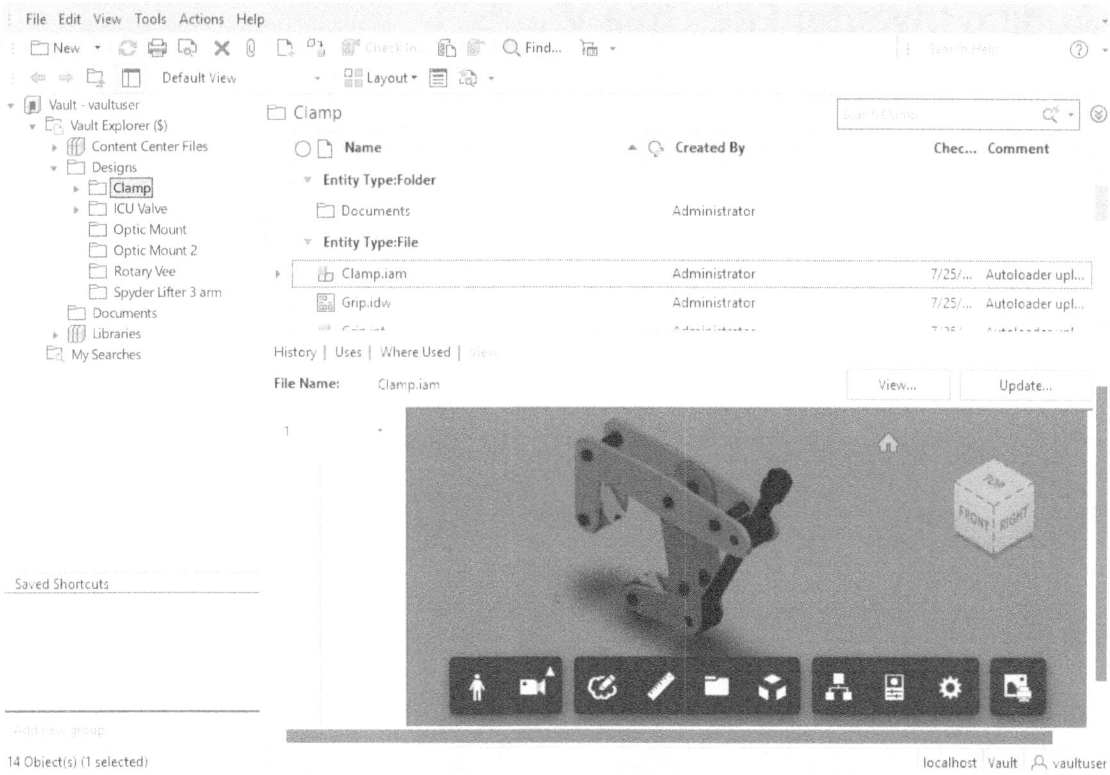

Figure 3–6

Hint: Visualization File Administration

If your Vault administrator has disabled the visualization attachment options in order to save space in the vault, Vault does not automatically create the visualization files.

Adding Inventor Files to a Vault

Autodesk Autoloader guides you through the process of organizing and uploading files to the vault. It ensures that all related Autodesk Inventor files in the project can be resolved prior to uploading to the vault. You can filter the files that are uploaded, including non-Inventor files in the selected folder and its subfolders.

Autodesk Autoloader helps you resolve any file relationship problems and find duplicate files before uploading the files to the vault. All errors must be resolved before Autodesk Autoloader can upload the files to the vault. Examples of errors are shown in Figure 3–7.

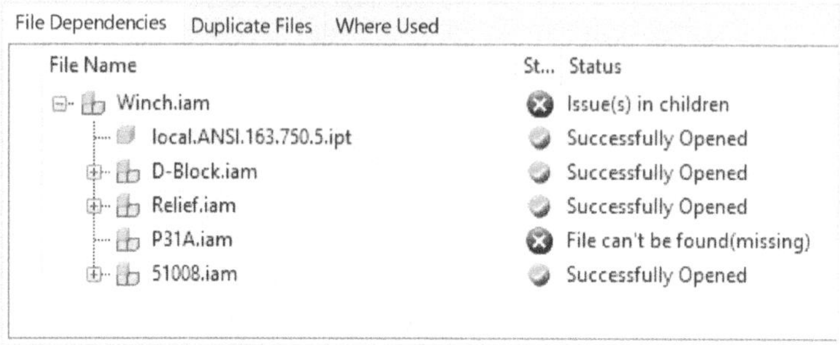

Figure 3–7

How To: Upload to Vault with Autodesk Autoloader

The following steps detail how to upload existing Autodesk Inventor designs to the vault using Autodesk Autoloader.

1. Note the top-level folder of your existing designs, as shown in Figure 3–8.

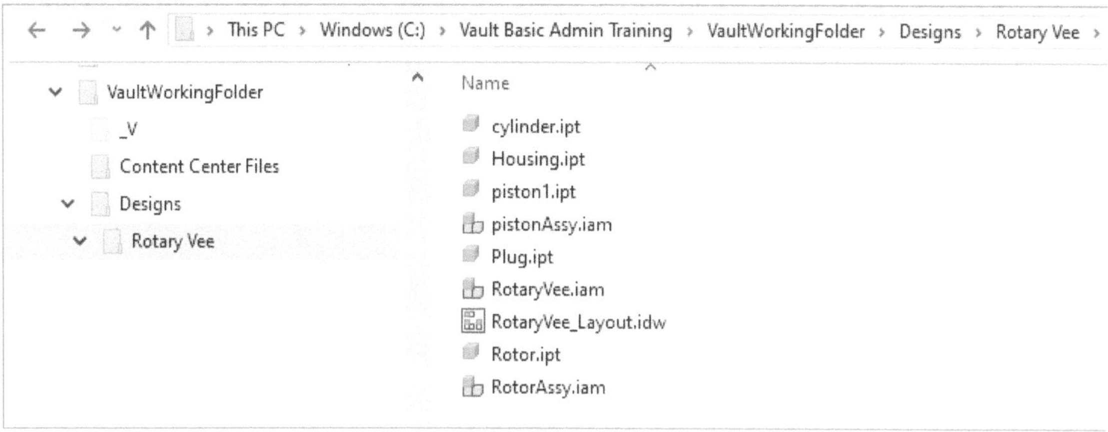

Figure 3–8

2. Start Autodesk Autoloader (**Start>All Programs>Autodesk>Autodesk Data Management> Autodesk Autoloader 2025 for Vault**).
3. Click **Next**.
4. Click **Select Folder**.
5. In the *Browse For Folder* dialog box (shown in Figure 3–9), select the top-level folder for the designs you want to upload to the vault and click **OK**.

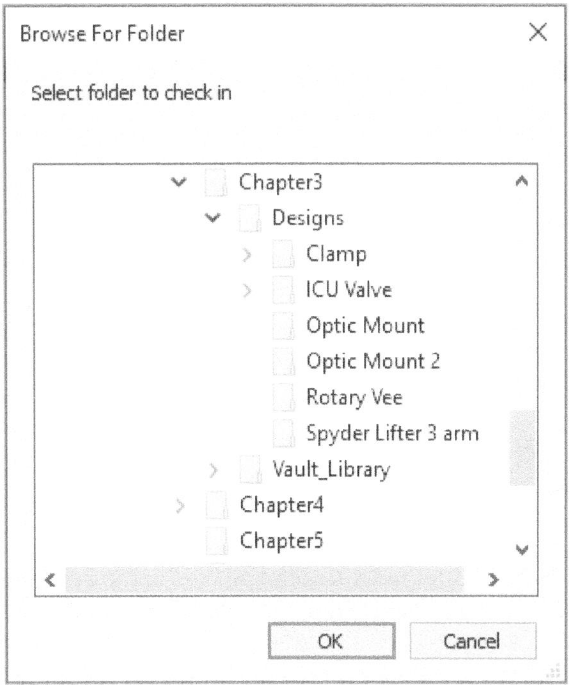

Figure 3–9

6. Select the existing project file that Autodesk Autoloader uses to determine the files to upload to the vault, as shown in Figure 3–10. Click **OK**.

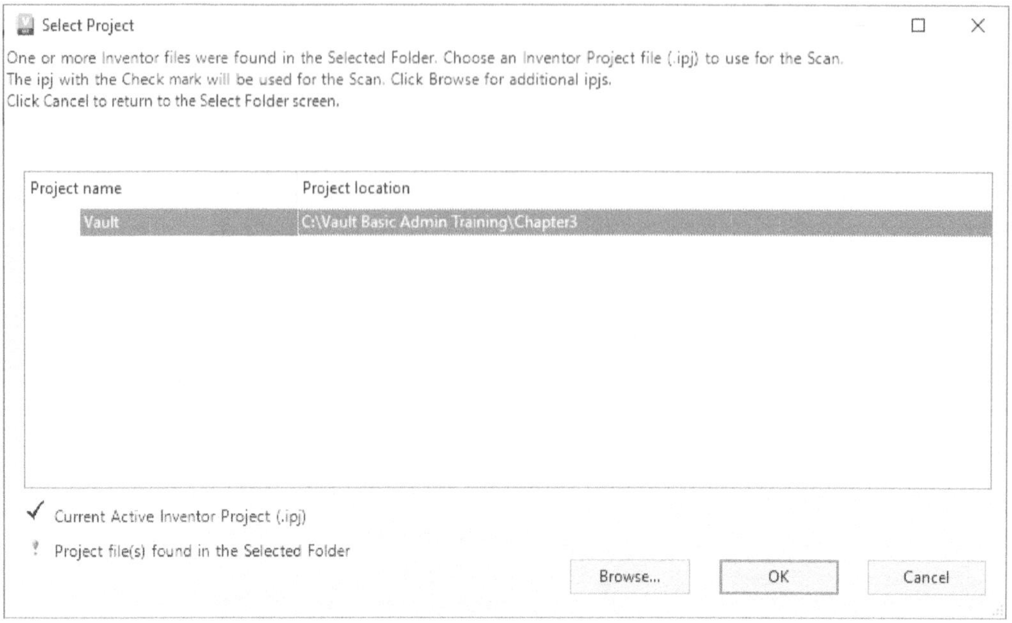

Figure 3–10

7. Click **Next**.
8. Click **Scan** to set Autodesk Autoloader to scan all files in the selected folder and subfolders, as shown in Figure 3–11. File relationships are confirmed during the scan and other referenced files, such as library parts, are added to the list of files to upload. If required, fix any reported problems and then restart Autodesk Autoloader. To resolve issues, you can also open files from within the Autoloader. Rerun the scan to recheck the files.

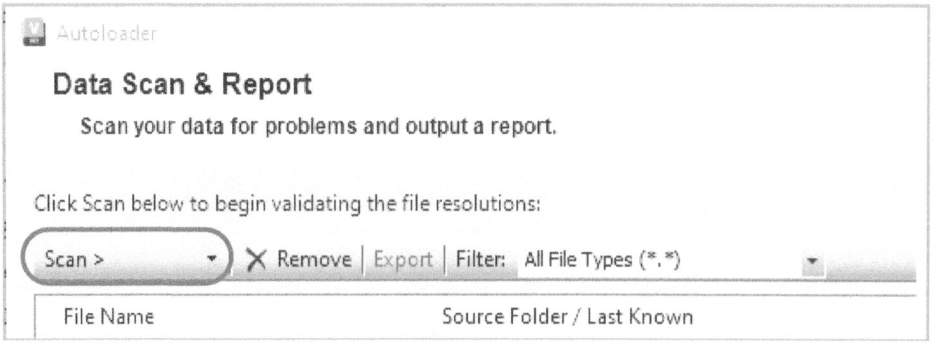

Figure 3–11

9. Click **Next**.

10. Log in to the vault.
11. Map the generated folders in the vault to the corresponding folders in the existing project folder, as shown in Figure 3–12.

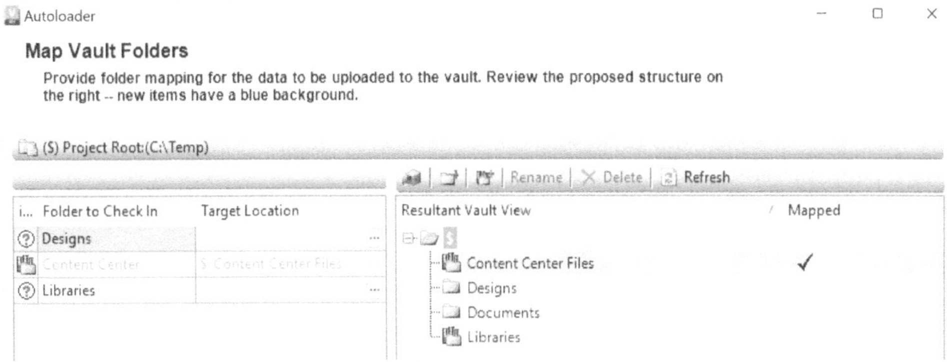

Figure 3–12

12. Click **Next**.
13. Optionally, filter the files to be uploaded to the vault. You can include or exclude specific Inventor file formats and non-Inventor files, as shown in Figure 3–13.

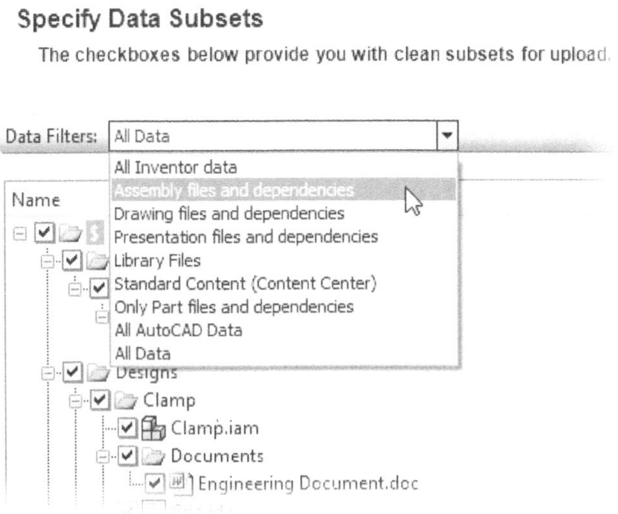

Figure 3–13

14. Upload the files to the vault. You can optionally generate a visualization file of each Inventor file before it is uploaded to the vault.

Practice 3a
Add Inventor Files to Vault Using Autoloader

Practice Objective

- Add Inventor files to a vault using Autodesk Autoloader.

In this practice, you will use Autodesk Autoloader to add Autodesk Inventor files to a vault. The completed practice is shown in Figure 3–14.

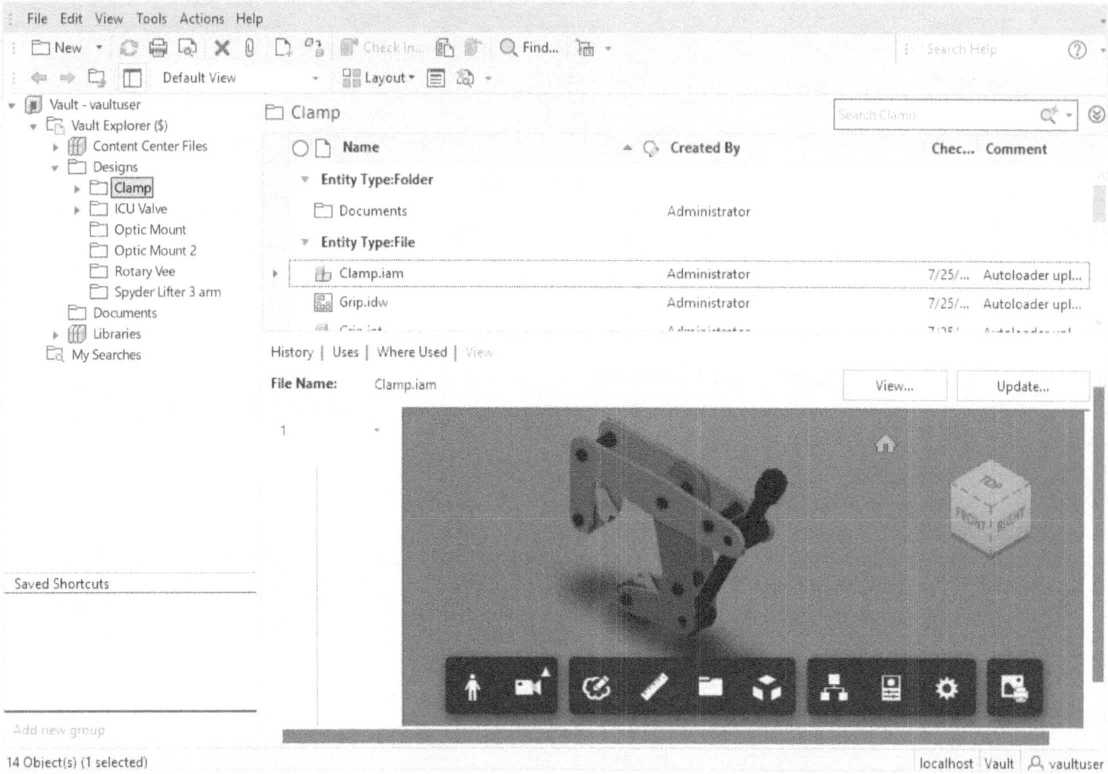

Figure 3–14

Task 1: Prepare existing designs.

1. Start Autodesk Autoloader (**Start>All Programs>Autodesk>Autodesk Data Management>Autodesk Autoloader 2025 for Vault**).
2. On the *Welcome* page, click **Next**.
3. On the *Select Data Source* page, click **Select Folder**.
4. Browse to *C:\Vault Basic Admin Training\Chapter3\Designs*.

5. Click **OK**.
6. In the *Select Project* dialog box, click **OK** to accept **Vault.ipj** as the project file, as shown in Figure 3–15. If required, click **Browse** to select the Vault.ipj project file.

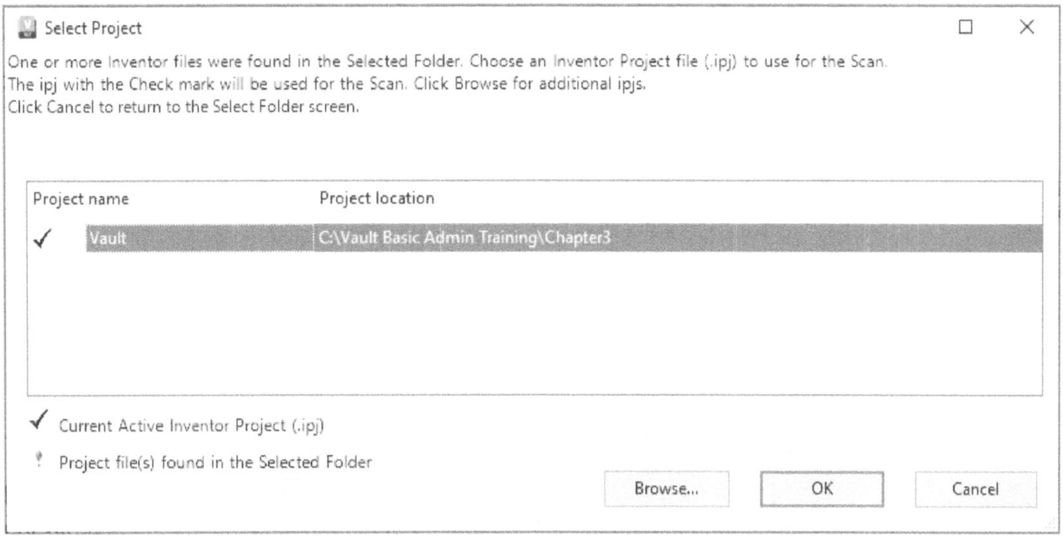

Figure 3–15

7. On the *Select Data Source* page, the folders beneath the *Designs* folder are displayed, as shown in Figure 3–16.

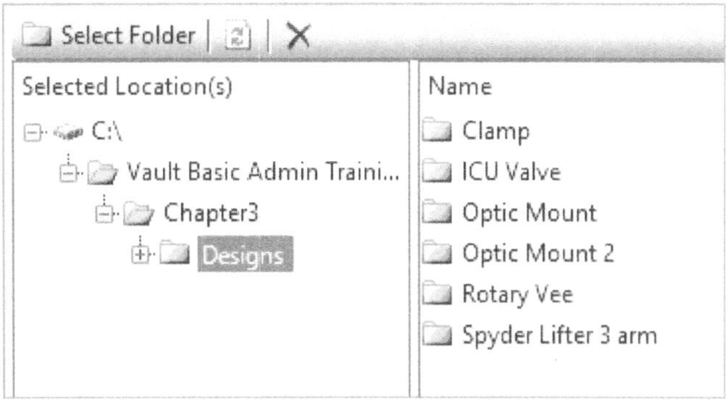

Figure 3–16

8. Click **Next**. The files to be scanned are displayed on the *Data Scan & Report* page, as shown in Figure 3–17.

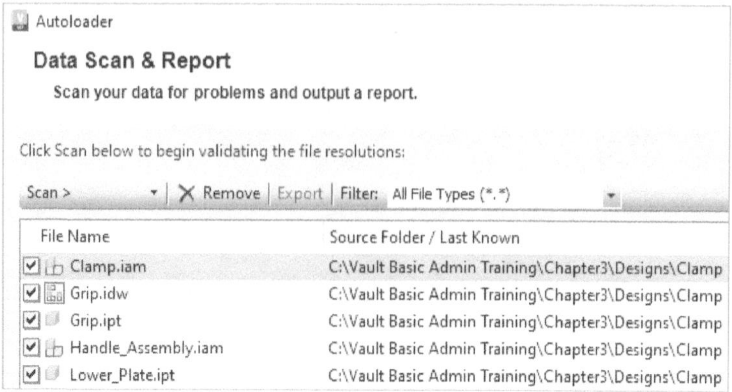

Figure 3–17

Task 2: Add designs to the vault.

1. Click **Scan**.
2. When the scan is complete, click **OK**. Scroll through the results. All files should have opened and resolved successfully.
3. Click **Next**.
4. Log in to the vault using the following information (as shown in Figure 3–18):
   - For *User Name*, enter **Administrator**.
   - For *Password*, leave the box empty.
   - For *Vault*, select **Vault**.
     - You might have to click the browse button next to the *Vault* field to open the *Vaults* dialog box. Select **Vault** and click **OK** to select the database.

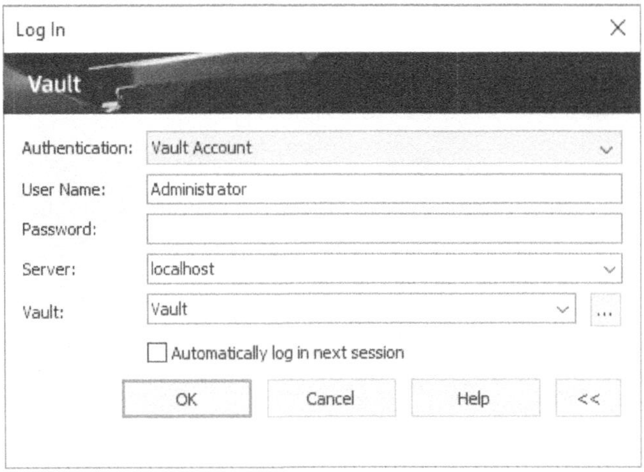

Figure 3–18

5. On the *Map Vault Folders* page, mappings from project folders to vault folders are listed on the left. The vault hierarchy is listed on the right, as shown in Figure 3–19.

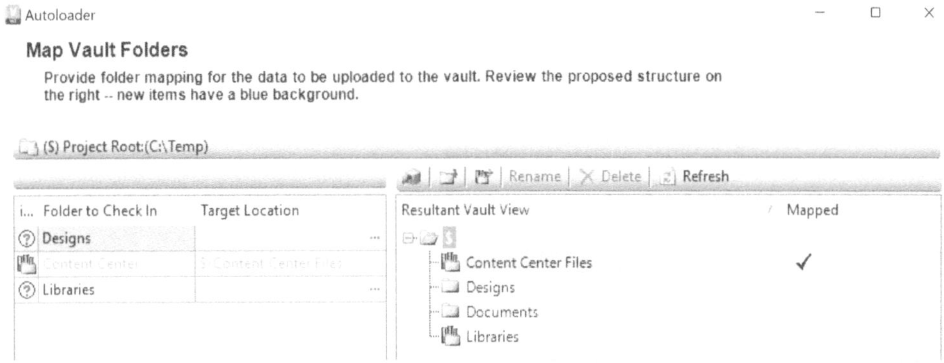

Figure 3–19

6. In the *Folder to Check In* list, double-click on **Designs**.

7. In the *Browse Vault For Folder* dialog box (shown in Figure 3–20), do the following:
    - Click **Designs**.
    - Click the **Direct Mapping** checkbox to toggle it on.
    - Click **OK**.

    The *Designs* folder on the local computer is mapped to the *\Designs* folder in the vault.

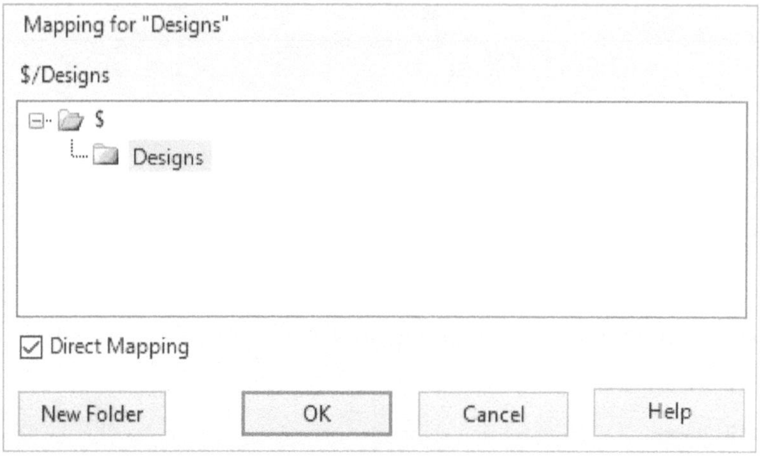

Figure 3–20

8. In the *Folder to Check In* list, double-click on **Libraries**.
9. In the *Mapping for Libraries* dialog box, select the ***Libraries*** folder and click **OK**.
10. In the *Map Folder Target Location* column, *Designs* should be mapped to **$/Designs**, and *Libraries* should be mapped to **$/Libraries**.
11. Click **Next** to start the Copy & File Redirection Progress process.
12. When the process is complete, click **Next**.
13. On the *Specify Data Subsets* page, review the list of files selected for upload. Note that non-Inventor files are included in the list.
14. Select the **Create Visualization Attachment** checkbox to toggle on the creation of visualization files from the uploaded files. A confirmation dialog box will warn that the selection could impact performance. Click **Yes** to confirm that you want Vault to create visualization files.
15. Click **Upload**.
16. The files are uploaded to the vault as reported in the *Autoload Progress & Report* dialog box.

    Note: *Vault creates all visualization files before the files are uploaded to the vault. This might take a few minutes to complete.*

17. When the process is complete, note the location of the report file on the *Autoload Progress and Report* page under *Status*.

18. In File Explorer, navigate to the report file (XML format). Open the report in Excel selecting the Open file with the following style sheet applied option to view. Review the report, then close the file.
19. In the *Autoloader* dialog box, click **Done**.
20. Launch the Vault Client.
21. Expand the *Designs* folder in the navigation pane and click on a couple of subfolders. Note that the files are displayed that were loaded with the Autoloader.

End of practice

Chapter 4

Organizing and Populating a Vault

In this chapter, you will learn how Autodesk® Inventor® files are organized for best results with Autodesk® Vault. You will then learn how to prepare existing projects and upload them to a Vault using Autodesk Autoloader.

Learning Objectives

- Describe how Autodesk Inventor project files work with a vault.
- Describe how Autodesk Inventor model files are organized for best results with Autodesk Vault.
- Describe how library files are organized for best results with Vault.
- Describe how Content Center files are organized for best results with Vault.
- Prepare existing models to use Autodesk Autoloader.
- Upload models to a vault using Autodesk Autoloader.

4.1 How Autodesk Inventor Files Are Organized

In this section, you will learn how Autodesk Inventor project files, model files, and library files are organized for the best performance with Vault. A typical Autodesk Inventor design includes a large number of files. You can use Autodesk Autoloader to help organize your existing models before uploading them to the vault, or you can organize the files manually before you upload them. Whichever method you use, you should know how Autodesk Inventor uses the project file to find files and how regular model files and library files are organized.

Figure 4–1 displays a number of designs added to a vault. The files are organized in the vault to match the local working folder structure when the files were uploaded to the vault.

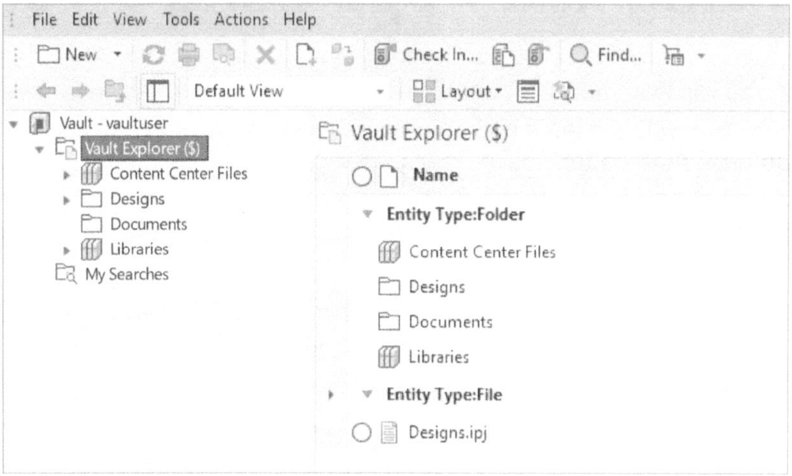

Figure 4–1

About Project Files

Autodesk Inventor uses project files to organize and locate related files. Before you upload files to a vault or try to fix resolution issues, you must learn how Autodesk Inventor uses the project file to locate the files in a design.

Project Files Defined

Autodesk Inventor uses project files to organize storage locations for related files in a design. For example, when you open an assembly in Autodesk Inventor, it looks for the component files relative to the locations specified in the project file. When you place a part from the Content Center, the generated part is stored in a folder relative to the top-level folder specified in the project file. A project file is set up to correspond with the way the files are organized in the vault.

You must create a Vault project file, as shown in Figure 4–2, when you want to work with designs that will be managed using Autodesk Vault. This project file format is only available if you have Autodesk Vault installed. The workspace, libraries, and Content Center files entries specify where Inventor searches for files. All paths are defined relative to a project file location.

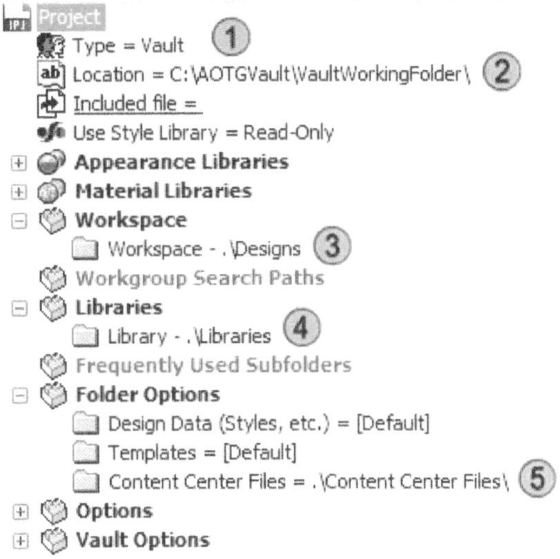

Figure 4–2

1. A Vault project file is required for managing designs stored in the vault.
2. The local working folder is mapped to the root folder in the vault. All files in the design are typically located under this folder.
3. The *Workspace* folder is the top-level folder for the models and drawings you create for all designs stored in the vault. You create subfolders under here to organize your designs.
4. Library files in the vault are copied to folders under this local folder. Files in these folders cannot be edited.
5. Files generated from the Content Center are stored under this folder when copied from the vault.

Autodesk Inventor uses the copy of the project file in the local working folder when you work with files you have checked out from the vault. Therefore, the paths in the project file must correspond to the way that files are organized in the local working folder. When you get files from the vault, the vault structure is reproduced in the local working folder.

Project File Location

The project file should be located one folder above all other model and library file folders. A folder beneath the project file folder holds all designs with folders for each design.

Figure 4–3 displays the layout of a typical vault working folder. The project file, **Designs.ipj**, is located in the root folder (*VaultWorkingFolder*). The *Designs* folder is the workspace folder in the project file and is located under the project file. It contains folders for different designs. The *Content Center Files* and *Libraries* folders are also located under the project file but outside of the workspace folder.

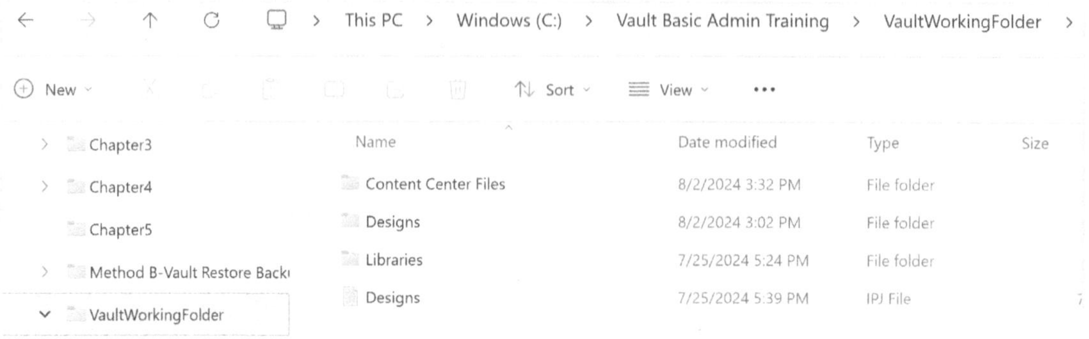

Figure 4–3

Use a Single Project File

There are many ways to organize Autodesk Inventor project and model files. Some users have one project file for all designs; other users have one project file for each design. With Vault, a single project file should be used so you need to manage just one project file and do not have to switch project files when moving from one design to another.

Frequently Used Subfolders

Frequently used subfolders are shortcuts defined in the project file to give you quick access to designs and library parts in your local working folders. In Figure 4–4, a project file is displayed in the project file editor. The ***Frequently Used Subfolders*** entry of the project file contains paths to frequently used design and library folders.

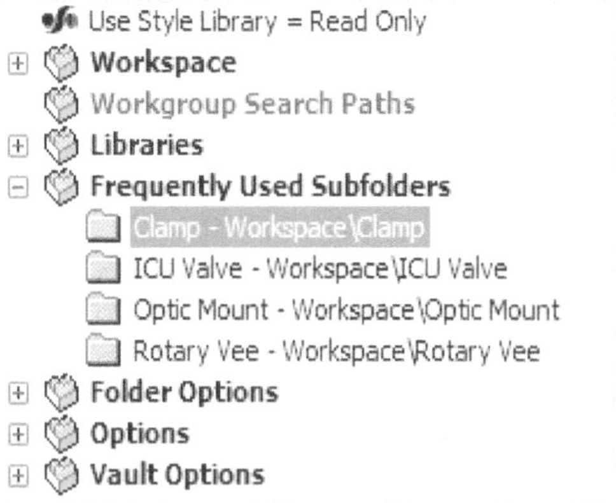

Figure 4–4

Frequently used subfolders are displayed when you browse for a file in Autodesk Inventor, making it easier to navigate to specific designs or libraries.

Mapping Project Folders

When you check in files or add new files to the vault, the files are copied from the local working folder to folders in the vault. Inventor determines where to copy the files by looking in the project file. The vault folders are specified by mapping each local search path to a vault folder.

A typical folder mapping is shown in Figure 4–5. The *Project Root* folder is where the project file is stored. In the example shown, the local *Project Root* folder is mapped to the root folder of the vault. Therefore, the project file is copied to the root of the vault, and model files will be copied to their respective folders relative to the root folder in the vault. Each library path in the project file is also mapped to a vault folder. In Figure 4–5, files in the local path named *Library* are copied to the *Libraries* folder in the vault, and files in the local *Content Center Files* path are copied to the *Content Center Files* folder in the vault.

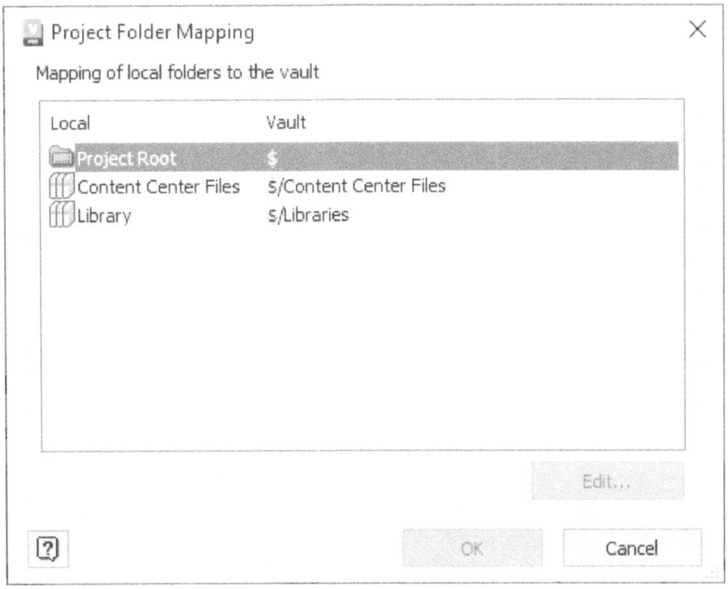

Figure 4–5

The mapping information is stored as XML data in the project file. For example, the mapping for the *Library* folder corresponding to the previous image is displayed in Figure 4–6. The local path and the vault path are both specified.

```
<ProjectPath pathtype="Library">
  <PathName>Library</PathName> (1)
  <Path>.\Libraries</Path> (2)
  <VaultPath>$/Libraries</VaultPath> (3)
</ProjectPath>
```

Figure 4–6

1	Path name in project file.
2	Local folder path. This folder is relative to the folder containing the project file.
3	Corresponding vault folder path. The folder structure under this folder matches the folder structure under the local folder path.

About Model Files

There are many ways to organize model files. The method you select must be compatible with the project file and with Vault. In this section, you will learn how model files are organized for the best results with Autodesk Vault.

How Inventor Model Files Are Organized

For best results, model files are organized in folders under a single project file, as shown in Figure 4–7.

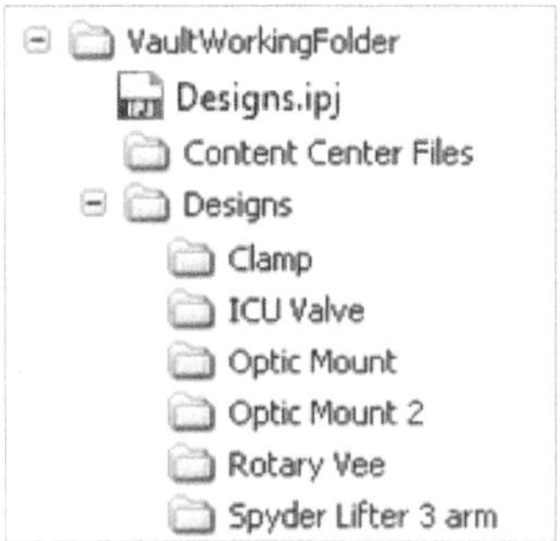

Figure 4–7

The same folder structure is used in the vault. When you retrieve files to your local working folder, they are copied to the same relative location and they open successfully in Inventor. For example, the corresponding vault is organized as shown in Figure 4–8. A single project file is located in the root of the vault.

Folders for the designs, libraries, and Content Center parts are one level below. You can further organize your files using subfolders under these top-level folders. When you get files from the vault, they are copied to the local working folder with the same structure and can be opened successfully.

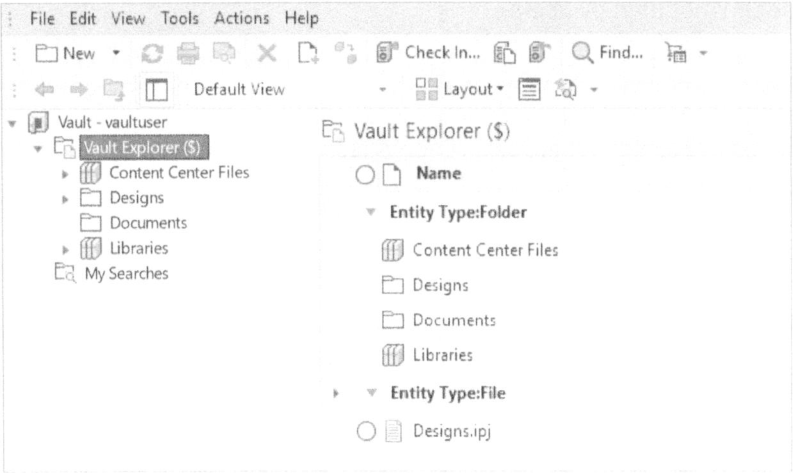

Figure 4–8

Project File Settings for Model Files

The ***Workspace*** path specifies the location of a top-level folder for all non-library model files. Files for different designs are stored in folders under the *Workspace* folder. If model files are saved outside of the *Workspace* folder, Autodesk Inventor will not find them.

In the project file, the workspace is set as a relative path to the folder that contains the project file, as shown in Figure 4–9.

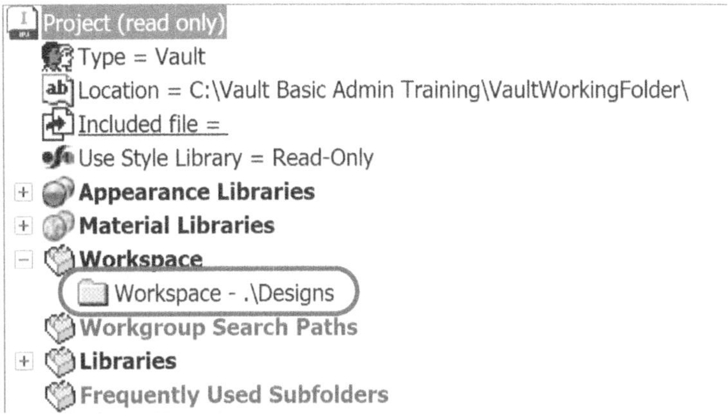

Figure 4–9

How Common Parts Are Organized

If a part or subassembly is used in more than one design, the file should be stored in a separate folder from the designs in which the part is used, and then it should be referenced in each design. If the part or assembly rarely or never changes, the file can be stored in a library folder so that it cannot be modified by users.

The vault is used as a centralized storage area for all of your files, including common parts and library parts and assemblies. Upload all of your library and common components to the vault so that Inventor users can place them in their designs using the **Place from Vault** command. Figure 4–10 displays a folder named *Common Parts*, which contains parts that are included in a number of designs.

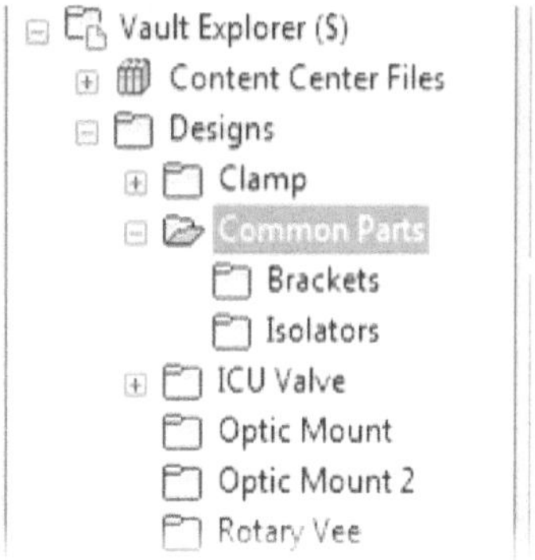

Figure 4–10

About Library Files

Library files are parts or subassemblies that do not normally change. In Autodesk Inventor, library files are treated as read-only files that are not normally versioned.

Typically, library files are used in more than one design. Common purchased components, Content Center files, and iParts are typical library components. Autodesk Inventor includes a wide selection of library parts in the Content Center libraries. You can also get library parts and assemblies from component manufacturers or create them yourself. You must set up and organize library components correctly so that they work with the vault.

About Library Files

Library files are parts or subassemblies that do not normally change and are used in more than one design. You store library files in library folders. Files stored in library folders are treated as read-only and cannot be modified by users. Any file can be designated as a library file, including regular Inventor parts and assemblies and AutoCAD® drawing files.

About Library Folders

Files that are stored in library folders in the vault are designated as library files. Library folders are similar to regular folders except that files in library folders are treated as library files and cannot be modified while stored in a library folder. Library folders must be created directly under the root of the vault, because you cannot create them under a regular folder.

Library folders use a different icon than regular folders. Note that subfolders are used to group library parts into meaningful categories. You can create any level of nested library folders to help organize the files, as shown in Figure 4–11.

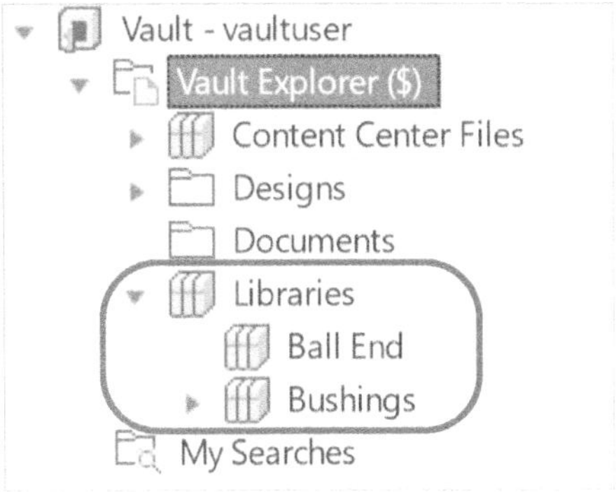

Figure 4–11

When a user retrieves a design from the vault and the design contains library files, the library files are copied into the working folder to the same relative location and folder as in the vault.

iParts in the Vault

In Figure 4–12, an iPart factory, **Heim Bushing.ipt**, is displayed in a library folder. Note that a unique icon is used to distinguish a factory from other file formats. iPart children also have unique icons.

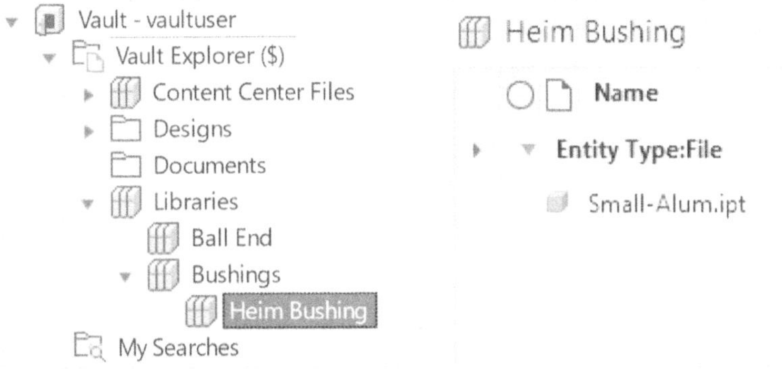

Figure 4–12

Project Files Settings for Library Parts

When you open a model, Autodesk Inventor looks for library files in the locations specified in the project file. Figure 4–13 shows a project file with a single library path that points to the top-level library folder. The library path is relative because the library folder is beneath the folder containing the project file.

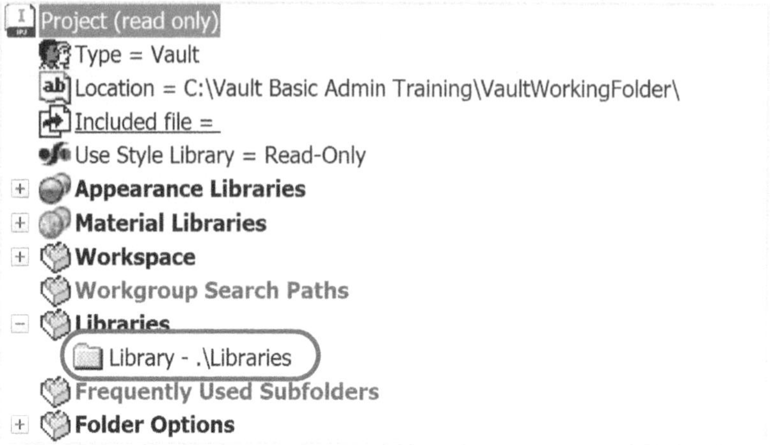

Figure 4–13

Importance of Relative Paths

Because all design files, including library files, are stored in the vault, all paths in a vault project file should be defined relative to the folder containing the project file. When you use relative paths, the entire local working folder structure is portable; it can be located in any location on a user's computer. If you use absolute paths to local folders such as *G:\Libraries*, or UNC names such as *\\PartServer\Libraries*, each user must have the same setup on their computer if they want to share the same project file from the vault.

About Content Center Files

Content Center files are parts that you often use in more than one design. They are similar to other library files and you need to set them up correctly to work with Autodesk Vault.

About Content Center Files and Vault

Content Center files are parts that are placed from the Content Center libraries. The Content Center libraries are databases that store definitions of parts. A part file is not created until you first place the selected part in your design. Because many designs use identical instances of a part (for example, a common fastener), you normally store the resulting part file in a common folder that is outside of your designs so that many designs can reference one copy of the library part. When you place the part from the Content Center in another model, the folder in which you store Content Center parts is checked before a new part file is created. If the part already exists, the design references the existing part instead of creating another.

When you use Autodesk Vault to manage documents for a design team, you should install the Content Center libraries with the Autodesk Data Management Server (ADMS) rather than as Inventor Desktop Content.

How Content Center Files Are Organized

As with user-defined library components, you share Content Center files between designs but you do not modify them. In the same way that you use the top-level *Libraries* folder, you specify a storage location for Content Center parts in the project file that is outside the *Designs* folder. Because you cannot modify parts generated from the Content Center, you store them in library folders in the vault. When you store a design in the vault or get versions of a design, parts placed from the Content Center act in a similar manner to other library parts.

You can organize Content Center files in many ways. However, for best results when using the vault, you should organize these files in the same way that you organize library files. The recommended folder structure for storing Content Center files is shown in Figure 4–14. The *Content Center Files* folder is located directly under the project file but outside of the folder where regular design files are stored.

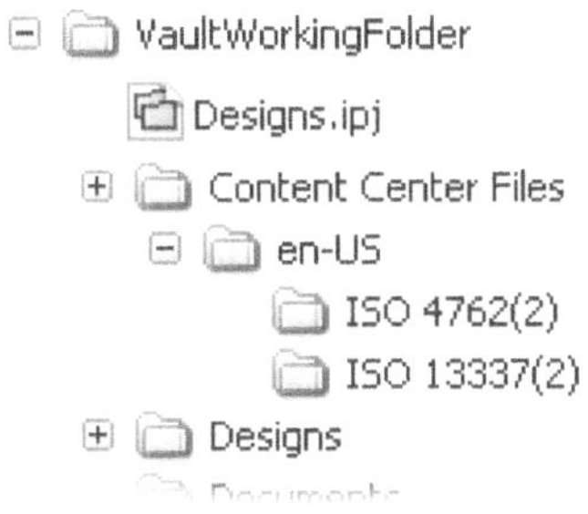

Figure 4–14

Content Center Files in the Vault

Parts generated from the Content Center libraries are stored in the vault using the same folder structure below your working folder. When you create a part from the Content Center, the part is placed in a folder below the *Content Center Files* folder. The folder name reflects the family name of the part in the Content Center. In the vault, the local *Content Center Files* folder is mapped to a library folder one level below the root folder in the vault, as shown in Figure 4–15.

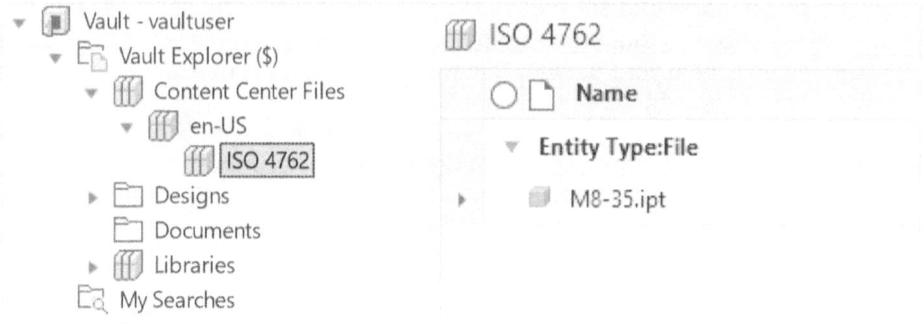

Figure 4–15

Project File Settings for Content Center Parts

In the Autodesk Inventor project file editor, the *Content Center Files* path is set to the folder that you created for the Content Center files. Because the *Content Center Files* folder is beneath the project file, the path is relative to the project file, as shown in Figure 4–16. The *Content Center Files* folder should be located outside the folder specified for user-defined library components.

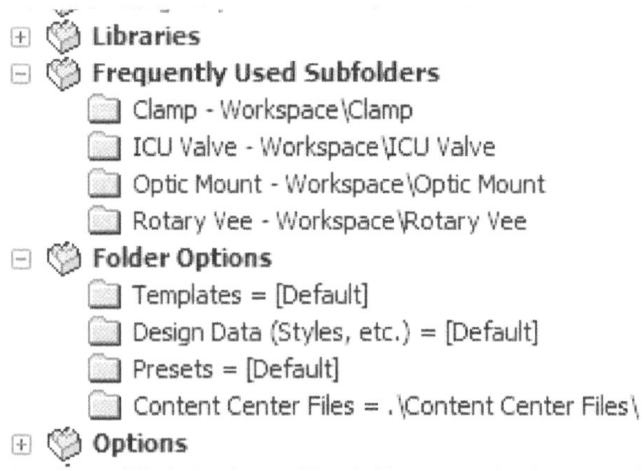

Figure 4–16

4.2 Adding Existing Models to a Vault

In this section, you will learn how to prepare existing designs and add them to a vault using Autodesk Autoloader, a software that prepares, analyzes, and uploads Autodesk Inventor files to a vault. Many companies have existing Inventor designs that they need to add to the vault. You can use several methods to add your existing designs to the vault, depending on whether you want to manually prepare and upload the designs or use a more automated method such as Autodesk Autoloader.

Preparing Models

The method you use to prepare data depends on the method you use to upload data to the vault. When you use Autodesk Autoloader to upload data, there is little preparation required because Autoloader reorganizes the files for you. If Autodesk Autoloader finds problems with some file relationships, you are required to fix the problems before using Autoloader to upload the files to the vault.

Planning the Vault Structure

Before you upload existing model data, you must plan how you want to store your model files, library files, Content Center files, non-model files, and other data in the vault. If you use Autodesk Autoloader to upload your data, the software creates a single project file and the top-level vault folders for you. All that you need to create are subfolders to organize the files for each design. The structure and project file that Autoloader creates ensures that you can successfully work on your designs in Autodesk Inventor.

It is not a requirement that you have a single project file for all your designs before uploading files to a vault with Autodesk Autoloader. You can run Autoloader for each project file to upload the designs managed by the project file. It is highly recommended that you place all designs uploaded to the vault under the single vault project file created when you first upload files to a new vault using Autoloader.

Preparing Project Files

When you run Autodesk Autoloader, you select an existing folder to upload. You then select a project file associated with the designs in the selected folder and its subfolders. The selected project file is used to validate file references in the designs in the selected folder before they are uploaded to the vault. Autodesk Autoloader reads any type of project file including Single-User, Shared, Semi-Isolated, and Vault.

Autoloader uses all defined paths in the project file to determine which files to upload. Each design in the selected folder and its subfolders is examined for dependent files. Autoloader checks that all dependent files can be found in the scope of the search paths so that models correctly resolve after uploading to the vault. All dependent files are added to the list of files to upload. Because Autoloader supports all project file formats, it locates all referenced files in the *Workspace*, *Workgroup*, *Libraries*, and *Content Center Files* search paths.

Existing projects can be organized in many different ways. Because Autoloader works with one project file at a time, run Autoloader once for each project file. If you already use a single project file for all of your designs, all designs can be uploaded at once using Autoloader. If you use multiple project files, you must run Autoloader for each project file.

You do not need to convert your existing project files to a Vault-type project file before you work with Autoloader. Autoloader creates a new Vault project file for you and adds it to the vault. The new project file is ready to use, including the correct search paths and folder mappings.

Common Project File Problem

Although your existing projects can resolve correctly when you open the file in Autodesk Inventor, you might have to add additional search paths if Autodesk Autoloader cannot find files. For example, in Figure 4–17, the project file is located in the same folder as the main assembly, **Winch.iam**. The project file has *Workgroup* search paths to the *Motors* and *Hydraulics* folders, which are not located below the project file location. The project file does not contain a *Workspace* path. The main assembly opens successfully in Autodesk Inventor. However, when Autodesk Autoloader searches for files, the main assembly is not found because none of the search paths in the project file include the location of the main assembly file.

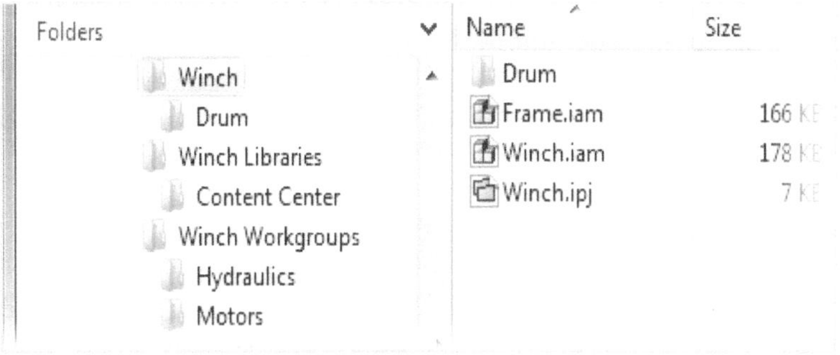

Figure 4–17

To fix the project file, add a *Workspace* path to the existing project file, and then run Autodesk Autoloader again.

Solving File Resolution Problems

You cannot upload designs that fail to fully resolve. If Autoloader cannot find child files, you must either locate them and resolve the problem or remove the child part's reference from the parent file.

You can check your designs by opening each master assembly, drawing, and presentation file in Autodesk Inventor to ensure that all files are found. This can be a lengthy process, especially for large designs with many parent files. Alternatively, use Autodesk Autoloader to find resolution problems because it identifies just the issues that you need to resolve. Resolve the problem files and then run Autoloader again to recheck the data.

Duplicate File Names

Although you can store files with the same name in the vault, it is recommended that you use unique file names. If files are different, they should have different names. If the same file is used in more than one model, place the file in a common folder from which you can use the file in many designs, as shown in Figure 4–18. If the file is used by many designs and is rarely or never modified, move the file to a library folder so that it is protected from unintended changes.

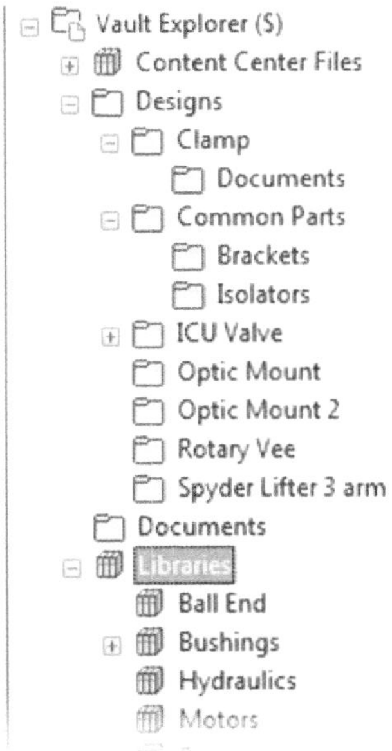

Figure 4–18

If you need to rename files, upload the files to the vault and then use the Vault renaming utility to rename the files rather than renaming the files in File Explorer and manually repairing the references. To add files with duplicate names to the vault, toggle off the **Enforce unique file name** setting in the vault and then add the files. In Vault, search for duplicate file names. If the files are different, rename them. After renaming, toggle on **Enforce unique file name**. The option to enforce unique file names in a vault is located in the *File Name Options* dialog box (**Tools>Administration>Vault Settings**, then click **Define...** on the *Files* tab). If using Autoloader, the **Enforce unique file name** option must be disabled, as shown in Figure 4–19.

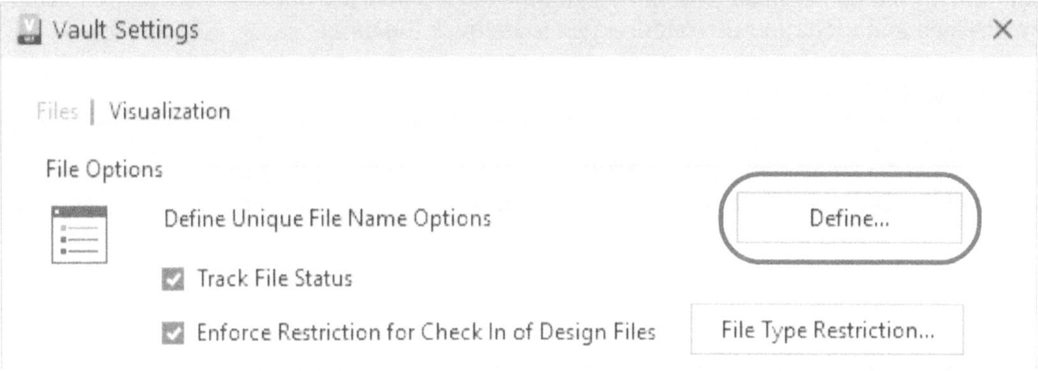

Figure 4–19

To consolidate duplicate files into one shared file, add your designs to the vault and then reorganize the files. Vault understands file relationships; therefore, you can move files without breaking links. To find where a file is used, view the *Where Used* information in Vault Explorer and record where each file is used. Delete all but one copy of the file, move the one copy from its current folder to a common folder, and then check out each dependent file and resolve the links. Use the **File Replace** operation where appropriate.

Migrating Files

If you want to migrate your design files to the latest release of Autodesk Inventor, you can migrate the files before or after you add them to the vault. To migrate files, schedule a migration task using the Task Scheduler in Inventor. The scheduled task opens all files from a local or vault folder, migrates the files, and saves them back to the same local or vault location.

You are not required to migrate Autodesk Inventor files before uploading them to the vault; however, Autoloader will not upload Inventor files older than R10 (must be migrated first) and AutoCAD files older than R14.

Uploading Models

When you have prepared your data for uploading, you use Autodesk Autoloader to upload the models to the vault. Autoloader checks file dependencies, consolidates files, creates the vault folder structure, uploads the files, and creates a vault project file. The resulting vault folder structure and project file ensure that you can successfully work with Autodesk Inventor and Vault.

How To: Upload to Vault with Autodesk Autoloader

The following steps describe how to upload an existing Autodesk Inventor design to the vault using Autodesk Autoloader.

1. Organize the folder structure of your existing designs in the local folder as you want them to display in the vault. The associated Inventor project file is shown in Figure 4–20.

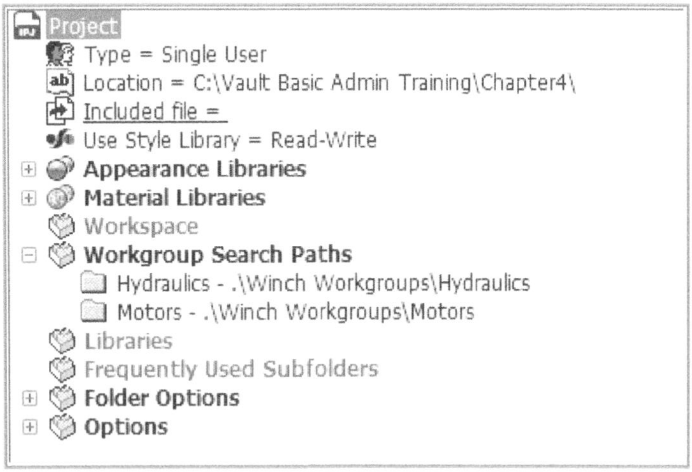

Figure 4–20

2. Start Autodesk Autoloader.
3. Select the top-level folder containing the designs you want to upload to the vault.
4. Select the project file that manages the files to be uploaded, as shown in Figure 4–21.

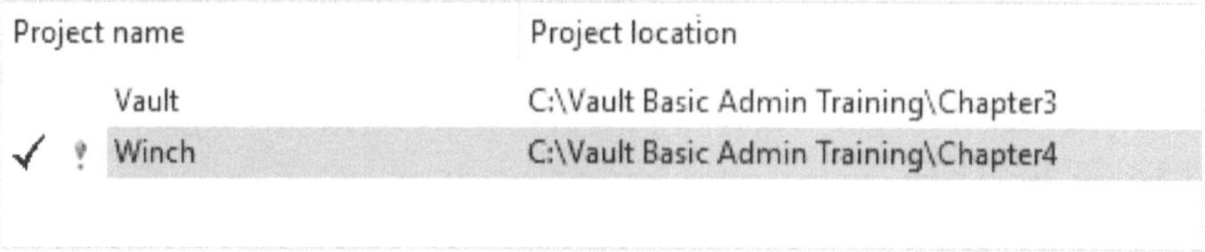

Figure 4–21

5. Click **Scan**, as shown in Figure 4–22, to scan all files in the project folders and confirm file relationships.

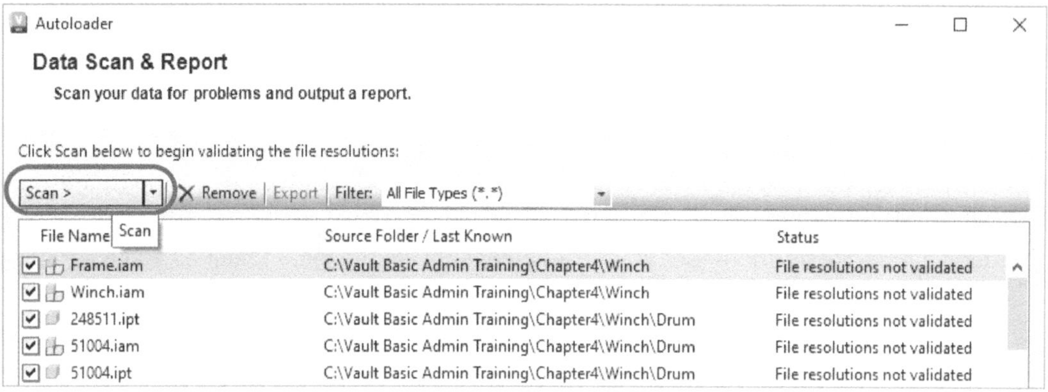

Figure 4–22

6. If required, fix any reported problems, as shown in Figure 4–23. Missing files and file resolution issues are reported. You are not required to abandon the Autoloader session. Open the files in their associated CAD application and repair the reported issues.

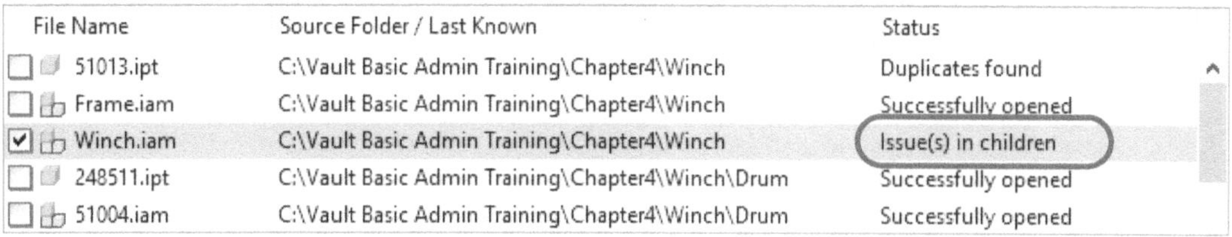

Figure 4–23

7. Return to Autoloader and rescan the files. You can only proceed when all reported issues have been resolved. The problem files can also be excluded from the selection set and loaded by hand later.

8. In the drop-down list, select **Find duplicates**, as shown in Figure 4–24. This will help identify any identical files that might cause confusion later in the process.

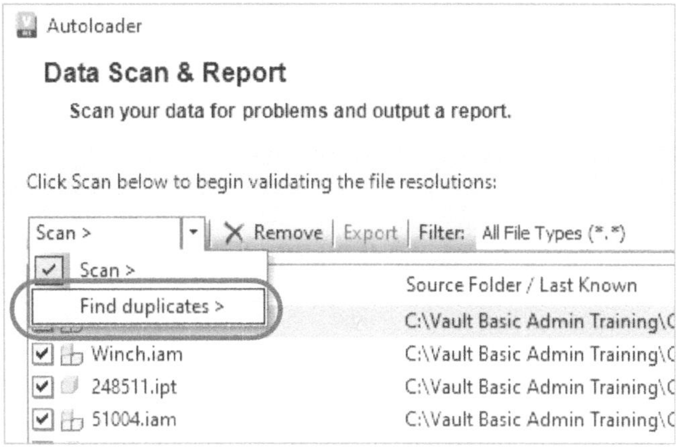

Figure 4–24

9. Once all issues have been resolved, click **Next**.
10. Log in to the vault.
11. Map the generated folders in the vault to the corresponding folders in the existing project folder. If your project file contains multiple workgroup or library search paths, you must map each one to a corresponding folder in the vault. You can create additional vault folders below the three Autoloader-generated folders to help organize the data in the vault.

*Note: During the mapping step, selecting to map 'Winch' to 'Products' in the vault will put 'Winch' under 'Products'. If mapping the 'Winch' folder to a 'Winch' folder in the vault, select the **Direct Mapping** option at the bottom of the Browse Vault For Folder dialog box (shown in Figure 4–25).*

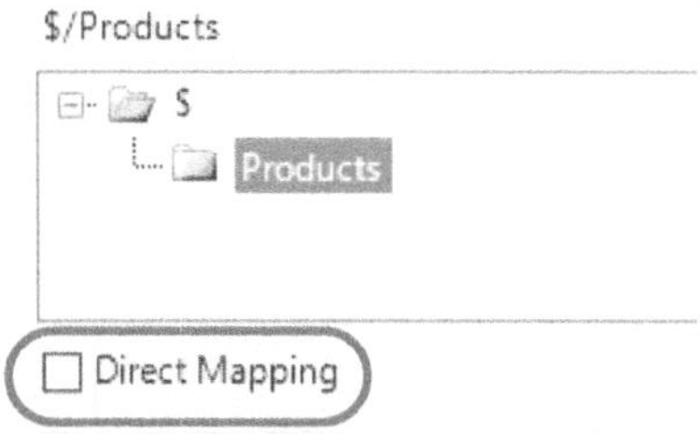

Figure 4–25

12. Click **Next**.
13. On the *Copy & File Redirection Progress* page, wait until the operation is complete, then click **Next**.
14. Upload the files to the vault. You can optionally generate a visualization file of each CAD file before it is uploaded to the vault. Once the files are uploaded, the *Autoloader Progress and Report* page notes the report location and file name to review the details of the upload.

Autoloader Results

When you use Autoloader to upload files to a new vault, Autoloader organizes the files based on the recommended vault structure. The results of using Autoloader to upload several designs is shown in Figure 4–26. Autoloader creates a new Vault project file, and creates two top-level library folders, *Content Center Files* and *Libraries*, along with a single top-level *Designs* folder. The project file contains the correct search paths and folder mappings. You should not have to edit the project file unless you want to add frequently used subfolders. You can get a copy of the project file to your working folder and immediately start working with the model files.

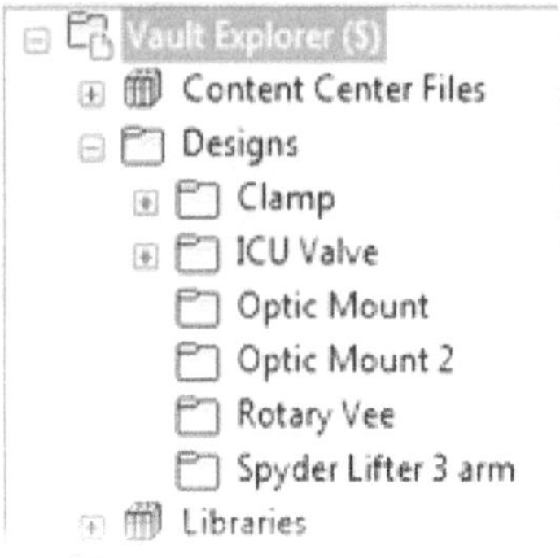

Figure 4–26

Uploading Non-Inventor Data

By default, all files in and below the selected folder are uploaded to the vault. File relationships between Autodesk Inventor documents are maintained, as are external reference relationships between .DWG files. Other files, such as images, documents, and spreadsheets, are also uploaded, but are not automatically attached to other documents in the vault. If required, you must manually attach them to the appropriate file after you upload the files to the vault.

In Autoloader, you can upload all files found in or below the selected folder or limit the upload to Autodesk Inventor files or DWG-based files, as shown in Figure 4–27. You can also control the upload status for each file.

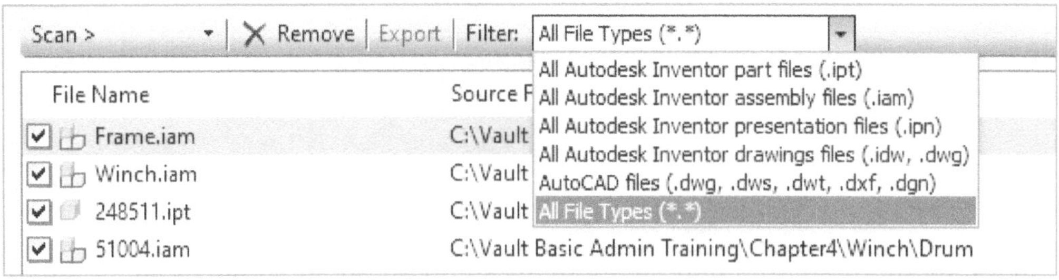

Figure 4–27

Adding Visualization Files

You can also generate .DWF or .DWFx files for all CAD files uploaded to the vault. This can take a considerable amount of time for large datasets. You can run Autoloader multiple times with subsets filtered by file format to reduce the time for any one upload.

Another approach is to use the Task Scheduler to check out and then immediately check in all files after you have uploaded all files without .DWF attachments. The .DWF files are created when the files are checked back in to the vault.

Practice 4a
Add Existing Projects to a Vault

Practice Objectives

- Prepare a project to be uploaded to a vault.
- Upload the project to a vault using Autodesk Autoloader.

In this practice, you will prepare a project for uploading and then upload the design to an empty vault using Autodesk Autoloader. The completed practice is shown in Figure 4–28.

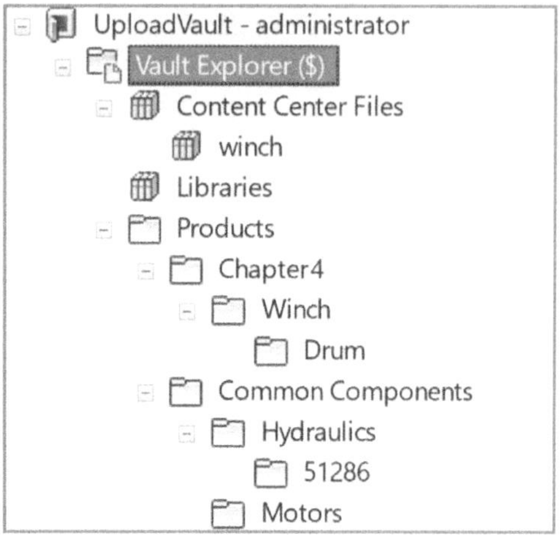

Figure 4–28

Task 1: Add existing projects to a vault.

1. Exit Autodesk Inventor if it is running.
2. Start the Autodesk Data Management Server Console. Log in as **Administrator** and leave the password blank.
3. Right-click on the *Vaults* folder and select **Create**, as shown in Figure 4–29.

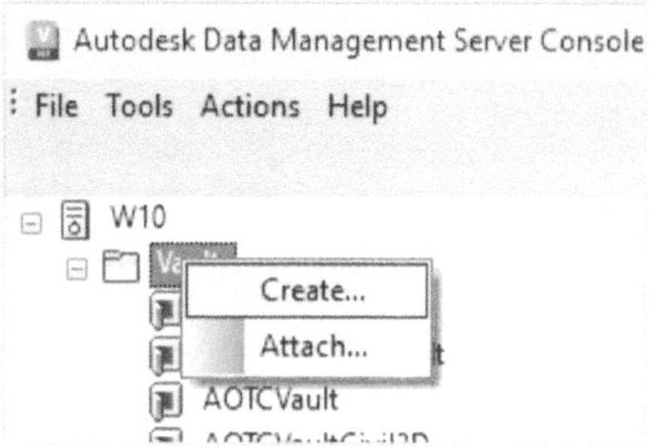

Figure 4–29

4. In the *Create Vault* dialog box, for *New Vault Name*, enter **UploadVault**, as shown in Figure 4–30. Click **OK**. When the vault is created, click **OK** to close the message box.

Figure 4–30

5. Exit the Autodesk Data Management Server Console.
6. In File Explorer, navigate to the *C:\Vault Basic Admin Training\Chapter4* folder. Right-click on **Winch.ipj** and select **Edit**.
7. In the Inventor *Project File Editor* dialog box, view the project file's entries for ***Workgroup Search Paths***, as shown in Figure 4–31. The *Hydraulics* and *Motors* workgroup folders are located below the folder containing the project folder.

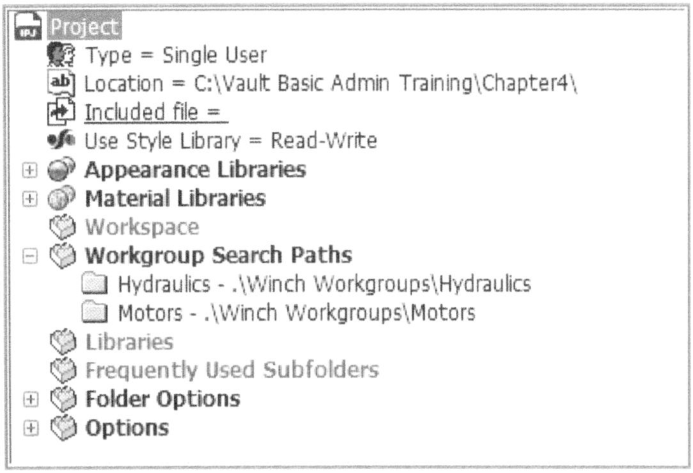

Figure 4–31

8. Right-click on **Workspace** and select **Add Path**.

9. In the location, enter **.\Winch** (a period, followed by \Winch) and press <Enter>. The path should appear as shown in Figure 4–32.

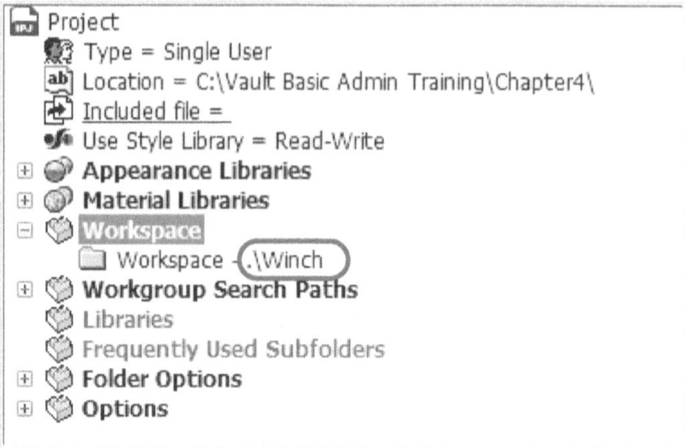

Figure 4–32

10. Click the plus sign (+) to expand **Folder Options**.
11. View the *Content Center Files* path, as shown in Figure 4–33.

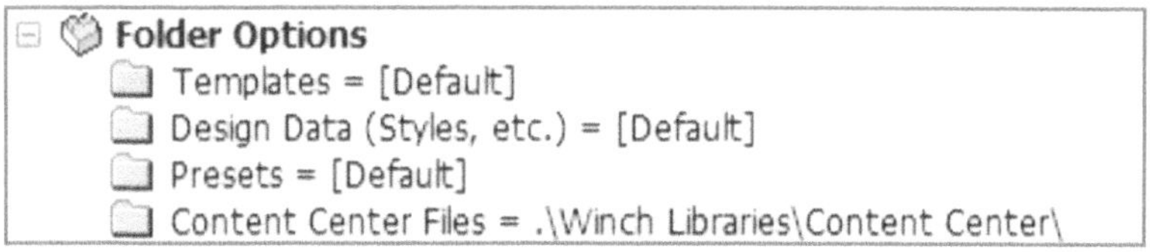

Figure 4–33

Note: *If the supplied data folders were not installed to their default location, you might have to select a new path for the Content Center files.*

12. Click **Save**. Close the *Project File Editor* dialog box.

Task 2: Check file dependencies.

1. Start Autodesk Autoloader. On the *Welcome* page, click **Next**.
2. On the *Select Data Source* page, click **Select Folder**. Browse to and select the *C:\Vault Basic Admin Training\Chapter4* folder.
3. Click **OK**.

4. In the *Select Project* dialog box, ensure that the **Winch** project file is shown as the active project file. If not, activate it, as shown in Figure 4–34.

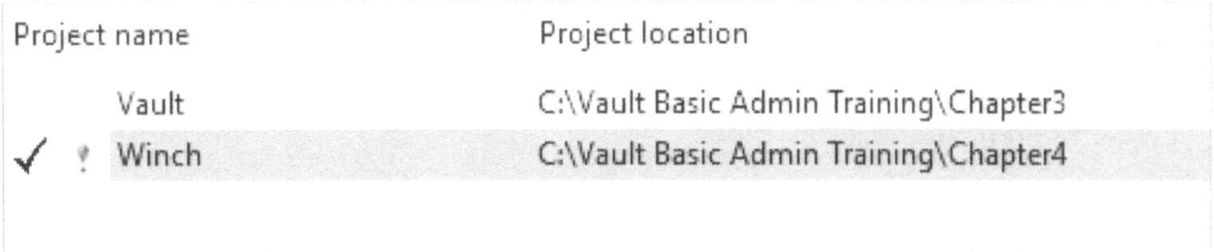

Figure 4–34

5. Click **OK**.
6. Click **Next**.
7. On the *Data Scan & Report* page, click **Scan**.
8. When the scan is complete, click **OK** to close the message box.
9. Note that **Next** is unavailable, indicating that there was a problem in one or more files. Click the *Status* column header to sort by status, and then scroll through the files and view the *Status* column, as shown in Figure 4–35.

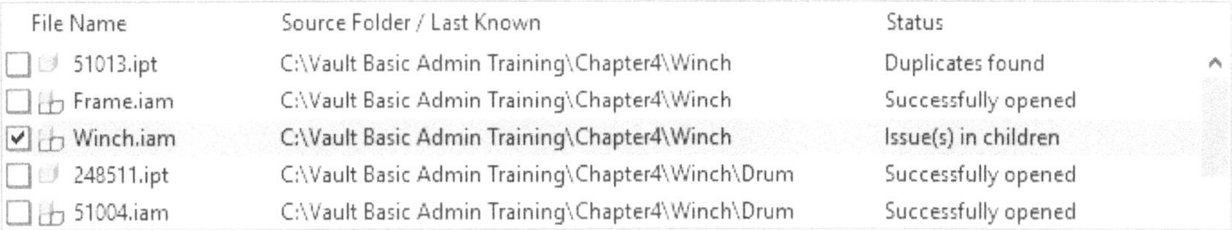

Figure 4–35

10. Under *File Name*, click **Winch.iam**. Click **>>** to expand the *Autoloader* dialog box, if not already expanded.
11. On the *File Dependencies* tab, scroll down to **P31A.iam**. The file resolution issue for Winch.iam is that P31A.iam cannot be found, as shown in Figure 4–36.

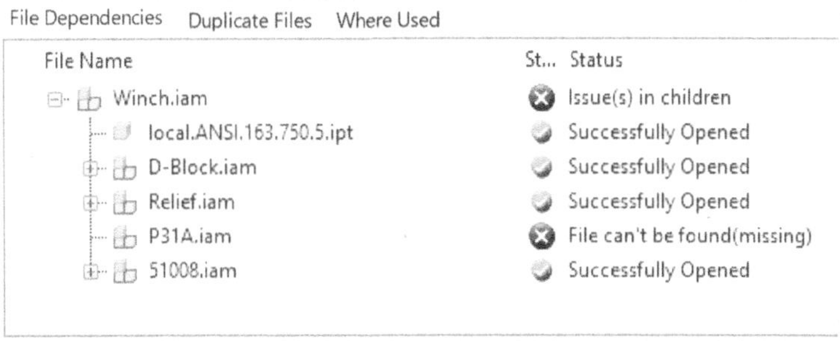

Figure 4–36

Task 3: Solve file resolution problem.

1. Start Autodesk Inventor.
2. Ensure that **Winch.ipj** is the active project file (select **File>Manage>Projects**).
3. Open **Winch.iam** from the local folder.
4. In the *Resolve Link* dialog box, resolve the link error by selecting the **P31B.iam** file from the *Winch Workgroups\Motors* folder, as shown in Figure 4–37. Click **Open**. Click **Yes** if you are prompted to update the assembly.

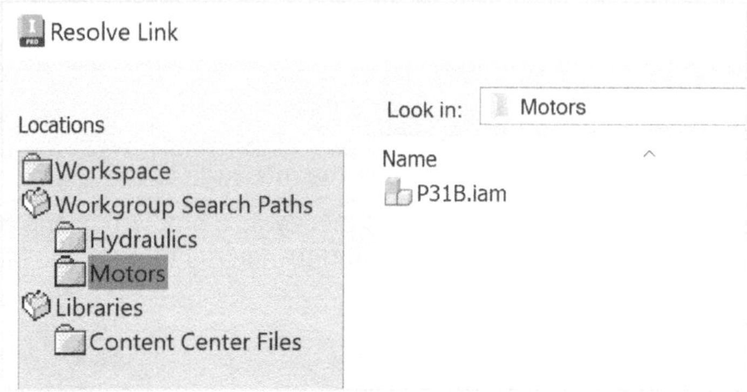

Figure 4–37

5. Click **Save**. In the *Save* dialog box, click **Yes** to All>OK. Update the data format if prompted.
6. Close the file.

Task 4: Solve duplicate files problem.

1. Switch to Autodesk Autoloader. Click **Scan**. If you cannot restart the scan, click **Back** and **Next** again to return to the *Data Scan & Report* page. Click **Scan** to rescan the files. The Winch.iam file is now resolved without errors.

   The scan reports that two different 51013.ipt files are referenced in the examined files, as shown in Figure 4–38.

File Name	Source Folder / Last Known	Status
51013.ipt	C:\Vault Basic Admin Training\Chapter4\Winch	Duplicates found
51013.ipt	C:\Vault Basic Admin Training\Chapter4\Winch\Drum	Duplicates found

Figure 4–38

2. Under *File Name*, click the first **51013.ipt** row. In the details pane at the bottom of the dialog box, click the *Duplicate Files* tab. The location of each 51013.ipt file is displayed, as shown in Figure 4–39.

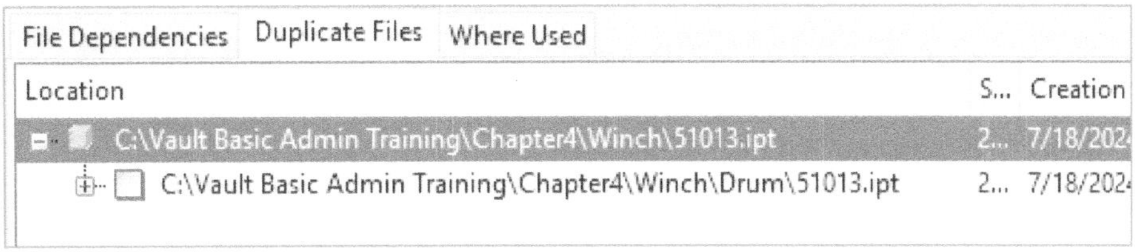

Figure 4–39

3. Switch to Autodesk Inventor. Open ***...\Winch\Frame.iam***.
4. In the browser, select **51013:3**. In the *Assemble* tab>*Component* panel in the ribbon, select **Replace>Replace All**, as shown in Figure 4–40.

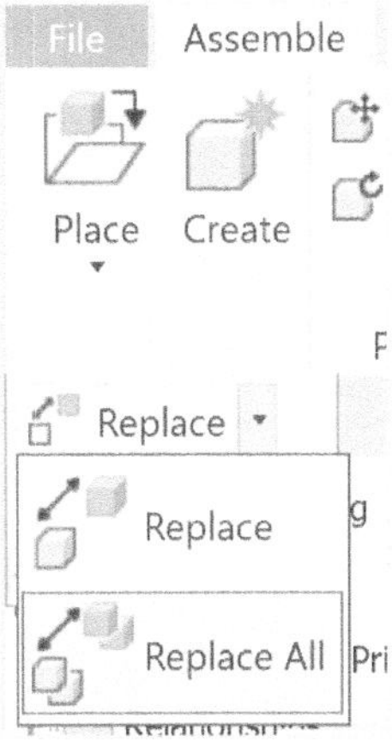

Figure 4–40

5. In the *Place Component* dialog box, browse to the *Drum* folder. Select **51013.ipt** and click **Open**.
6. Save the file. Close Frame.iam. Update the data format if prompted.
   - The original ...\Winch\51013.ipt file is no longer referenced in the assembly.
7. In File Explorer, browse to the *C:\Vault Basic Admin Training\Chapter4\Winch* folder. Delete **51013.ipt**.
8. Switch to Autodesk Autoloader. Scan the files again. All files are opened and resolved successfully. No duplicate files are found.

Task 5: Complete the upload.

1. Click **Next**. Log in to the vault.
   - For *User Name*, enter **Administrator**.
   - Leave the *Password* blank.
   - For *Vault*, select **UploadVault**.
   - Click **OK**.
2. On the *Map Vault Folders* page, note that the project file's search paths are listed on the left and the new vault folders are on the right. Note that three new folders are created below the root folder in the vault.
3. Under *Resultant Vault View*, select the *Designs* folder. Click **Rename**. In the *Rename Folder* dialog box, enter **Products**, as shown in Figure 4–41. Click **OK** to rename the vault folder.

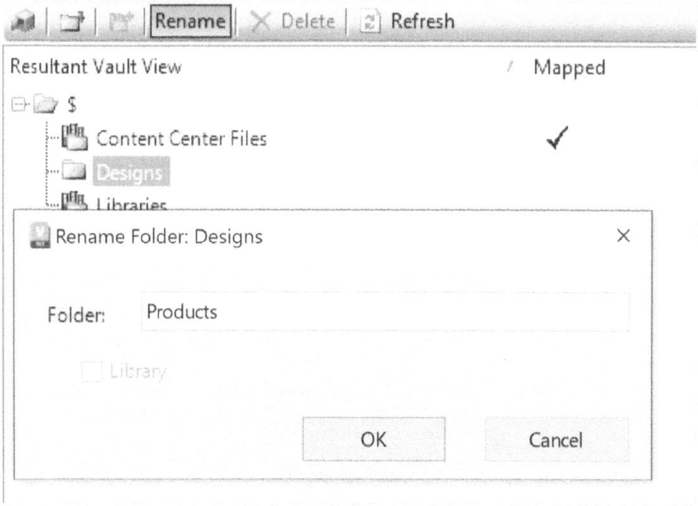

Figure 4–41

4. Under *Folder to Check In*, double-click on **Chapter4**.

5. In the *Browse Vault For Folder* dialog box, select the *Products* folder. Ensure that the **Direct Mapping** checkbox is not checked, as shown in Figure 4–42.

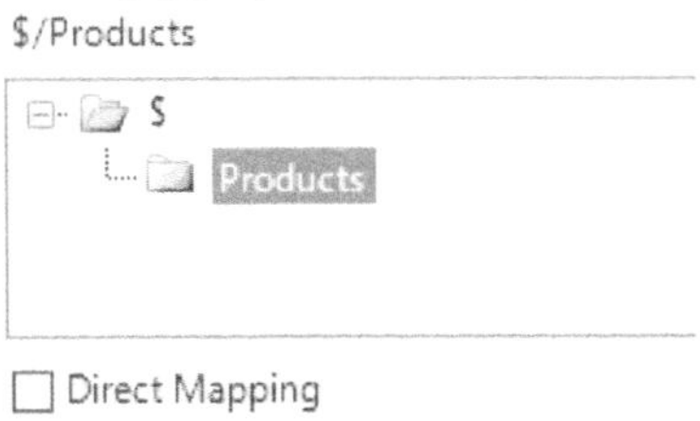

Figure 4–42

6. Click **OK**. The workspace folder from the project file is mapped to the new folder in the vault, as shown in Figure 4–43.

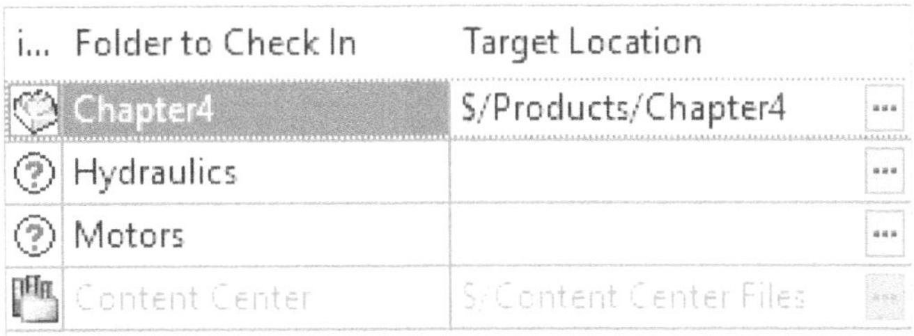

Figure 4–43

7. Under *Folder to Check In*, double-click on **Hydraulics**. In the *Browse Vault For Folder* dialog box, click **Products**. Click **New Folder**.
8. In the *Create Folder* dialog box, enter **Common Components**. Click **OK**.
9. In the *Browse Vault for Folder* dialog box, click **Common Components**. Click **OK**. A *Hydraulics* subfolder is created automatically, as shown in Figure 4–44.

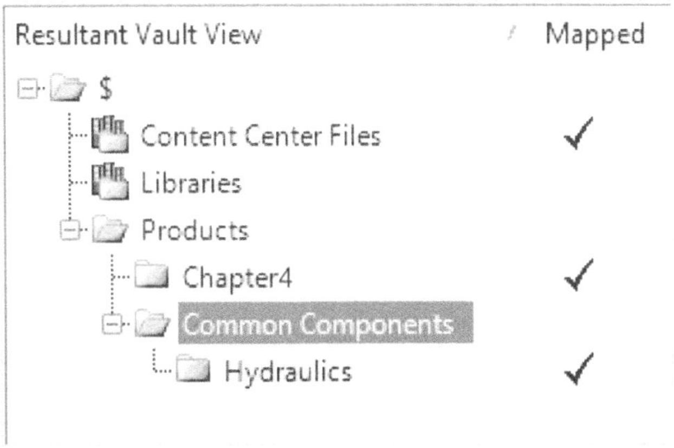

Figure 4–44

10. Under *Folder to Check In*, double-click on **Motors**. In the *Browse Vault For Folder* dialog box, click **Common Components**. Click **OK**. A *Motors* subfolder is created automatically, as shown in Figure 4–45.

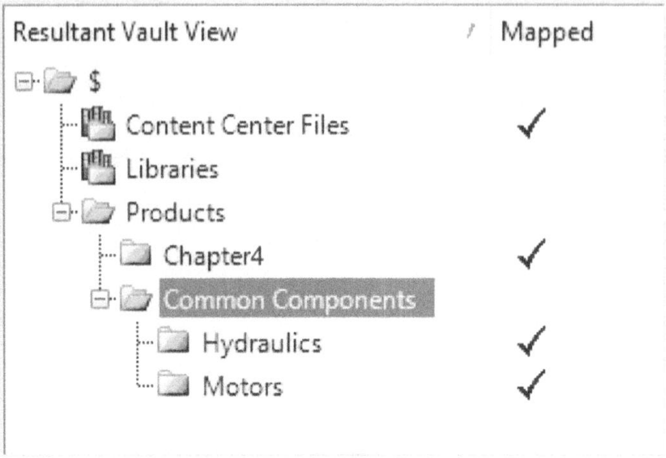

Figure 4–45

11. Click **Next**.
12. On the *Copy & File Redirection Progress* page, wait until the operation is complete. Click **Next**.
13. On the *Specify Data Subsets* page, examine the resulting structure of files in the vault, as shown in Figure 4–46.

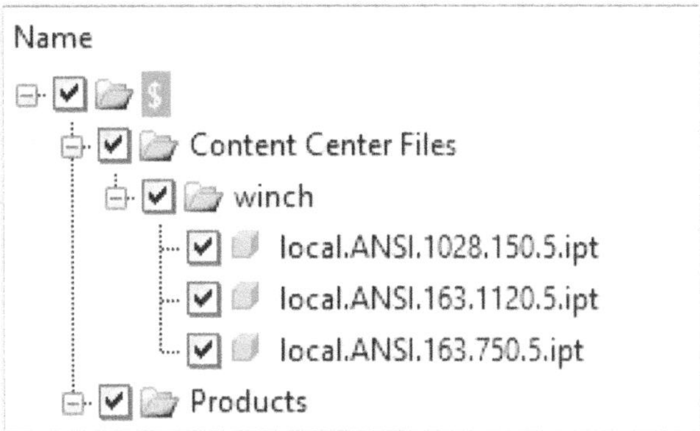

Figure 4–46

14. Click **Upload**.
15. On the *Autoloader Progress and Report* page, make note of the report location and file name.
16. Click **Done**.

Task 6: Review the results.

1. Start Autodesk Vault.
    - For *User Name*, enter **Administrator**.
    - Leave the *Password* blank.
    - For *Vault*, select **UploadVault**.
    - Click **OK**.
2. In the root folder of the vault, *Vault Explorer ($)*, note that there is a project file named **Designs.ipj**.
3. View the contents of the other folders, as shown in Figure 4–47.

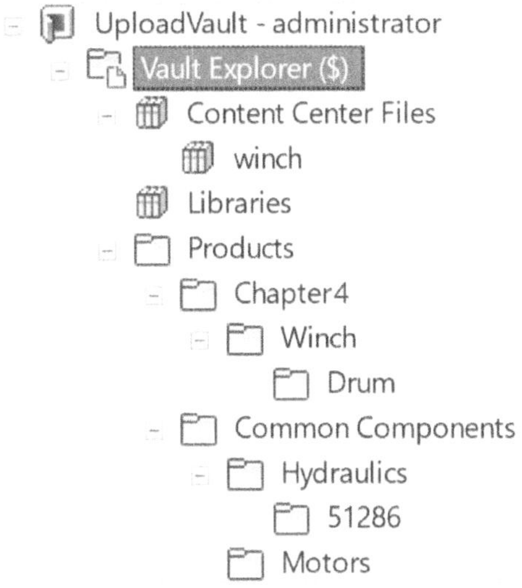

Figure 4–47

4. Exit the Autodesk Vault Client.

End of practice

Chapter 5

Managing Vault

As a Vault administrator, you are responsible for maintaining vaults and files, including managing user accounts and managing the integrity and performance of the vaults.

Learning Objectives

- Describe the components of an Autodesk® Vault installation.
- Create a new vault.
- Enable unique file names, set working folders, and enable visualization files.
- Describe how groups and roles are used to control user access.
- Create users and groups, assign roles, and grant access to vaults.
- Manage file properties (including renaming properties and removing properties from a vault).
- Map user-defined properties to indexed file properties.
- Add AutoCAD block attributes to a vault as properties.
- Re-index vault databases to reflect property changes.
- Back up and restore vaults.
- Maintain a vault.

5.1 Setting Up Vault

In this section, you will learn about the components of the vault server, typical Vault installation methods, how to create a vault, and how to set up the Vault environment.

Components of Autodesk Vault

When you install Autodesk Vault, several software applications and their associated data files are stored on the vault server. You should understand the purpose of each application and where each component is installed in order to correctly manage Vault.

Autodesk Vault consists of a server and one or more clients that access data on the server. The server manages the vault file store, where the files you add to the vault are stored. The server also manages the vault databases where the property data from the files and the files' relationships are stored. The components of Autodesk Vault are shown in Figure 5–1.

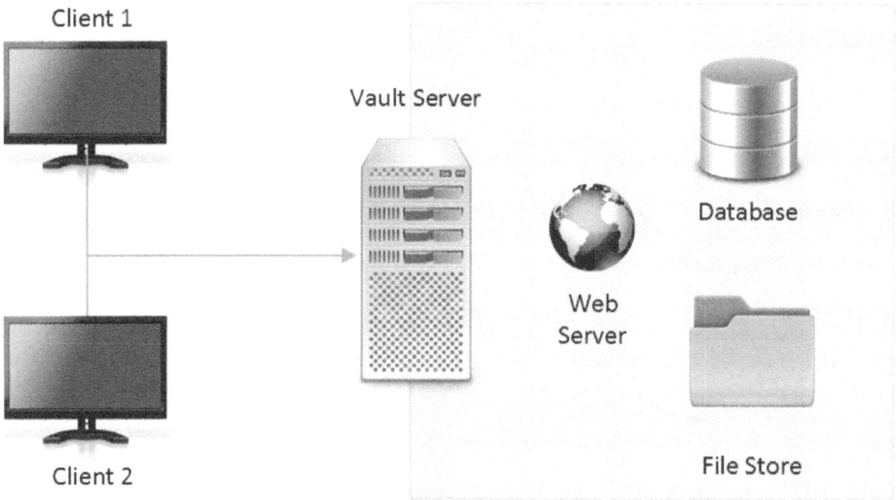

Figure 5–1

The vault clients are installed on each user's computer and are used to view, extract, and add files and data from the vault. The clients communicate to the vault server through XML-based web services using standard HTTP protocol.

About the Vault Server Software

The Autodesk Vault server consists of the hardware and software that receives transaction requests from clients, processes those transactions, and returns data back to the clients. The software on the Vault server consists of three applications working together to manage the Vault databases and file stores, as shown in Figure 5–2.

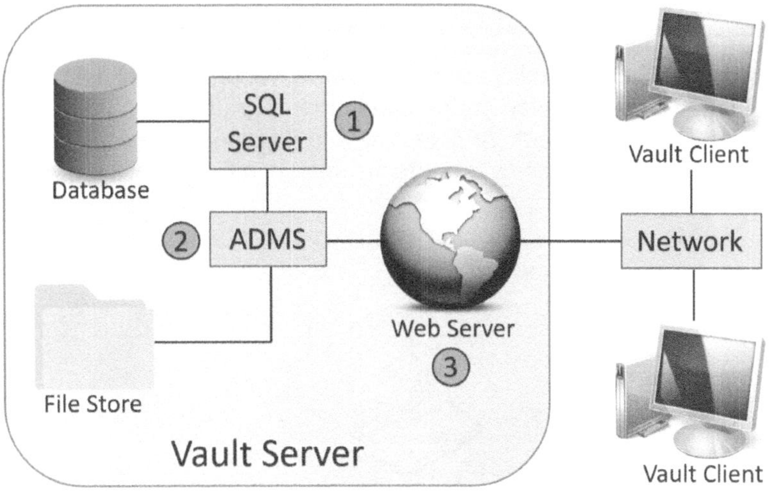

Figure 5–2

Components of the Vault server:

1. The database server manages the databases and handles requests for data. By default, Microsoft SQL Server Express, a free, but limited, version of Microsoft SQL Server is installed. Microsoft SQL Server Express has a limit on the size of the databases. The limitations outside the metadata limit are one processor and concurrent users might be limited by the operating system. The full version of SQL Server supports multiple processors and many concurrent users, and it has no limit on the database size. If you install Microsoft SQL Server before you install Vault, you can use it instead of Microsoft SQL Server Express. In a true production environment, SQL Express is not ideal from a performance perspective.
2. Autodesk Data Management Server (ADMS) manages all requests from clients, such as receiving client requests, sending requests to the database server, packaging and returning data back to the clients, and storing and retrieving files from the file store.
3. The web server manages web requests and responses between vault clients and the vault server. Microsoft Internet Information Services (IIS) is required for the installation of Vault on a stand-alone workstation or on a server that more than one user accesses. You must install IIS before you install Autodesk Data Management Server.

Setup Scenarios

You must make several decisions before you install Autodesk Vault. The software and hardware you use and how you configure your network are dependent on the number of users, the size of the databases, the size of the file store, and the expected network activity. The typical scenarios outlined below are general guides. Before you install Autodesk Vault, review the Autodesk Vault installation documentation located at https://help.autodesk.com/.

Single-User Setup

To use Vault in a single-user, single-workstation environment where you do not need to share data with other users, you can install Vault on the same workstation as the CAD application. All components required will be installed during installation of Autodesk Vault. This is typical of a training installation. The Vault Client, Vault Server, and CAD application software are installed on the same workstation in a single-user setup, as shown in Figure 5–3.

Figure 5–3

Multi-User Setup

When two or more users need to share design data, the Vault must be installed on a computer that is on a network and is accessible to the design team.

For smaller teams, you can use either one of the design team's workstations, a dedicated workstation, or a dedicated server. Install Vault on either a Windows server operating system or a Windows desktop operating system. You must install Microsoft Internet Information Services (IIS) before you install Vault because more than one user will be accessing the vault. You can start with Microsoft SQL Server Express and then upgrade to Microsoft SQL Server when your vault databases approach the size limit.

For larger teams, consider using a dedicated server running a Windows server operating system. For more than 10 users, you should install Microsoft SQL Server.

Creating Vaults

Most Vault installations use just one vault for their master design data, because data and mappings cannot be shared across vaults. However, you might want to create additional vaults for training so that users can become familiar with Vault procedures without affecting the main vault. You can also use more than one vault to isolate design data. For example, a contractor might want to isolate data from different clients who each have separate libraries and shared content.

After you create a new vault, you need to grant permissions to existing users. If you are creating the vault for training, consider creating different user accounts for training that are granted access to just the training vault so that users do not accidentally add data to the wrong vault.

How To: Create a Vault

The following steps describe how to create a vault.

1. Start the Autodesk Data Management Server (ADMS) Console. Expand the node in the left pane to reveal Vaults. Click **Vaults**. Select **Actions>Create**.
2. Enter a name for the vault, as shown in Figure 5–4. Accept the default file store location or specify a location.

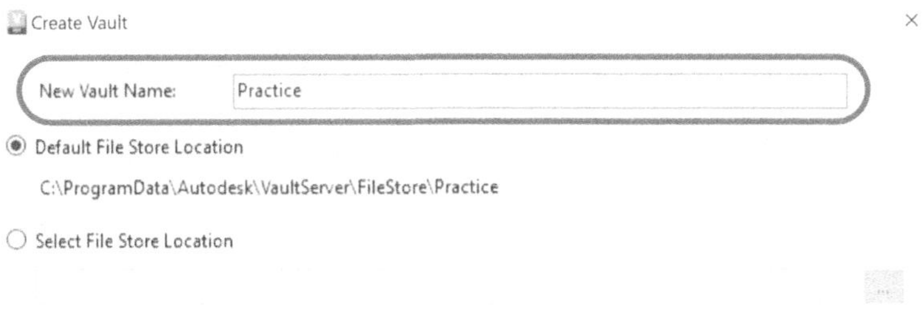

Figure 5–4

3. Expand the **Vaults** node to reveal the new vault and select it. Review the new vault's properties, as shown in Figure 5–5.

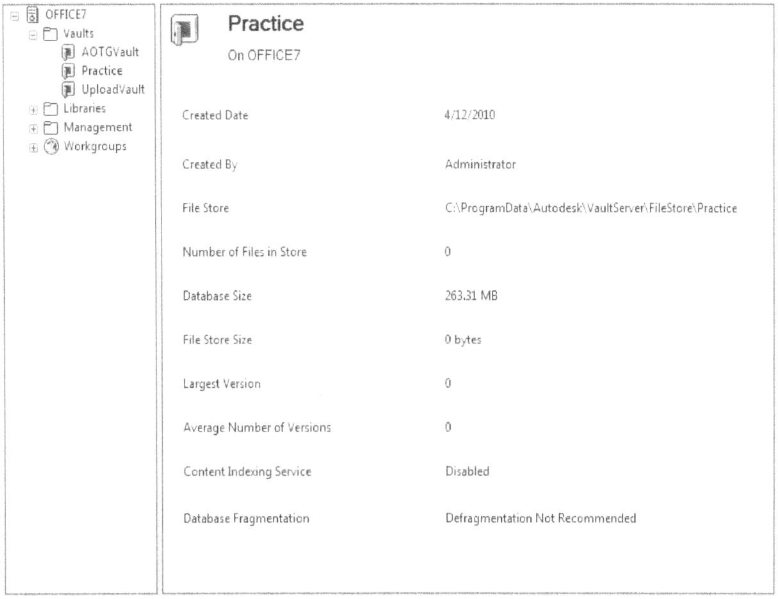

Figure 5–5

4. To grant users access to the vault, select **Tools>Administration**, then in the *Global Settings* dialog box, select **Manage Access...**, as shown in Figure 5–6.

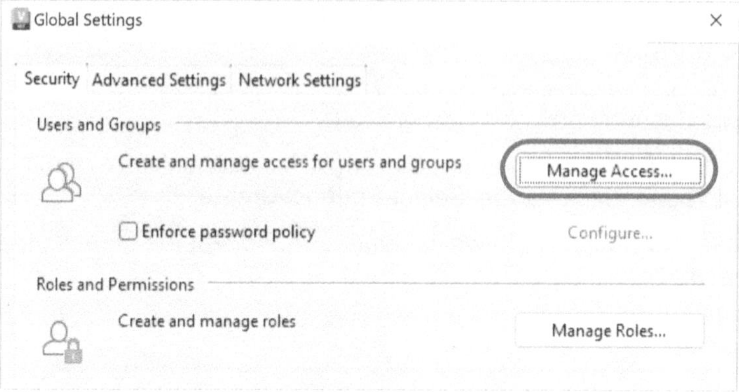

Figure 5–6

5. In the *User and Group Management* dialog box, use the *Users* and *Groups* tabs, as shown in Figure 5–7, to add users and groups to the vault.

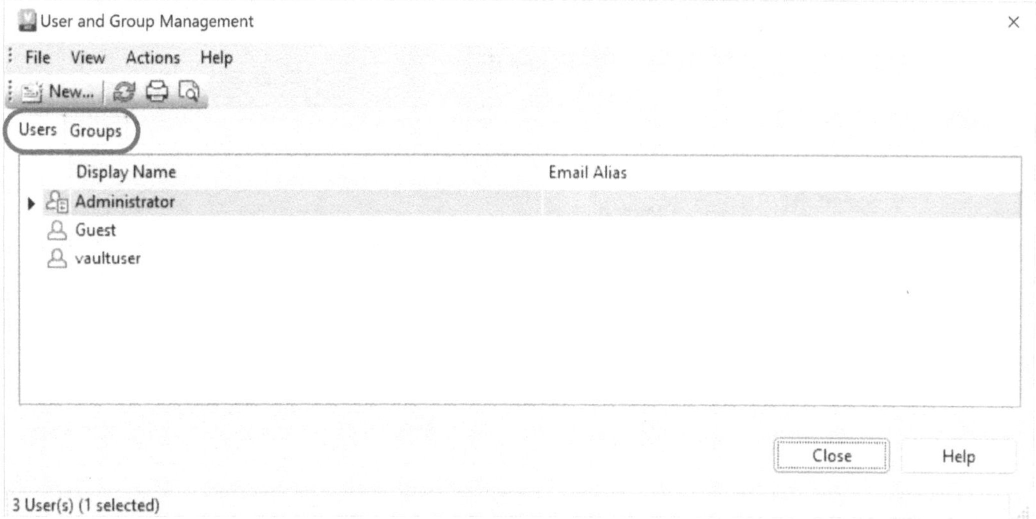

Figure 5–7

Setting the Environment

When you create a new vault, you must decide whether to enforce unique file names and to define a working folder for all users or enable users to define their own working folders, and whether or not to enable or disable automatic visualization file attachments.

Enforcing Unique File Names

When unique file names are enforced, files in the vault must each have a unique, identifying name. This is a highly recommended best practice.

This rule is enforced when files are added to the vault, renamed in the vault, or restored to the vault. If unique file names are going to be enforced, it is recommended that you set this option before any files are added to the vault, although it can be toggled on at any time.

If unique file names are enforced, and you want to add a project that contains files with names that match files in the vault, you can temporarily disable unique file names. After you add the project to the vault, locate the duplicate file names and then rename the duplicate files. When you have finished renaming the files, enforce unique file names again.

Disabling the Checking In of Design Files in Vault

CAD files should always be added to the vault using the Vault add-in in the CAD application so that file relationships are preserved. By default, users are prevented from adding CAD files using Autodesk Vault Client. If you want to enable users to add CAD files using Vault, CAD files that have relationships to other files will not maintain those relationships in the vault.

Defining a Working Folder and Autodesk Inventor Project File

A default working folder for all new vaults is predefined as *My Documents\Vault*, allowing users to immediately begin working with a vault. The default working folder location can be changed by a user to another location. The vault administrator can also enforce a working folder for all users so that users cannot define their own working folder, eliminating the need for users to create a working folder and making a consistent location for vault files on user workstations.

The enforced working folder path can be the following:

- Network path: \\ *designco\users\pdollan*
- Local path: *C:\users\bdunn*
- Path containing a system variable for a directory: \\ *designco\users\%username%*
- Path beginning with My Documents: *My Documents\Vault*

When the working folder is enforced, any previous working folder settings are replaced with the new path. If an enforced working folder location cannot be applied to a user's settings, the previous user-defined location is used. If there is no previous user-defined location, the default location *My Documents\Vault* is used.

The default Autodesk Inventor project file can be set by a user unless the vault administrator enforces a consistent project file for all users. Enforcing a consistent project file for all users can help ensure successful file resolutions when renaming files, for example.

Visualization Options

Vault uses visualization files (typically .DWF and .DWFx) to display CAD files in the vault. By default, visualization files are automatically created and attached to the corresponding CAD file when you check files in to the vault. Automatic creation can be disabled if you want to reduce the size of the vault or if you do not plan to use visualization files.

Visualization files can also be generated and stored in a folder outside of the vault so that other users who do not have access to the vault can see your designs. As an administrator, you can specify a default folder location for the published files.

If you enable the automatic creation of visualization files, as shown in Figure 5–8, users are not forced to create visualization files each time they check in or add a file. Enabling creation enables the settings in the add-ins so that users can toggle creation on or off. If you disable automatic creation, the settings in the add-in are disabled so that users cannot create visualization files.

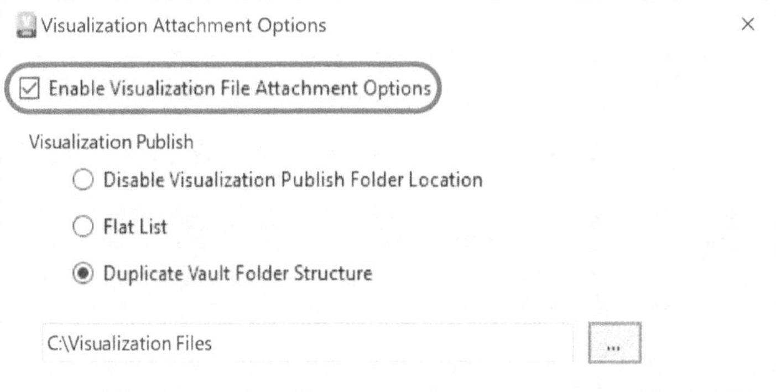

Figure 5–8

Visualization Publishing Options

A variety of options are available for you to specify what gets published, select the type of visualization file, and fine-tune the output of visualization files. The settings are available on an application basis, as shown in Figure 5–9. For example, you can specify different settings for AutoCAD® files, 2D Inventor files, and 3D Inventor files for various releases in the case of Inventor.

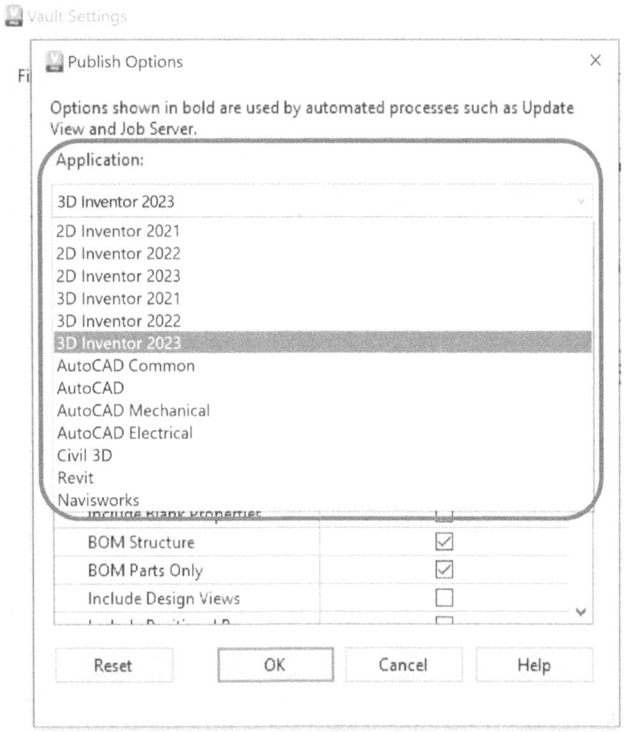

Figure 5–9

Visualization Commands

The visualization commands options (shown in Figure 5–10) enable you to specify which commands break the link between a data file in the vault and its corresponding visualization file. When an operation causes a file to be versioned forward, the link to the visualization file is removed, preventing an out-of-date visualization file from being attached to the data file.

If a command is unchecked, then when that command is performed, the *Visualization Compliance* property for the data file is set to **Not Synchronized** to indicate that the visualization file attached to the data file is out of date and might not accurately represent the contents of the data file. When the data file is viewed, you are warned that the visualization file is not synchronized. You can either update the visualization file or manually verify that the visualization file is correct. When a visualization file is verified, the *Visualization Compliance* property for the data file is set to **User Verified**.

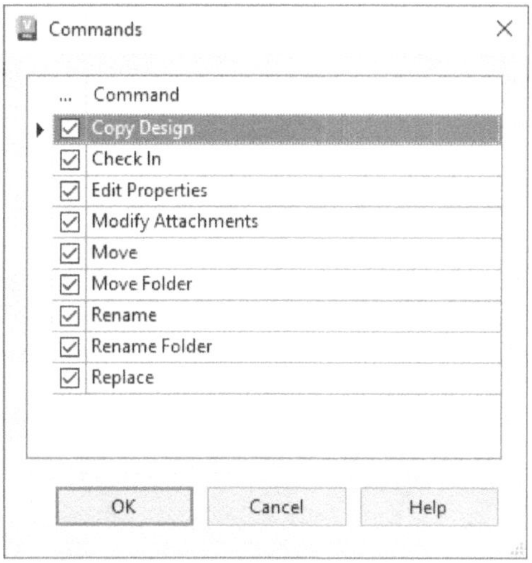

Figure 5–10

How To: Set the Vault Environment

The following steps describe how to enforce unique file names, set the working folder, and configure visualization files.

1. Log in to Autodesk Vault as an administrator.

2. Select **Tools>Administration>Vault Settings**, as shown in Figure 5–11.

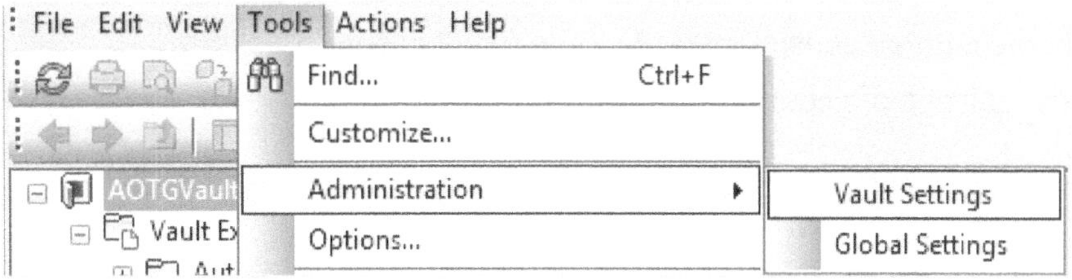

Figure 5–11

3. The *Vault Settings* dialog box is displayed.
4. To enforce unique file names, on the *Files* tab, select **Define**. In the *File Name Options* dialog box, select the **Enforce unique file name** checkbox, as shown in Figure 5–12.

Figure 5–12

5. To enforce a working folder for all users, in the *Vault Settings* dialog box, select **Define** under *Working Folder*. In the *Working Folder Options* dialog box (shown in Figure 5–13), do the following:
   - Select the **Enforce consistent working folder for all clients** checkbox.
   - Enter or select a folder name.

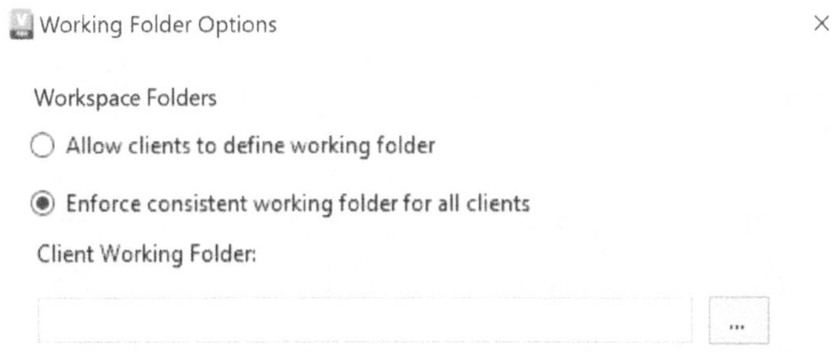

Figure 5–13

6. To enforce a consistent project file for all users, in the *Working Folder Options* dialog box (shown in Figure 5–14), do the following:
   - Select the **Enforce consistent project file for all clients** checkbox.
   - Enter or select a project file.

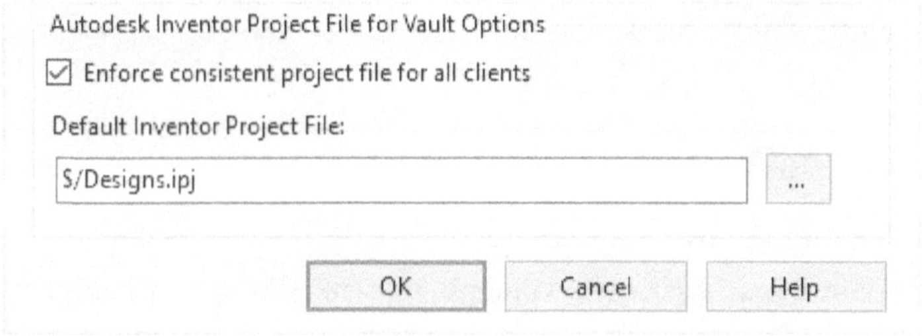

Figure 5–14

7. To set visualization options, click the *Visualization* tab in the *Vault Settings* dialog box, as shown in Figure 5–15.

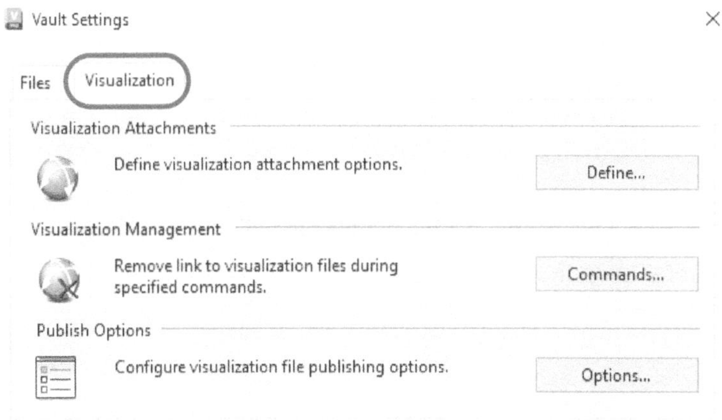

Figure 5–15

8. To set visualization file attachment options:
   - Under *Visualization Attachments*, click **Define**.
   - In the *Visualization Attachment Options* dialog box, select **Enable Visualization File Attachment Options** to enable or disable the attachment options in Vault add-ins.

- To publish visualization files to a location outside of the vault, under *Visualization Publish*, select **Flat List** or **Duplication Vault Folder Structure**, as shown in Figure 5–16. Browse to a folder or enter a folder name, if appropriate.

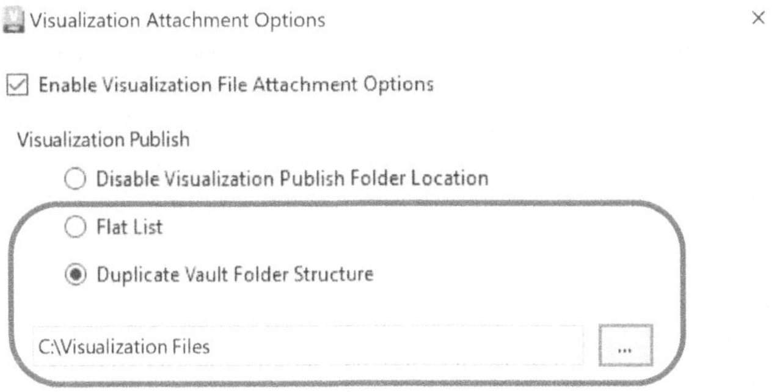

Figure 5–16

9. To remove the link between a visualization file and its underlying file when a specified command is executed, do the following:
   - In the *Vault Settings* dialog box, on the *Visualization* tab, under *Visualization Management*, click **Commands**.
   - In the *Commands* dialog box (shown in Figure 5–17), select which commands should cause the link to be removed.

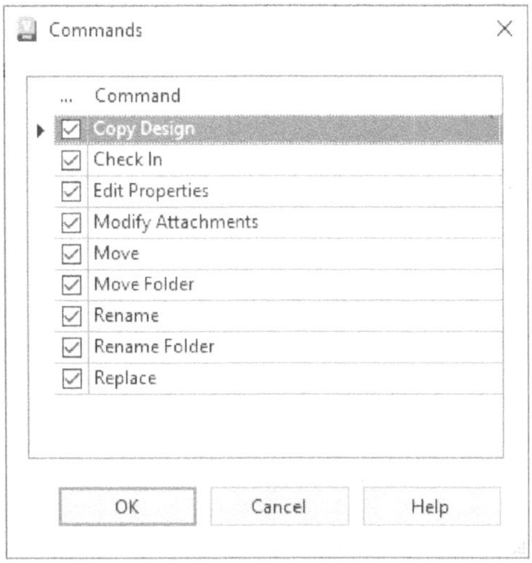

Figure 5–17

10. To specify the visualization file format, select what is included in visualization files and tune visualization file settings:
    - In the *Vault Settings* dialog box, on the *Visualization* tab, under *Publish Options*, click **Options** to display the *Publish Options* dialog box (shown in Figure 5–18).
    - Select the *Application* to which the visualization settings will apply.
    - Select the appropriate settings.
    - Repeat for all of the applications you are using.

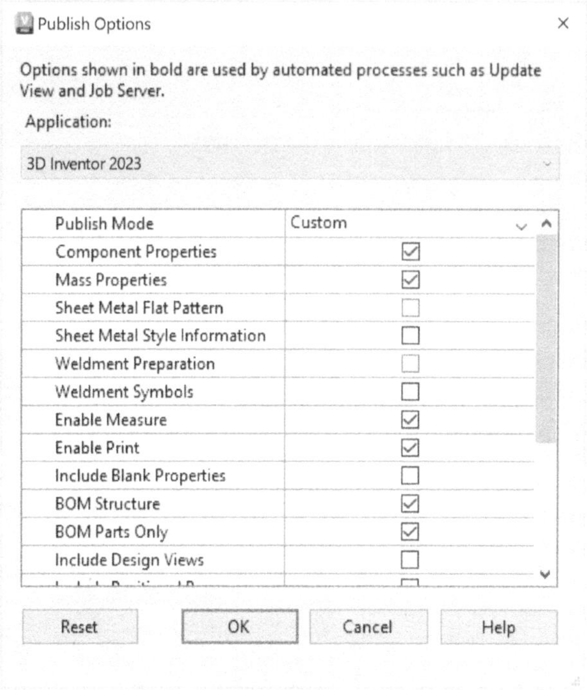

Figure 5–18

Practice 5a
Create and Set Up a Vault

Practice Objectives

- Create a vault.
- Review vault settings and set a common working folder.
- Add a file to the vault.

In this practice, you will create a vault, review vault settings, and set a common working folder. You will then add a file to the vault and examine both the vault databases and vault file store. The completed practice is shown in Figure 5–19.

Figure 5–19

1. Start the Autodesk Data Management Server (ADMS) Console. Log in as **Administrator** and leave the password blank.
2. In the list of vaults, expand the *Vaults* folder. View the existing vaults.
3. Right-click on the *Vaults* folder and select **Create**, as shown in Figure 5–20.

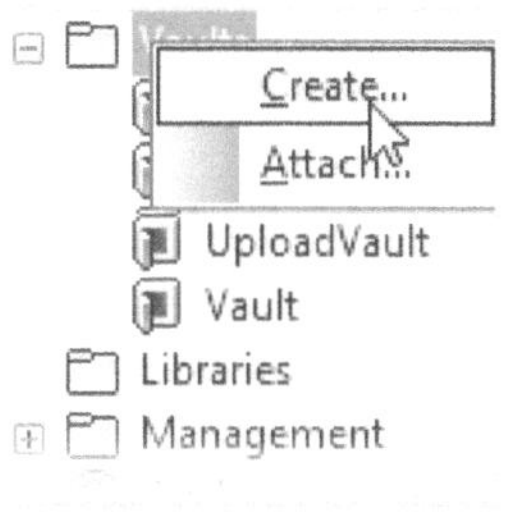

Figure 5–20

4. Enter **TestVault** for the new vault name. Review the default file store location. Click **OK**.

5. When the message box is displayed to indicate that the vault was successfully created, click **OK** to close the message box.
6. In the list of vaults, select **TestVault**. Review the database size and the file store location, as shown in Figure 5–21.

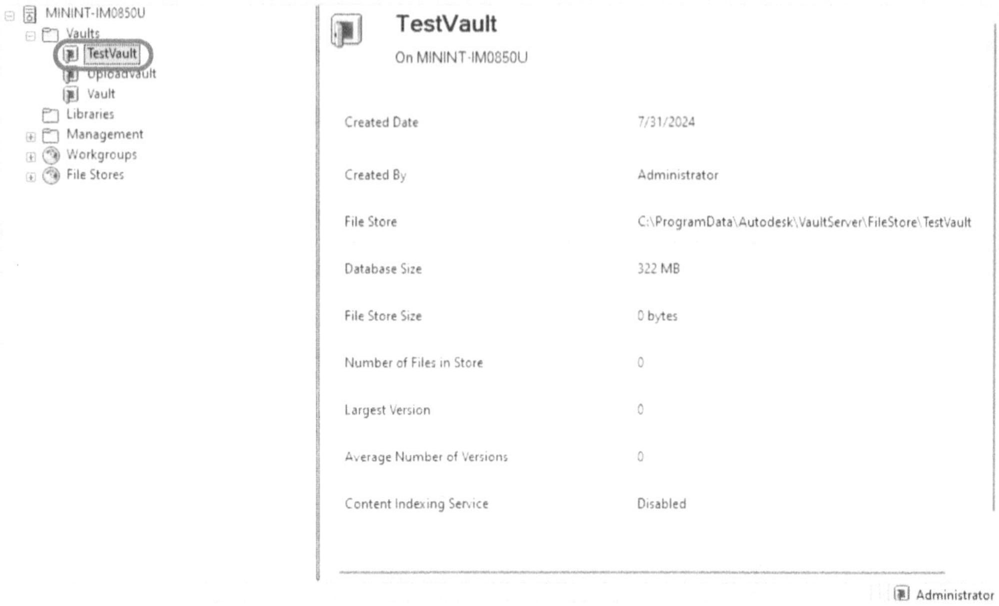

Figure 5–21

7. Start Autodesk Vault. Log in as **Administrator** to **TestVault**, as shown in Figure 5–22. Leave the password blank. If you were already logged in to Autodesk Vault, log out and then log back in.

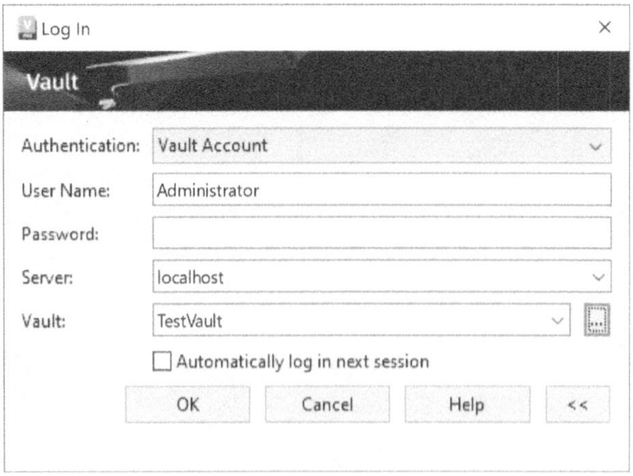

Figure 5–22

8. Select **Tools>Administration>Vault Settings**.
9. In the *Vault Settings* dialog box, on the *Files* tab, under *File Options*, select **Define**.
10. In the *File Name Options* dialog box, select the **Enforce unique file name** checkbox to toggle it on, as shown in Figure 5–23, and click **OK**.

Figure 5–23

11. In the *Vault Settings* dialog box, under *Working Folder*, click **Define**.
12. In the *Working Folder Options* dialog box, click **Enforce consistent working folder for all clients**. For *Client Working Folder*, click [...]. Create the folder **TestVault** under *C:\Users\Public* so that the *Client Working Folder* is *C:\Users\Public\TestVault*, as shown in Figure 5–24.

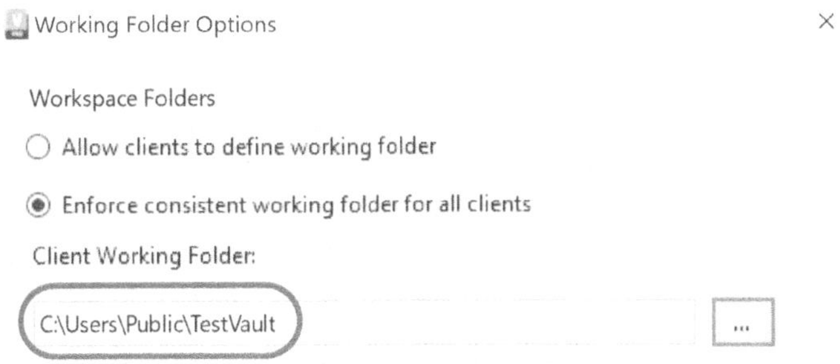

Figure 5–24

13. Click **OK** to close the *Working Folder Options* dialog box.
14. In the *Vault Settings* dialog box, select the *Visualization* tab. Under *Visualization Attachments*, click **Define**.
15. In the *Visualization Attachment Options* dialog box, select **Disable Visualization Publish Folder Location**, as shown in Figure 5–25, if not already selected. Click **OK**.

Figure 5–25

16. In the *Vault Settings* dialog box, under *Visualization Management*, click **Commands**. In the *Commands* dialog box, confirm that all checkboxes are selected, as shown in Figure 5–26, and click **OK**.

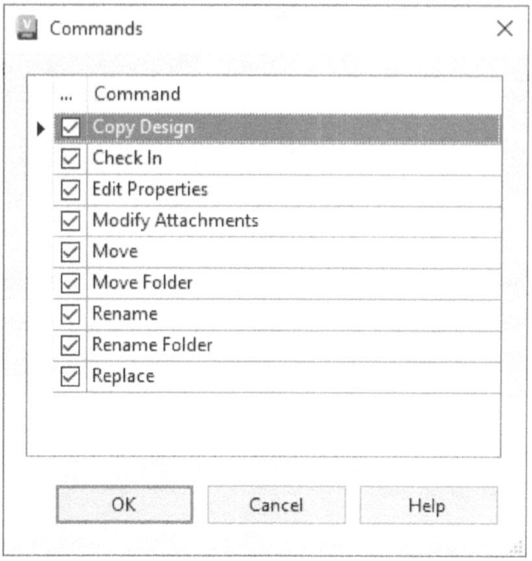

Figure 5–26

17. In the *Vault Settings* dialog box, under *Publish Options*, click **Options**. In the *Publish Options* dialog box, under *Application*, select **3D Inventor 2025**. Select the **Include Positional Reps** checkbox, as shown in Figure 5–27, to include positional reps in .DWF files. Click **OK**.

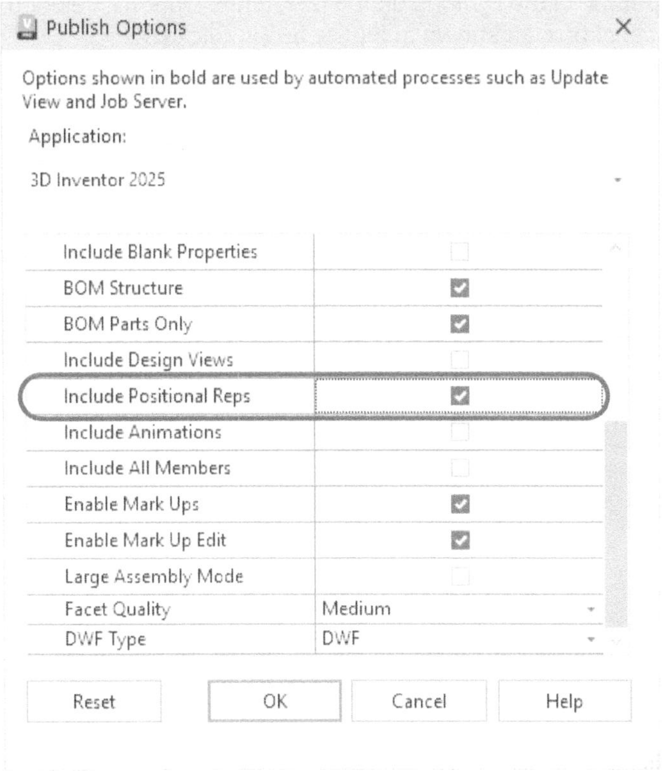

Figure 5–27

18. Click **Close** to dismiss the *Vault Settings* dialog box.
19. Select **Tools>Administration>Global Settings** to display the *Global Settings* dialog box.
20. Under the *Users and Groups* section, click **Manage Access...**. Note that you can access the same *User and Group Management* dialog box as you did from the ADMS Console.
21. Close the *User and Group Management* dialog box and then close the *Global Settings* dialog box.

22. Select **Tools>Options**. In the *Options* dialog box, under *Options*, select the **Show working folder location** checkbox, as shown in Figure 5–28. Click **OK**.

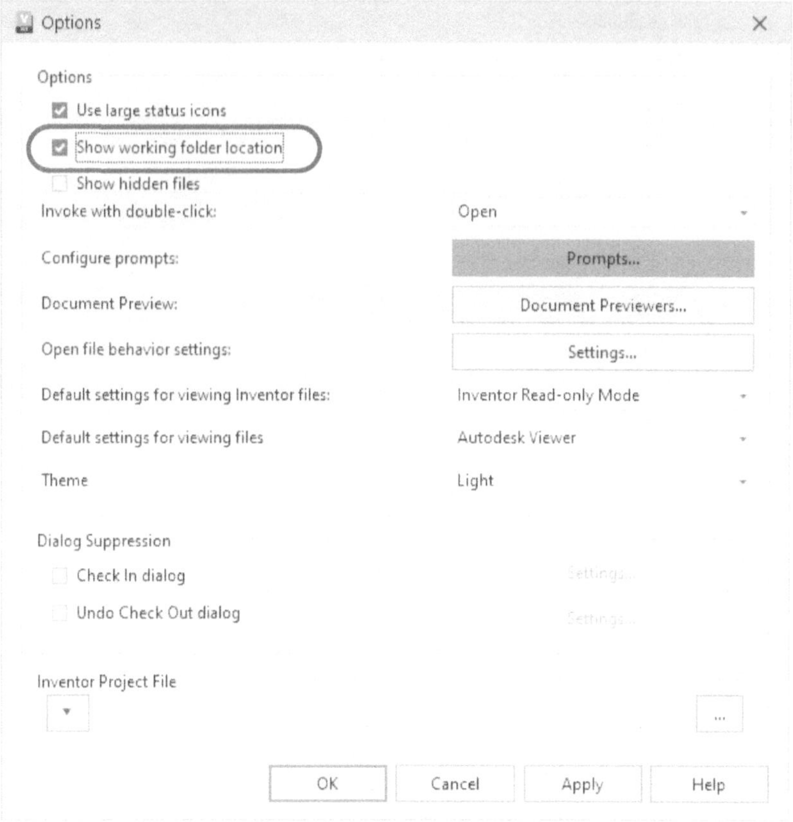

Figure 5–28

23. Select **File>Log Out**. Log in again as **Administrator**.
24. Click **OK** to close the *Enforce Working Folder* dialog box (shown in Figure 5–29).

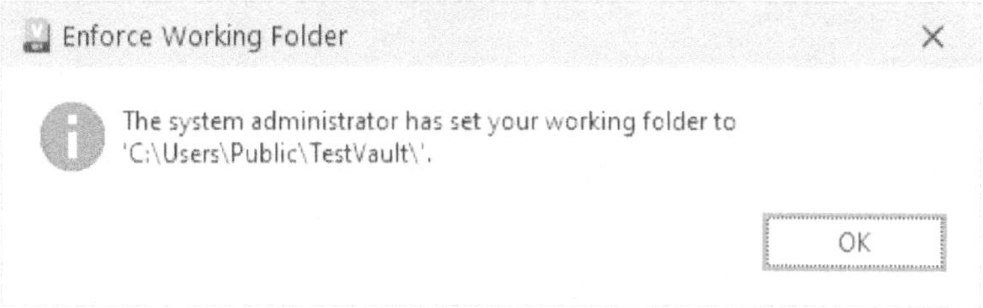

Figure 5–29

25. Confirm that the working folder is displayed in the title bar, as shown in Figure 5–30.

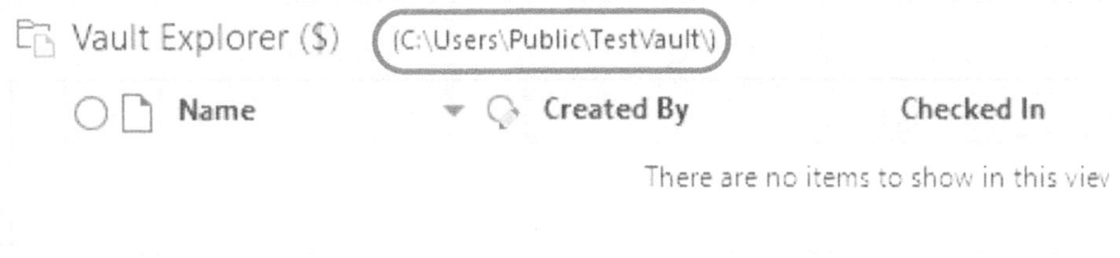

Figure 5–30

26. Add a non-CAD file to the vault using any of the methods you have learned in previous practices. Use a simple file such as a Microsoft Office document or text document.

Tip: Drag the file into the vault. Due to vaulting restrictions, you will not be able to drag a CAD file into the vault.

27. In Windows File Explorer, navigate to the file store for TestVault and continually expand the folders until you locate the file that you added, as shown in Figure 5–31. Note that the file was renamed but the file is stored in its native format.

Tip: The location of the file store is displayed on the property page in the ADMS Console.

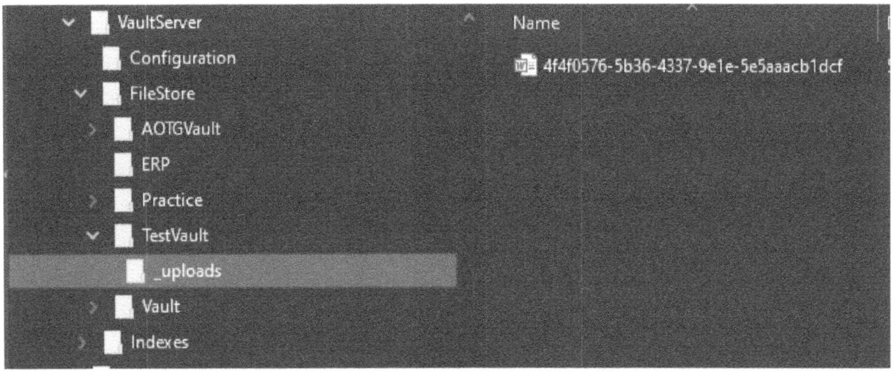

Figure 5–31

Note: Do not rename, delete, move, or change files in the file store.

28. Close both Autodesk Vault and the ADMS Console.

End of practice

5.2 Managing Users and Access

A user must have an account before logging in to a vault. The administrator is responsible for creating new user accounts, creating groups of users, assigning roles to users or groups, and granting access to vaults.

Hint: Windows Authentication

In this section, you employ the user authentication that is built in to Autodesk Data Management Server. If you use Vault Professional, you can also use Windows authentication to manage user access. See Help for more information.

Creating Users and Groups

A user account is required before a user can log in and access vault data. The administrator can specify which vaults a user can access and the user's permissions. User permissions can be controlled for individual users or for groups of users.

The *Global Settings* dialog box, where you access tools to manage users and groups, is shown in Figure 5–32.

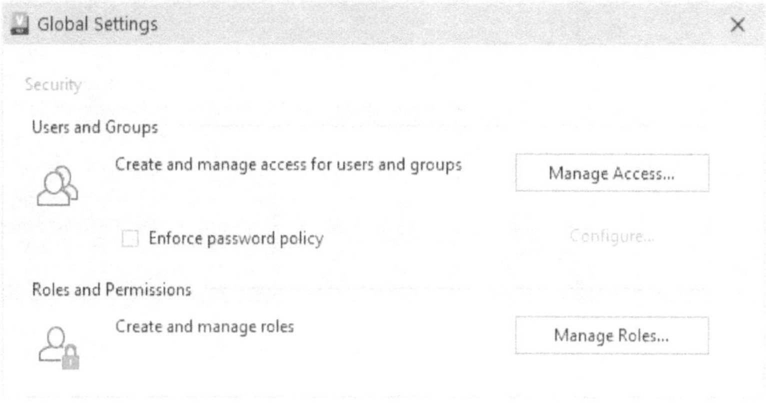

Figure 5–32

About User Accounts

To access a vault and its associated data, a user must have an account with the appropriate access permissions. As an administrator, you can add users, group users together for easy management, define roles, and assign access permissions. You should create unique user accounts for each user of Vault to ensure that Vault transactions are secure and can be tracked.

Note: *In Vault, permissions control the access at the vault level. If you assign a user or group to a vault, the permissions apply to all files and folders in the vault.*

About User Roles

You assign access permission to vaults by assigning one or more predefined roles to users or to groups of users. The permissions for that role apply to all files and folders in the vaults to which the user or group is assigned.

You can also create your own custom roles. You can do this by creating a new role, editing a role, or copying an existing role to then edit. For example, you can copy the Document Editor Level 2 role and then remove the Folder Create permission so that users cannot create their own folders within the vault.

You can assign users to several predefined roles. Some roles apply to users of Autodesk Vault and some apply to the Autodesk Inventor Content Center, as listed in the following table. Privileges are additive, so a user assigned multiple roles has all the privileges of the assigned roles.

Role	Permissions
Document Consumer	• Read folders and files • Read labels • Set Vault get options • Edit the user profile
Document Editor (Level 1)	Includes all the permissions of a Document Consumer plus: • Check out, create, and add files • Create folders • Create labels • Override file status • Modify visualization attachments
Document Editor (Level 2)	Includes all the permissions of a Document Editor (Level 1) plus: • Move, rename, and delete files • Rename and delete folders • Delete labels
Content Center Editor	Includes all the permissions of a Document Editor (Level 2) plus: • Add and delete categories • Publish content
Content Center Administrator	All tasks of the Content Center Editor plus: • Manage libraries
Administrator	All tasks listed above plus: • Manage users, vaults, and libraries • Log in to the ADMS Console

About Groups

Individual users have roles and permissions assigned to them that define what actions they can take and to which vaults they have access. To manage multiple users efficiently, you can create groups of users and assign roles and permissions to the group. As a member of a group, a user has all the permissions and roles assigned to the group.

Groups can be composed of users or other groups. Groups can be disabled, thereby toggling off all permissions assigned to the group.

Guidelines for Managing Users and Groups

Follow these guidelines to manage groups efficiently:

- **Assign most permissions at group level:** If you use groups, consider assigning most permissions at the group level and not for each individual user. For example, to assign most users the Document Editor (Level 1) role, create a group, add the users, and assign the group the Document Editor (Level 1) role. If one or two users also need to be Content Center Editors, either create another group for those users or assign the permissions at the user level. You will be able to manage users more easily if you are consistent with the way that you assign permissions.
- **Disable permissions at the group level:** If a group is no longer required or you want to stop access for all of the users that belong to just that group, you can disable the group, removing permissions assigned to the group.

How To: Add a New User

The following steps describe how to add a new user and assign the user to a group.

1. In Autodesk Vault, select the **Tools>Administration>Global Settings** or in the ADMS Console, click **Tools>Administration**. For access through ADMS, click the *Security* tab if not already displayed (there is only one tab when accessing through Vault).

   Note: *You can access the user management tools through either the ADMS Console or Autodesk Vault. By administering users through Autodesk Vault, you can manage users from any computer on which Autodesk Vault is installed rather than through the ADMS Console, which runs only on the Vault server.*

2. In the *Global Settings* dialog box, under *Users and Groups*, click **Manage Access...**, as shown in Figure 5–33.

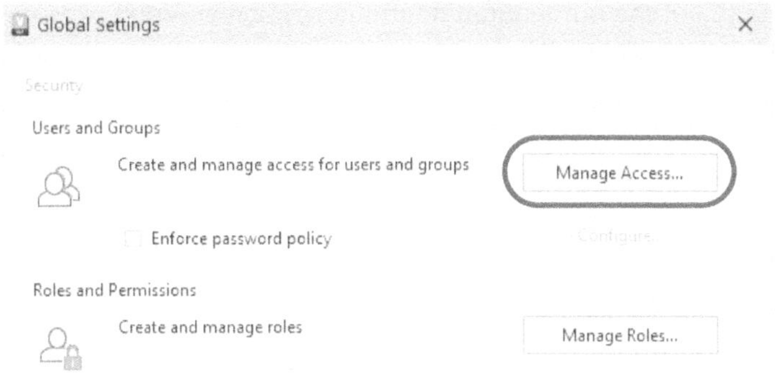

Figure 5–33

3. In the *User and Group Management* dialog box, on the *Users* tab, click **New...**, as shown in Figure 5–34.

Figure 5–34

4. In the *New User Profile* dialog box, enter the user data, such as *Display Name*, *Email Alias*, *First Name*, and *Last Name*, as shown in Figure 5–35.

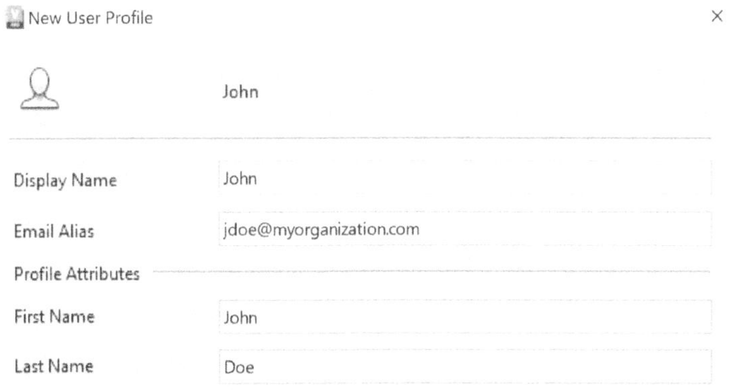

Figure 5–35

5. Select **Accounts** to set the authentication method, such as Vault Account or Autodesk ID. You can set the password as well.
6. If you are controlling permissions using groups, do not enter roles or vaults. If a few users require special permissions, specify the roles and vaults at the user level, as shown in Figure 5–36.

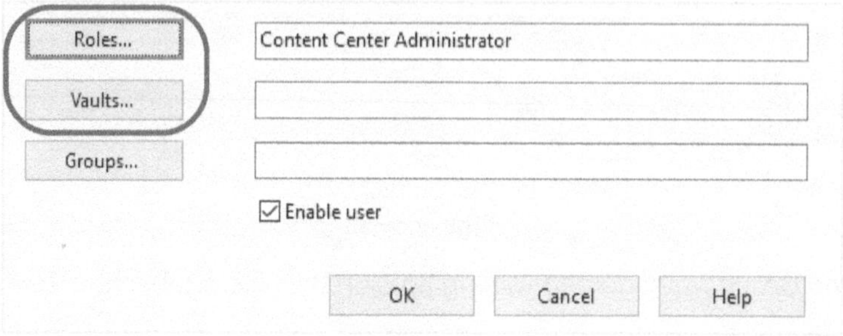

Figure 5–36

7. To create a new group, in the *User and Group Management* dialog box, select the *Groups* tab, then click **New...**, as shown in Figure 5–37.

Figure 5–37

8. In the *New Group Profile* dialog box (shown in Figure 5–38), enter the name for the group. Select the roles to apply to all members of the group. Select which vaults the group members can access with the selected roles.

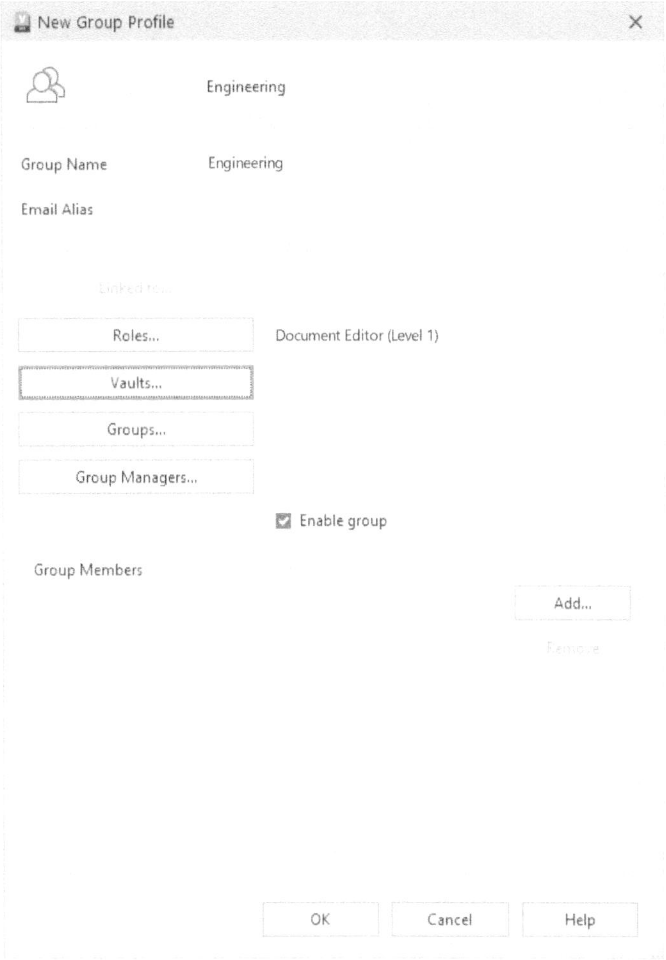

Figure 5–38

9. Add existing users to the group by selecting **Add** to display the *Add Members* dialog box (shown in Figure 5–39). A group requires at least one member to be added.

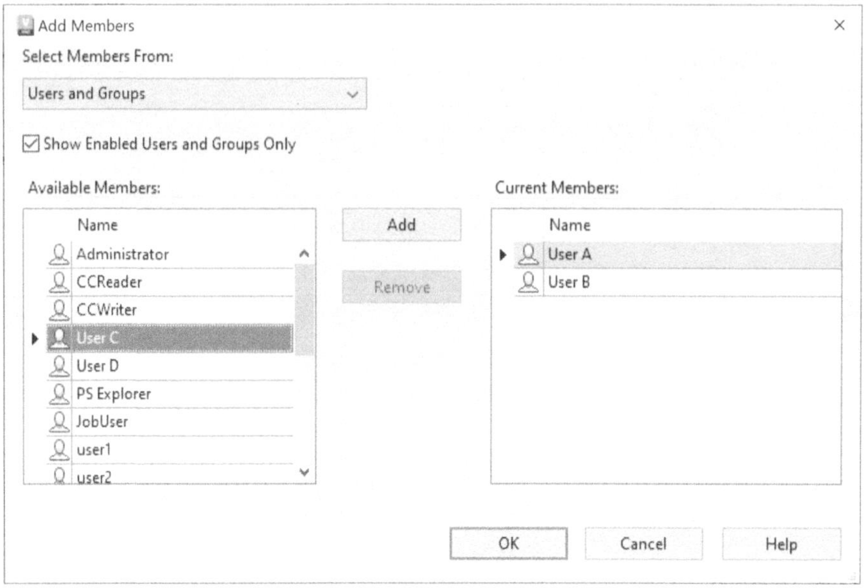

Figure 5–39

Practice 5b
Manage Users and Access

Practice Objectives

- Add users and groups to a vault.
- Set user permissions and manage user access to the vault.

In this practice, you will add users and groups to a vault. Users in engineering add models to the vault and require editor permission. One engineering user manages the Content Center libraries and must be given appropriate permission. All users in sales need read-only access to the vault in order to view models. The completed practice is shown in Figure 5–40.

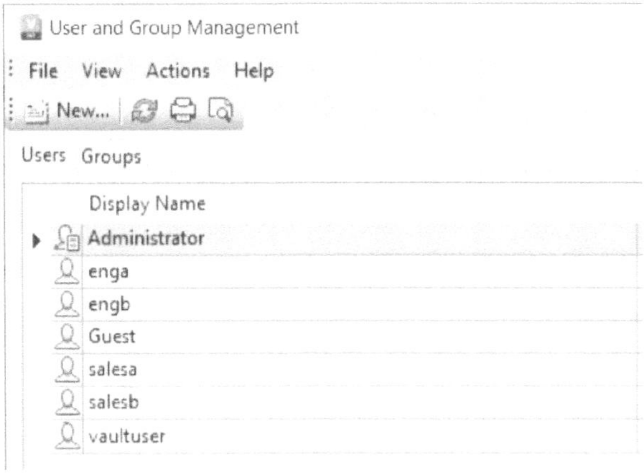

Figure 5–40

1. Start the ADMS Console. Log in as **Administrator** and leave the password blank.

   Note: *You can also administer users from Autodesk Vault.*

2. Select **Tools>Administration**.
3. In the *Global Settings* dialog box, on the *Security* tab, under *Roles and Permissions*, click **Manage Roles...**.
4. In the *Roles Management* dialog box, review the permissions for the Document Editor (Level 1) and Document Consumer roles. Select **Document Consumer** and click **Edit**. Review the list in *Selected Permissions*. Close the *Edit Role* dialog box. Select the **Document Editor (Level 1)** and click **Edit**. Review the *Selected Permissions* and note the differences compared to the Document Consumer role. Close the *Roles Management* dialog box.

5. In the *Global Settings* dialog box, under *Users and Groups*, click **Manage Access...**. In the *User and Group Management* dialog box, click **View>By Effective Vault**. Review the users for **TestVault**, as shown in Figure 5–41.

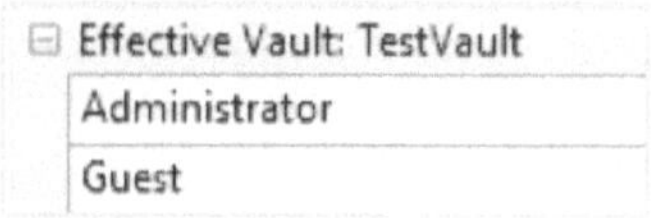

Figure 5–41

6. On the *Users* tab, click **New...**. Create a user with the following data:
   - *Display Name:* **enga**
   - *Email Alias:* leave the box empty
   - *First Name:* **Engineer**
   - *Last Name:* **A**
   - *Password:* **vault** (Select **Accounts** then **Vault Account**)
   - *Roles:* leave the box empty
   - *Vaults:* leave the box empty
7. Add another user with the following data:
   - *Display Name:* **engb**
   - *Email Alias:* leave the box empty
   - *First Name:* **Engineer**
   - *Last Name:* **B**
   - *Password:* **vault** (Select **Accounts** then **Vault Account**)
   - *Roles:* **Content Center Editor**
   - *Vaults:* leave the box empty
8. Add a third user with the following data:
   - *Display Name:* **salesa**
   - *Email Alias:* leave the box empty
   - *First Name:* **Sales**
   - *Last Name:* **A**
   - *Password:* **vault** (Select **Accounts** then **Vault Account**)
   - *Roles:* leave the box empty
   - *Vaults:* leave the box empty

9. Add a fourth user with the following data:
    - *User Name:* **salesb**
    - *Email Alias:* leave the box empty
    - *First Name:* **Sales**
    - *Last Name:* **B**
    - *Password:* **vault** (Select **Accounts** then **Vault Account**)
    - *Roles:* leave the box empty
    - *Vaults:* leave the box empty
10. Note that the users are not assigned to a vault.
11. On the *Groups* tab, click **New...**.
12. In the *New Group Profile* dialog box, enter the following data:
    - *Group Name:* **Engineering**
    - *Roles:* **Document Editor (Level 1)**
    - *Vaults:* **TestVault**
13. Under *Group Members*, click **Add**.
14. In the *Available Members* list, select **enga** and **engb**. Click **Add**. Click **OK** twice to close both the *Add Members* and *New Group Profile* dialog boxes.
15. Add another group named **Sales**. Grant **Document Consumer** access to TestVault. Add **salesa** and **salesb** as group members. Click **OK** twice.
16. In the *User and Group Management* dialog box, review the two groups, as shown in Figure 5–42.

Figure 5–42

17. Close the *User and Group Management* dialog box.
18. Close the *Global Settings* dialog box.
19. Start Autodesk Vault. Log in using the following information:
    - *User Name:* **salesa**
    - *Password:* **vault**
    - *Vault:* **TestVault**
20. Click **File>User Profile...**.

21. In the *User Profile* dialog box, select **Change Vault Account Password**. In the *Change Vault Account Password* dialog box, change the password from *vault* to **sales**, as shown in Figure 5–43. Click **OK**.

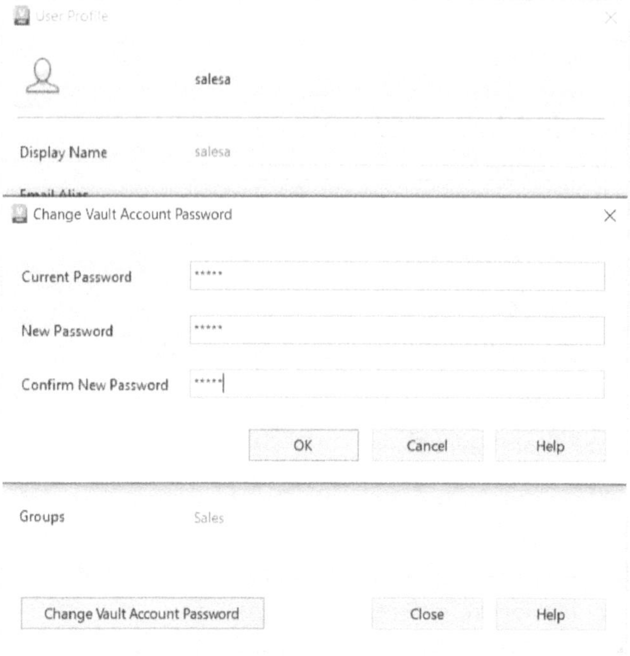

Figure 5–43

22. Log out of Autodesk Vault. Log back in to confirm that the password was changed to *sales*.
23. Try to create a new folder in the vault.
24. Because **salesa** does not have adequate permissions, the user cannot create a folder and receives the message shown in Figure 5–44.

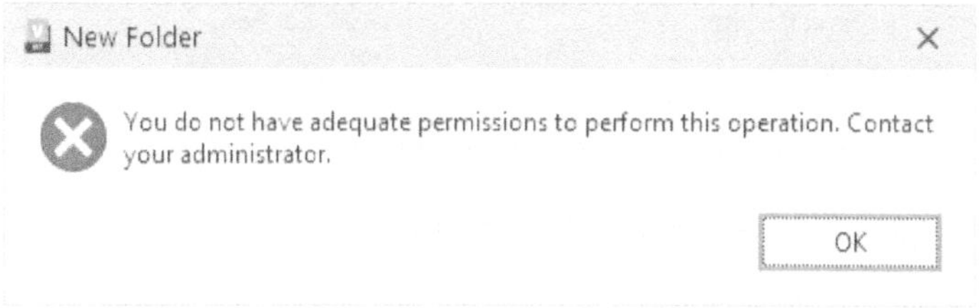

Figure 5–44

25. Log out and then close Autodesk Vault. Close the ADMS Console.

End of practice

5.3 Managing File Properties

When you add a file to the vault, the file's properties are stored in the vault database. The group of properties, called *metadata*, is used for tracking and finding files in the vault. It is important to manage properties so that users can efficiently use properties in their vault workflows.

Two types of properties are in Autodesk Vault. **System properties** are predefined and are included in every file's database record in the vault. A default set of **user-defined properties** are shipped with the system and mapped to the most common file properties. The values of these user-defined properties are automatically set when you add a file to the vault. As an administrator, you can add additional user-defined properties that are used in your company and map them to the file properties of common applications or change the mapping of the default set. The administrator can also rename file properties, select which file properties should be searched, and perform other property management tasks.

The *Property Definitions* dialog box (shown in Figure 5–45) is where you manage properties.

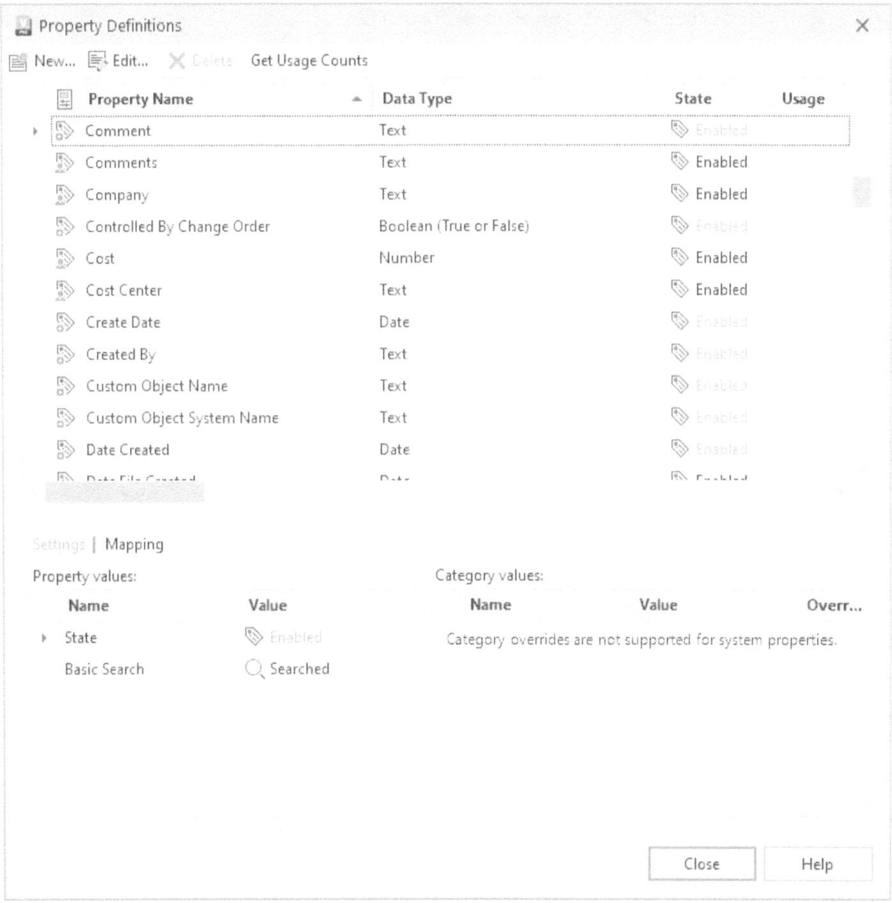

Figure 5–45

Renaming Properties

File properties are important for locating and organizing files in the vault. When a file is added to the vault, the file's properties are extracted from the file and stored in the vault database. The names of file properties (in the file) are determined by the company's standards. The names of user-defined file properties in the vault are determined by the vault administrator, also generally based on company standards. They can be the same as the actual file properties, or can differ to be more readable in Vault, for example. Vault adds several more properties, called system properties, whose names are predefined.

Each property has two names, the property name and the display name. If the property name for a file or system property is not meaningful to users or does not meet your company's standards, you can change the display name.

How To: Rename Properties

The following steps describe how to rename a property.

1. Log in to Autodesk Vault as an administrator.
2. Click **Tools>Administration>Vault Settings**. On the *Files* tab, click **Properties**.
3. In the *Property Definitions* dialog box, select the property to rename and click **Edit**, as shown in Figure 5–46.

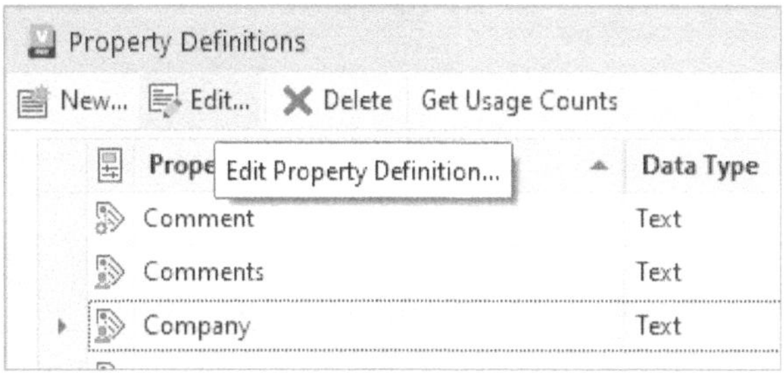

Figure 5–46

Note: You can click a column header to sort by that column.

4. Enter a new *Name* for the property, as shown in Figure 5–47.

Figure 5–47

Changing Property States

Vault properties are updated from the file when there is a mapping between the property of a file and that of the vault. Additionally, the Vault only extracts values of properties from files where a mapping exists between the file property and a vault property. All others are ignored. This keeps databases small for improved performance and reduces confusion by limiting the number of properties that users can access.

You can change the state of a file property from "Disabled" to "Enabled" if you plan to use the property for searching or reporting. The state of system properties cannot be changed; they are always in the database.

By default, the values of a property are searched when you perform a basic search from the *Find* dialog box. If there are many properties in a large database, this could impact the performance of the Find operation. You can change this default by setting the *Basic Search* value from "Searched" to "Not Searched." Later, if you find that you need to be able to search these, you can re-enable them so they are again searched. Note that you can always search an enabled property from the *Advanced* tab of the *Find* dialog box.

How To: Change Property States and Basic Search Values

The following steps describe how to change a property's *State* and *Basic Search* values.

1. Log in to Autodesk Vault as an administrator.
2. Click **Tools>Administration>Vault Settings**. On the *Files* tab, click **Properties**.
3. In the *Property Definitions* dialog box, select the property to change and click **Edit**, as shown in Figure 5–48.

   Note: *You can change the state of more than one property by selecting multiple properties before you click Edit.*

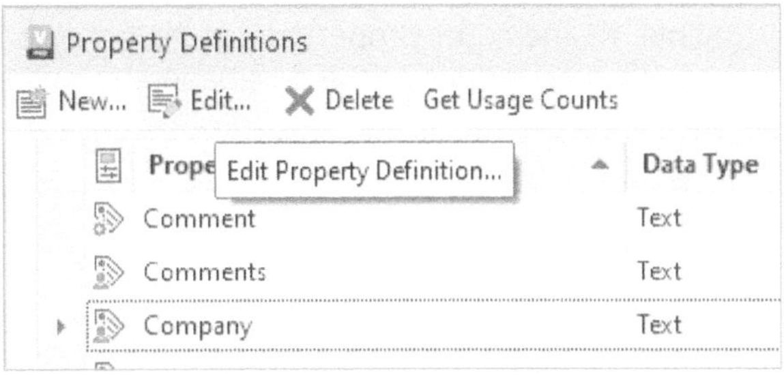

Figure 5–48

4. Change the state to **Enabled** or **Disabled**, as shown in Figure 5–49.

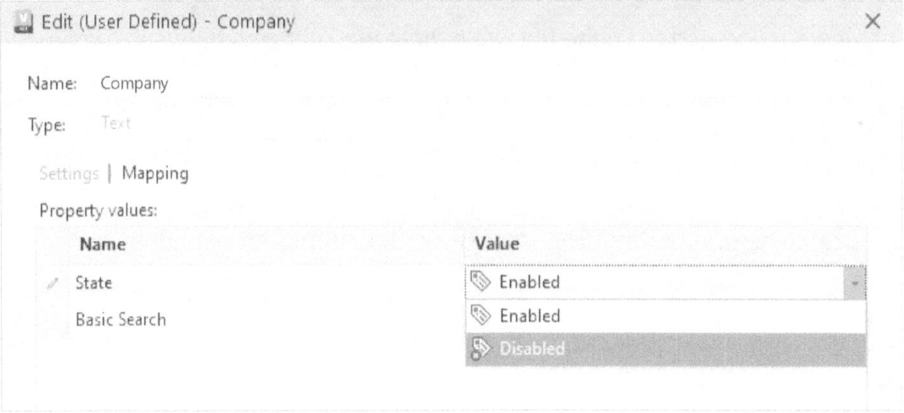

Figure 5–49

5. You can also make the property available in the Basic Search tool by changing the *Basic Search* field from **Not Searched** to **Searched**, as shown in Figure 5–50.

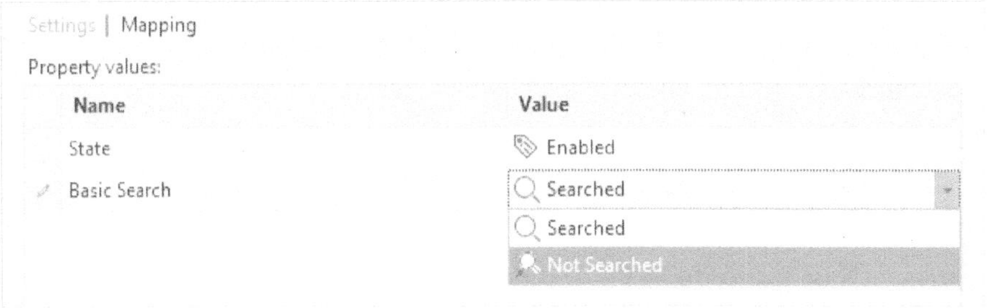

Figure 5–50

6. Log in to the ADMS Console. Re-index the properties for the corresponding vault so that the values of new in-use properties are added to the database and not-in-use properties are removed.

Mapping Properties

Many companies need to manage model files from different applications or with different standards. If a certain property is named differently in different files, you can map the different properties into one user-defined property.

About Mapping Properties

Different file formats use different names for similar properties. Also, some files include properties that are similar and it is difficult to determine which property holds the data.

You can manage several file properties as one Vault property by mapping them. When you map two or more file properties, the values of those properties are used to set the value of a single user-defined property. Conversely, if you edit a user-defined property value using the **Edit Property** command, mapping enables you to set the value of the mapped file properties from the new value of the user-defined property. That way, you can change the value of a mapped user-defined property in the Vault and when you check out the file in the authoring application, the file property value is correct. You can also control the order in which values are set. This is useful in cases where there is older data whose property name might be different for the same application. The first property value that is not blank is used to set the property value.

Figure 5–51 shows the results of merging the Engineer and Author properties into the user-defined property Engineer. It indicates how it is mapped from Autodesk Inventor and two different Word documents.

The user-defined property is mapped to the iProperty Engineer in Inventor. When an Inventor file is checked in, if the Engineer iProperty has a value, it will be used to set the value of the user-defined property.

Now take the case of a specification document written in Microsoft Word. Some of the Engineering groups have consistently used the standard Word property Author. However, another Engineering group has a template with a custom property Engineer that is used to specify the responsible engineer. In this case, Vault will first look to see if the custom property Engineer exists and has a value. If not, it then looks to see if the standard property Author has a value, as shown in Figure 5–51.

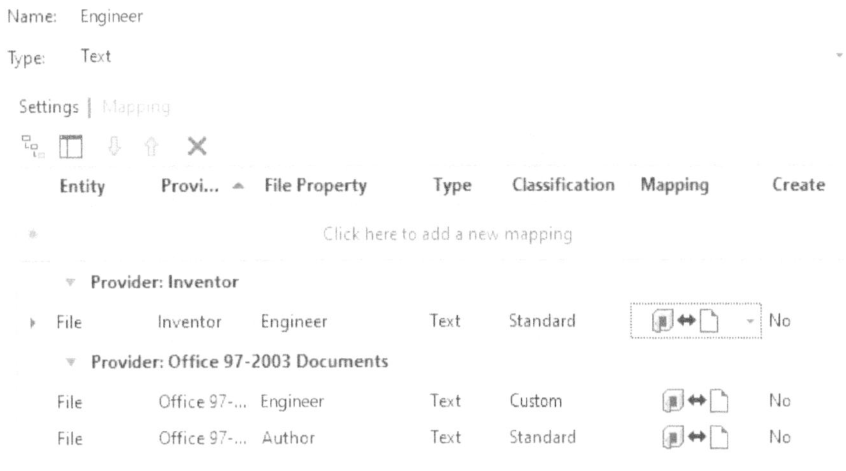

Figure 5–51

Note that in the case where there is no value, for either the Inventor or the Word document, the user-defined property value will not be set.

Mapping Property Rules

The following rules apply when you map properties:

- Generally, only user-defined (non-system) properties can be merged. *Originator*, *Original Create Date*, and *Thumbnail* are exceptions.
- Properties of different types can be mapped with some exceptions. There are special considerations when mapping properties of different types.
- Put the most important or most commonly used property first. The order of the merged properties is important. When a merged property is assigned a value, the merged properties are checked in the order in which they are defined. The first non-blank property is used for the merged property's value. The remaining properties are not checked.

How To: Map Properties

The following steps describe how to map property values for a new user-defined property.

1. Log in to Autodesk Vault as an administrator.
2. Click **Tools>Administration>Vault Settings**. On the *Files* tab, under *Properties*, click **Properties**.
3. In the *New (Property)* dialog box, create the user-defined property and ensure that it is enabled, as shown in Figure 5–52.

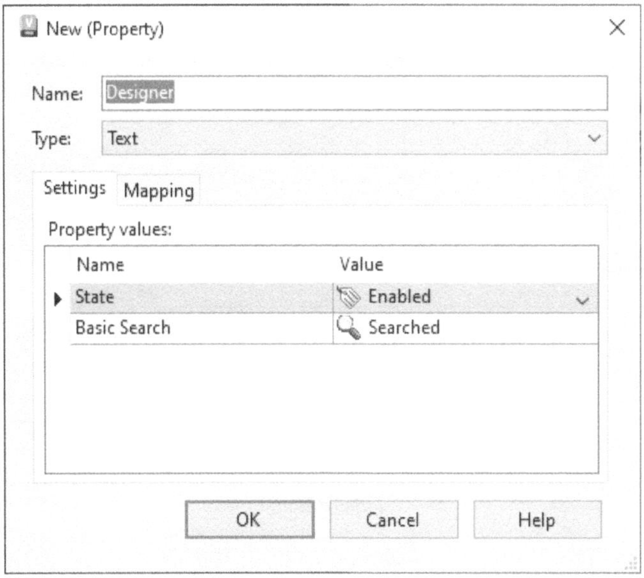

Figure 5–52

4. Select the *Mapping* tab and click on the space where it says *Click here to add a new mapping*, as shown in Figure 5–53.

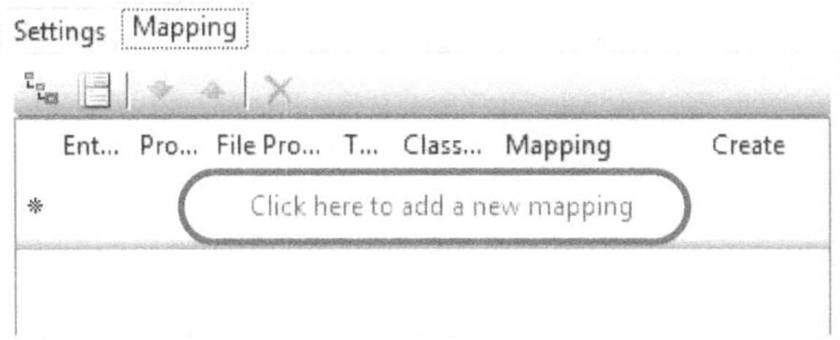

Figure 5–53

5. In the *Provider* field, select the application, as shown in Figure 5–54.

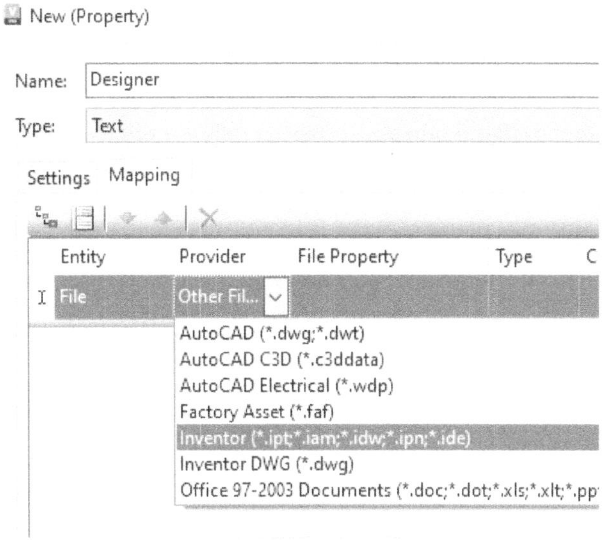

Figure 5–54

6. In the *File Property* field, select the property to map to, as shown in Figure 5–55. You will need to **Import Properties** from a representative file in the vault that contains a file property with a value.

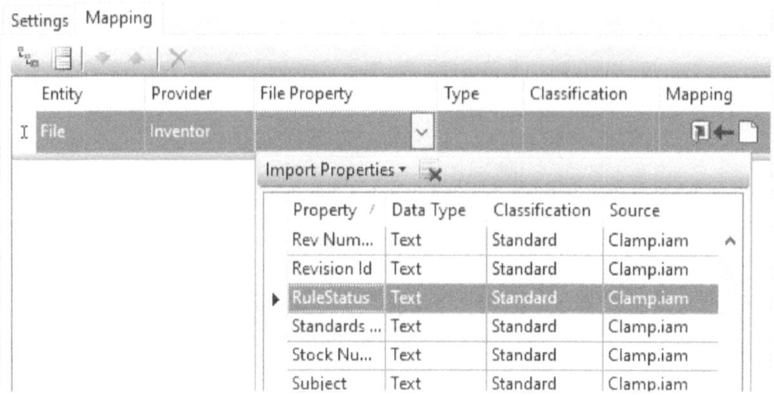

Figure 5–55

7. Specify the *Mapping*. Select if you want the file property to write to the user-defined property, the user-defined property to write to the file property, or both, as shown in Figure 5–56.

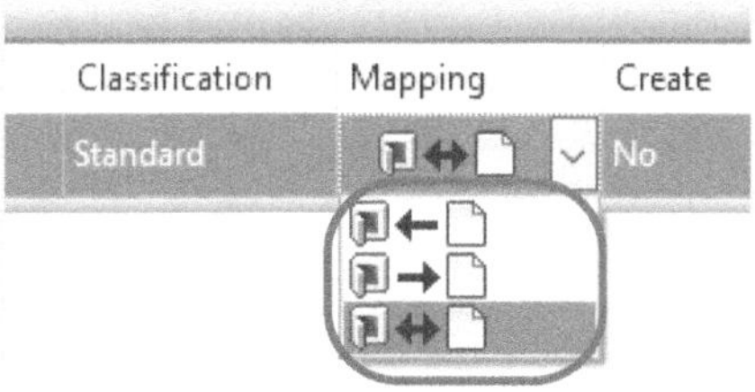

Figure 5–56

8. Specify the *Create* option. The *Create* option applies to write mappings; if the file property does not exist when a value is pushed to the file, the administrator can choose whether the file property is created or not, as shown in Figure 5–57.

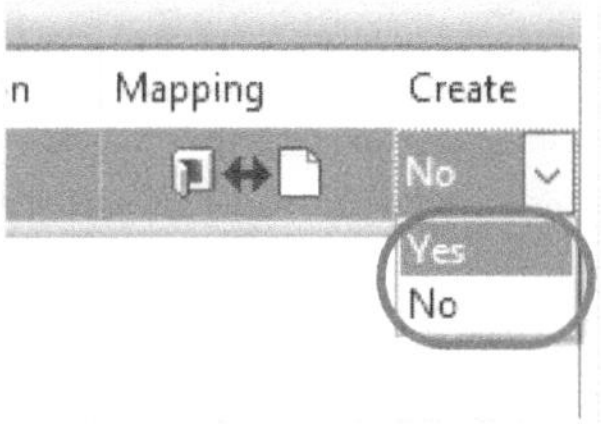

Figure 5–57

9. Specify the second application, if required, as shown in Figure 5–58.

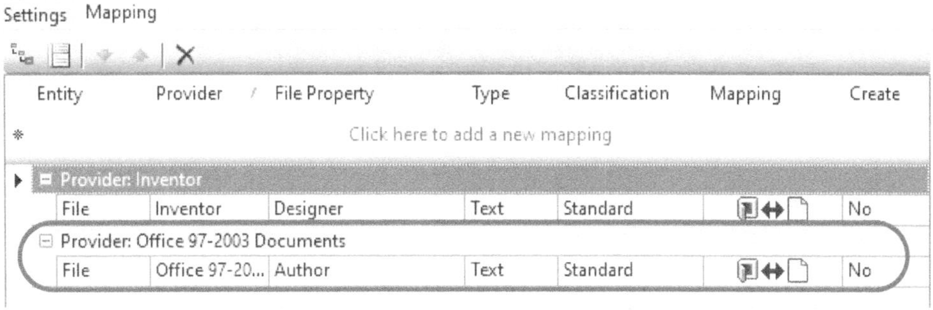

Figure 5–58

10. If there are files from the same application to be managed that have a file property that might be different than the ones mapped, specify it, as shown in Figure 5–59. Use the Up and Down arrows to specify which value to check first.

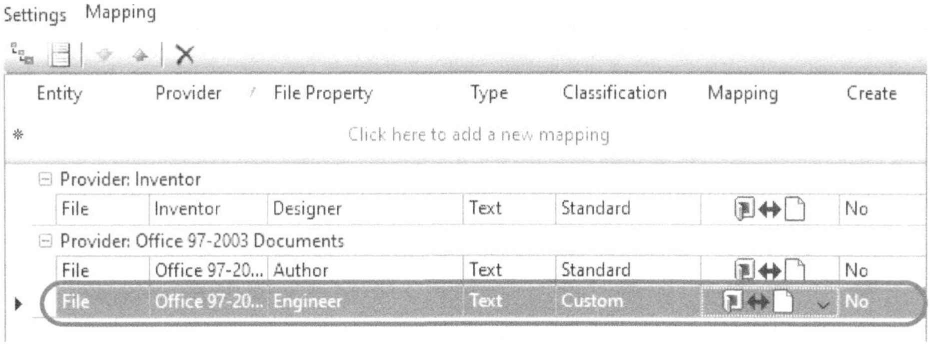

Figure 5–59

11. Click **OK** to create the user-defined property with the specified property mappings, as shown in Figure 5–60. You will need to re-index the properties in order to set any files with property values already in the vault.

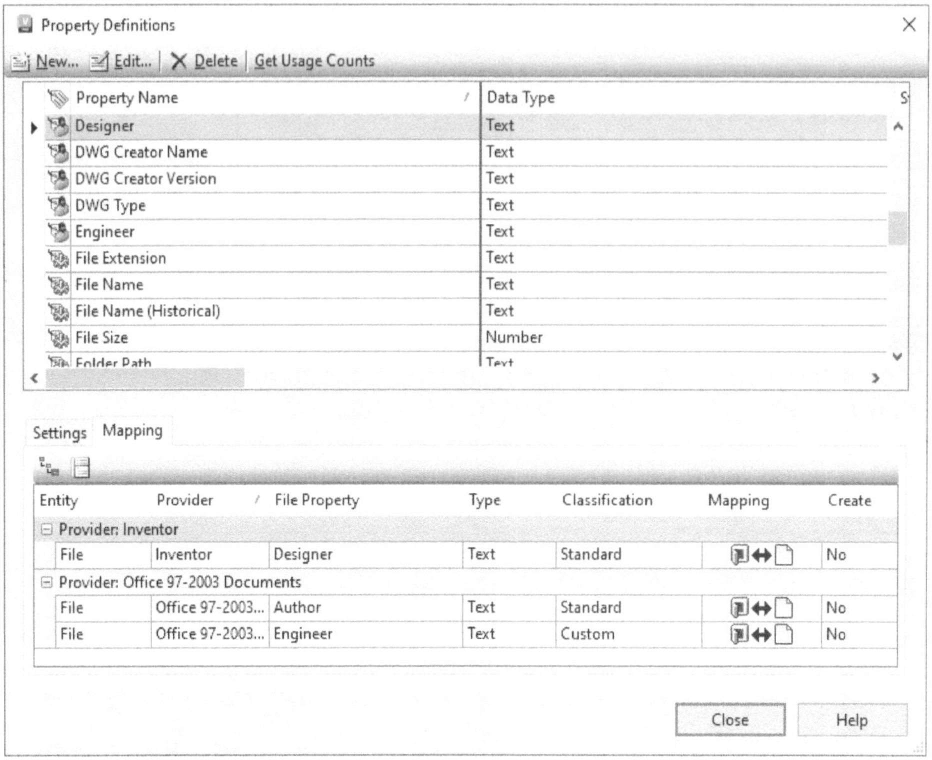

Figure 5–60

Adding AutoCAD Attributes

Many companies store important information about AutoCAD drawings in attributes. For example, the drawing number, description, designer, and latest revision are often stored in the title block. By default, attribute values are not extracted from AutoCAD files when the files are added to the vault; however, you can set up Vault to add block attribute values as properties.

In Vault, you can define a property, and name it as you see fit. You can then assign a mapping to an attribute in an AutoCAD titleblock. The names do not need to match. Attribute tag names are not always meaningful; therefore, you can also extract the attribute prompt and use the prompt as the property name.

An AutoCAD block can include more attributes than you want to use in Vault. If you do not need some of the properties, you can exclude them from the database indexes. If a property is similar to other properties in the vault, you can merge the new AutoCAD block property with the existing vault properties so that users see just one property for all files rather than having to view or search on different properties when they work on different file formats.

How To: Add AutoCAD Block Attributes Properties

The following steps describe how to add AutoCAD block attributes to the vault.

1. Open the drawing in AutoCAD and record the name of the block. Ensure that the case is correct.
2. Log in to the ADMS Console.
3. Select a vault.
4. Select **Tools>Index Block Attributes**.
5. In the *Index Block Attributes* dialog box, click **New**. Enter the name of the block. The case must match the name in AutoCAD, as shown in Figure 5–61.

   Note: *You can use the prompt instead of an attribute tag. To use the prompt when it is available, enable the* ***Extract attribute prompt when available*** *checkbox. If this checkbox is toggled on and there is no prompt, the attribute tag is used.*

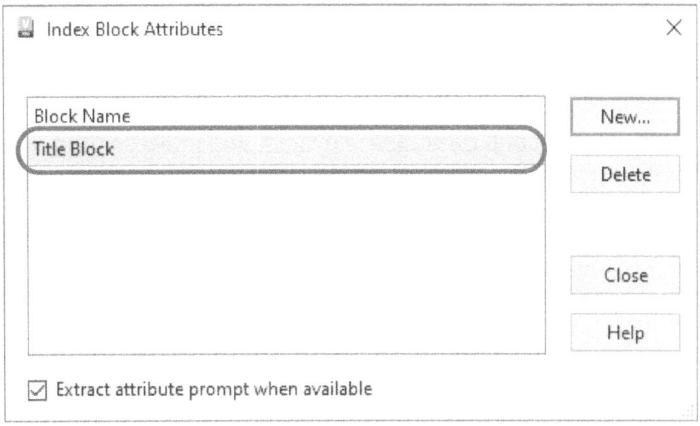

Figure 5–61

6. Close the *Index Block Attributes* dialog box.
7. Click **Actions>Re-Index File Properties** to re-index the properties.
8. Re-index the vault.

   You can create mappings to the attributes within the AutoCAD titleblocks in the same way you created mappings to Inventor iProperties and Word document properties.

Adding Other Properties

Autodesk Vault automatically adds properties from any application that has a Vault add-in. If you store other types of files in the vault, you can include their properties in the vault database by installing the appropriate iFilter. For example, if you store Adobe® Portable Document Format (PDF) files in the vault and need to organize and search for the files using properties, you can install the iFilter that supports PDF files. Some iFilters read just file properties while others read both a file's properties and the file's contents.

How To: Add Other Properties

To add properties from other file formats, do the following:

1. Purchase or download an iFilter for the appropriate file format.
2. Install the iFilter on the computer that hosts the vault server.
3. In the ADMS Console, re-index the vault database. If the iFilter can read the file contents and you want to search on file contents, enable the content indexing service.

Re-Indexing Vault Databases

Re-indexing scans the selected vault database, extracts, and indexes properties from the files in the vault database. The extraction and indexing process uses the latest available iFilters/Content Source Property Providers for the files. Only properties currently set to Enabled and properties that have read-mappings are re-indexed. During re-indexing, existing property (e.g., user-defined property) values are updated.

Reasons for re-indexing:

- New iFilters or Content Source Property Providers have been added that extract more relevant information.
- Property definitions have been set to **Enabled**.
- Read-mappings have been modified.

How To: Re-Index the Databases

The following steps describe how to re-index the vault databases.

1. Log in to the ADMS Console.
2. In the list of vaults, select a vault to re-index.
3. Select **Actions>Re-Index File Properties**.
4. In the *Re-Index File Properties* dialog box, select whether to re-index all files or just the latest and released versions only. Clicking **Status** lists the status of an active re-index procedure or the results of the last re-index procedure. It does not determine whether re-indexing is required.

5. Vault maintains re-index status for every file. Although certain criteria are selected for a re-index operation, it is not required that all files that fall under the criteria be re-indexed. This is because some files might already be up to date. However, the administrator can choose to force a re-index on all files that meet the selected criteria by selecting the **Force Re-Index** option. To force a re-index, click **>>** (Expand) and select the **Force Re-Index** checkbox.
6. To determine how many files will be affected, click **Calculate**, as shown in Figure 5–62.

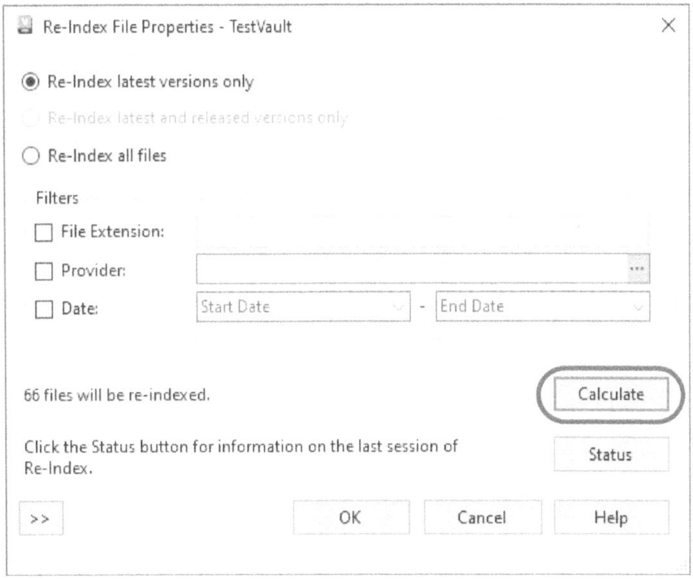

Figure 5–62

7. Click **OK** to run the re-indexing service.

   Note: *It might take a while to re-index the properties.*

8. To check if the re-indexing operation is complete, do one of the following:
   - Select the command again. If the operation is not complete, the *Re-Index File Properties Status* dialog box displays the status of the current re-indexing operation, as shown in Figure 5–63. If the operation is complete, the *Re-Index Properties* dialog box is displayed.

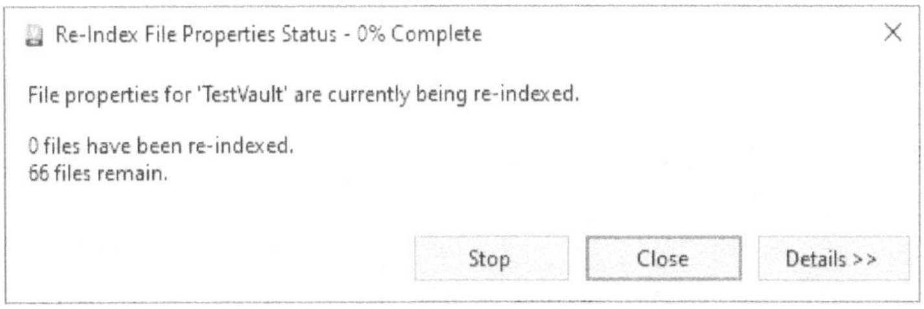

Figure 5–63

- Check the Server Log to see if the Property Re-index task is complete, as shown in Figure 5–64.

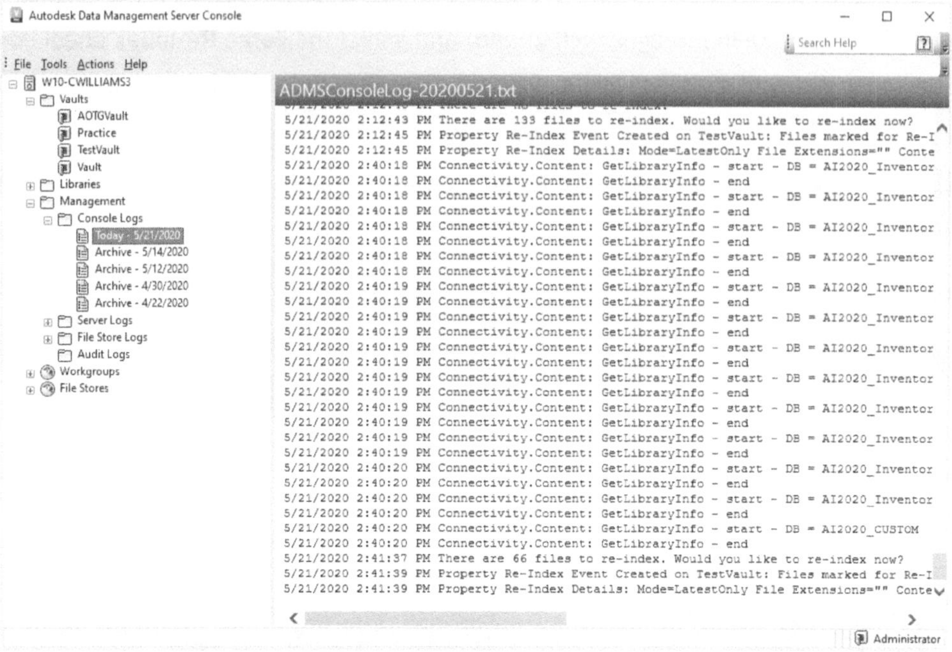

Figure 5–64

Practice 5c
Manage File Properties

Practice Objectives

- Add AutoCAD attributes as properties.
- Map and disable properties.
- Re-index the vault database to update the property indexes.

In this practice, you will add AutoCAD attributes as properties, map properties, disable properties, and re-index the vault databases to update the property indexes. The completed practice is shown in Figure 5–65.

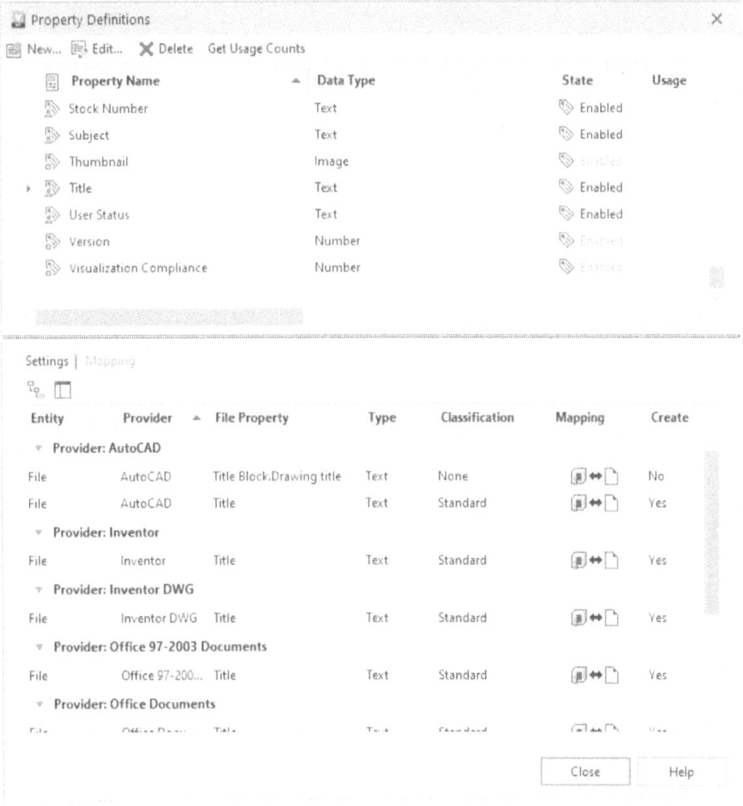

Figure 5–65

Task 1: Add an AutoCAD attribute as a property.

1. Start Autodesk Vault. Log in to **TestVault** as **Administrator** and leave the password blank.

2. Select **Tools>Administration>Vault Settings**.
3. In the *Vault Settings* dialog box, on the *Files* tab, clear the **Enforce Restriction for Check In of Design Files** checkbox.

   Note: *Normally, you should add design files using the vault client in the CAD application. For the purpose of this practice, the design file that you add to the vault is a drawing that is not related to other files so it can be added using Autodesk Vault.*

4. Close the *Vault Settings* dialog box.
5. Add the files **AutoCADBlockAttributes.dwg** and **Document.doc** from *C:\Vault Basic Admin Training\Chapter5* to the vault, as shown in Figure 5–66, using any method. The location does not matter.

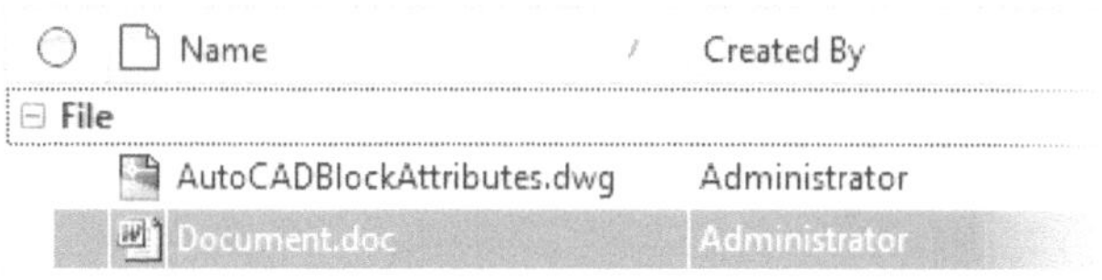

Figure 5–66

6. Start the ADMS Console. Log in as **Administrator** and leave the password blank.
7. Expand the list of vaults. Select **TestVault**.
8. Select **Tools>Index Block Attributes**.
9. In the *Index Block Attributes* dialog box, click **New**.
10. For *Block Name*, enter **Title Block**. Click **OK**.

    Note: *You must enter the block name with the correct case and a single space between the two words.*

11. Verify that the **Extract attribute prompt when available** checkbox is selected, as shown in Figure 5–67.

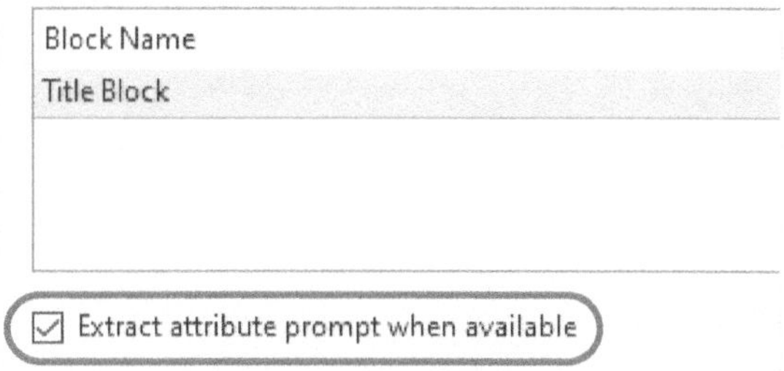

Figure 5–67

12. Click **Close**.

13. Select **Actions>Re-Index File Properties**.
14. In the *Re-Index Properties* dialog box, ensure that **Re-Index All Files** is selected. Click **>>** (Expand) and click **Force Re-Index**. Click **OK** and click **Yes** to re-index now.

    Note: *It might take a while to re-index the properties. To check if the re-indexing operation is complete, select the command again. If the operation is not complete, the status of the current re-indexing operation is displayed. If the operation is complete, the Re-Index Properties dialog box is displayed.*

Task 2: Map properties.

1. In Autodesk Vault, select **Tools>Administration>Vault Settings**.
2. In the *Vault Settings* dialog box, on the *Files* tab, click **Properties**.
3. Click on the *Property Name* column header to sort by property name. Hover over the *Data Type* column header until the filter icon displays. Select the Filter icon and select **Number**. Only properties with the **Number** data type are displayed. The filter is shown in Figure 5–68.

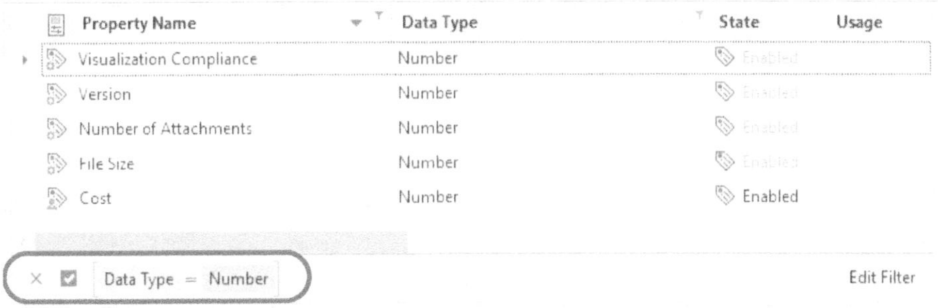

Figure 5–68

4. Click the X to remove this filter. All properties are displayed.

5. Select the **Title** property in the property list and the *Mapping* tab to reveal its mapping, as shown in Figure 5–69.

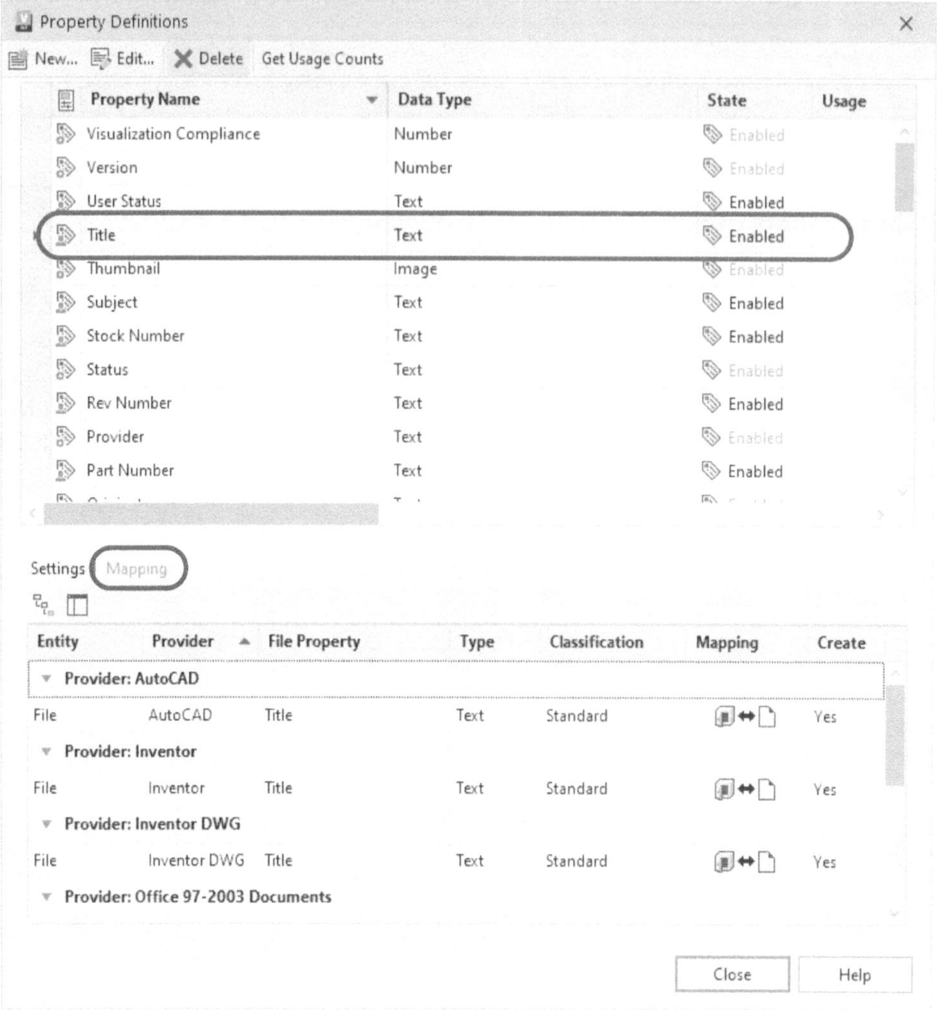

Figure 5–69

- *Title* is a standard attribute that is associated with many different document types. As such, the *Title* property is shipped as a default user-defined property with Vault and is mapped to the standard *Title* file property for Autodesk and Microsoft Office document types. However, for this example, you want to include a mapping to the block attribute *Drawing Title* in the AutoCAD file.

6. In the *Property Definitions* dialog box, select **Edit** to reveal the *Edit* dialog box for the *Title* property. Select the *Mapping* tab to display the default mapping, as shown in Figure 5–70.

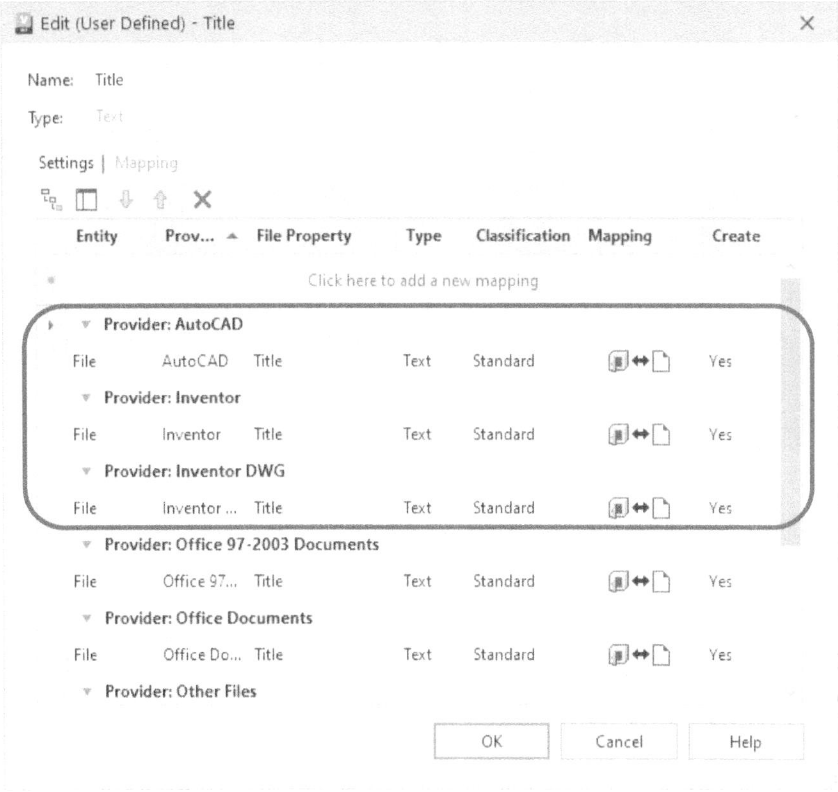

Figure 5–70

- Note again the default mappings. For AutoCAD, the property is already mapped to the *Title* file property. You will add a mapping that first looks in the *Title Block* attributes. If it does not find a value there it will then look for a value in the standard file property named *Title*.

7. Click in the *Click here to add a new mapping* area of the *Mapping* tab display. In the *Provider* drop-down list, select **AutoCAD (*.dwg;*.dwt)**, as shown in Figure 5–71.

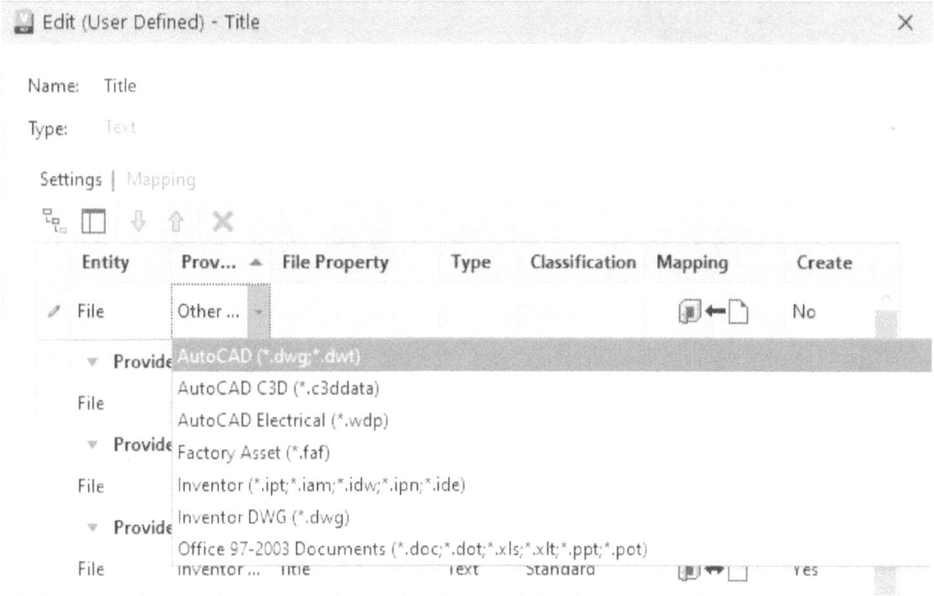

Figure 5–71

8. In the *File Property* drop-down list, select **Import Properties** and **Import From Vault**, as shown in Figure 5–72.

Figure 5–72

9. Select **AutoBlockAttributes.dwg**. From the list, scroll down until you find **Title Block.Drawing title**, as shown in Figure 5–73. Select this row and click **OK**.

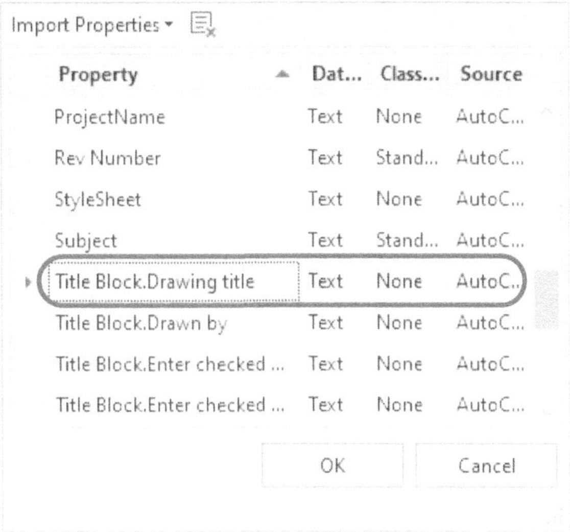

Figure 5–73

__Note:__ Drawing Title is an attribute in the title block of the AutoCAD drawing that you added to the vault. If Drawing Title is not in the list, you might need to run a repair of the Autodesk Data Management Server in Add/Remove Programs. Adding drawing attributes to the server can be affected if you installed AutoCAD products after installing ADMS.

10. Click on the **Provider: AutoCAD** row to display the new mapping, as shown in Figure 5–74.

- For AutoCAD files, the system will first look for the **Title** file property and then the **Title Block.Drawing title** block attribute.

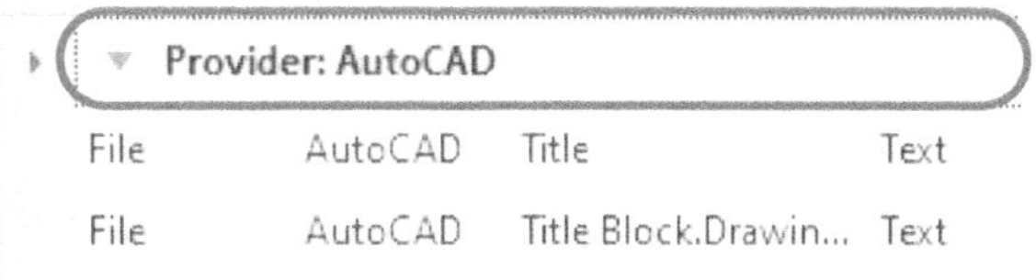

Figure 5–74

You want to change the order of the mapping so that the system first looks for a block attribute for the drawing title. If it does not find a value there, then look for the standard *Title* file property.

11. Select the second row in the *Provider: AutoCAD* section. Select the up arrow in the Mapping toolbar to move it before the *Title* file property, as shown in Figure 5–75.

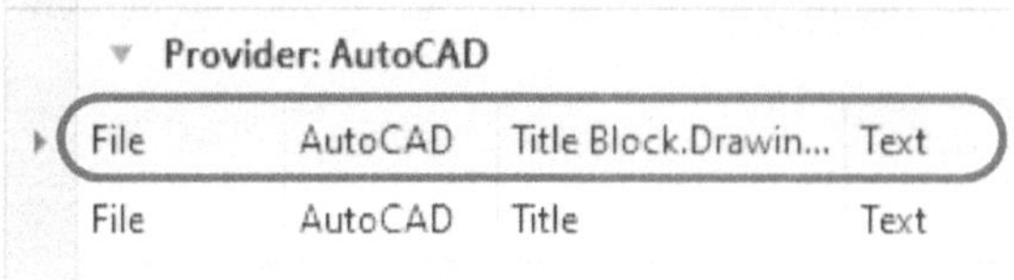

Figure 5–75

12. Select **OK** to dismiss the *Edit (User Defined) – Title* dialog box.
13. In the *Property Definition* dialog box, select **New** to create a new user-defined property.
14. In the *New (Property)* dialog box, enter **Project** for the *Name* of the new property. If the *Project* property already exists, select the **Project** property and click **Edit**.
15. Select the *Mapping* tab and click in the *Click here to add a new mapping* area.
16. In the *File Property* field, select **Import Properties**, as shown in Figure 5–76.

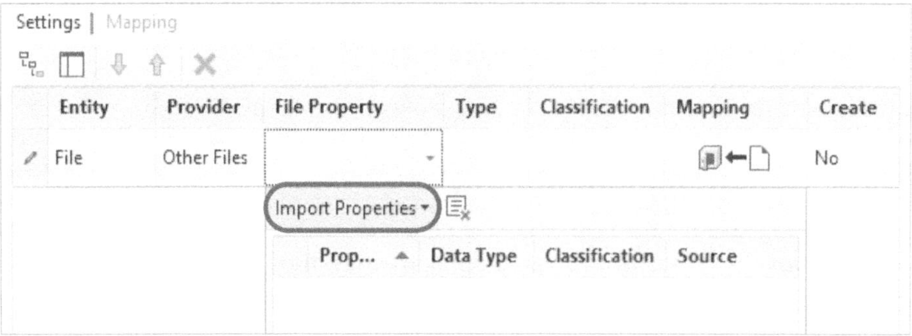

Figure 5–76

17. Select **Import From Vault** and browse to the Word document (**Document.doc**) you added to the vault. Click **Open**.
18. In the list of imported properties, scroll down to find the custom property **Project**, as shown in Figure 5–77. Select it and then dismiss the dialog by clicking **OK**.

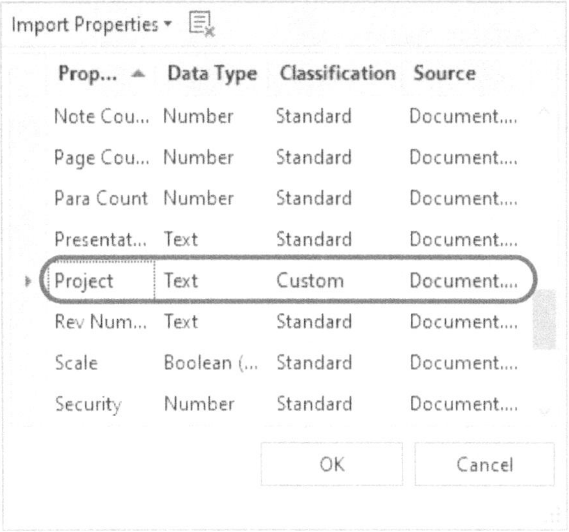

Figure 5–77

19. Click **OK** to create the user-defined property.

Task 3: Remove properties.

1. In the *Property Definitions* dialog box, select the properties with *Property Names* of **Company** and **Cost Center** by pressing <Ctrl>. Since these are not relevant to your organization, you will disable them. Click **Edit**.
2. In the *Edit – Multiple Properties* dialog box, in the *Value* drop-down list for **State (File Properties Only)**, select **Disabled**, as shown in Figure 5–78.

Figure 5–78

- The properties are disabled. In the future, if these properties are used and you want to include them in column customization or find/search workflows, they can be re-enabled.

3. Click **OK** to dismiss the *Edit – Multiple Properties* dialog box.

4. Click **Close**. Click **OK** to close the warning message that states that you must re-index the vault. Close the *Vault Settings* dialog box.
5. Switch to the ADMS Console. Ensure that **TestVault** is selected. Re-index the properties.
6. Below the list of vaults, expand the *Management* and *Server Logs* folders. Click **Today**, as shown in Figure 5–79.

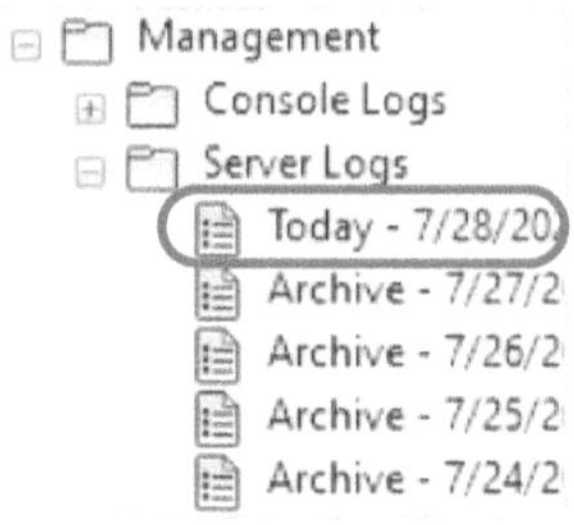

Figure 5–79

7. Scroll to the bottom of the log file. Confirm that the Property Re-index started and completed.

Task 4: Display properties in Vault Explorer.

1. In Autodesk Vault, navigate to the folder that contains the document and the AutoCAD drawing that you added to the vault earlier in the practice.
2. Click in the file pane. Click **View>Customize View**.
3. In the *Customize View* dialog box, click **Fields**.
4. In the *Customize Fields* dialog box, under *Select Available Fields From*, select **Any**. Review the properties. Properties whose states are set to **Disabled** (*Company*, *Cost Center*) are not displayed.
5. Under *Available Fields*, select **Title**. Click **Add** to add it to the list of fields to show. Select **Title** and **Project** from the *Show these files in this order list* and move them up until they are just after the *Name* field. Click **OK**.
6. Close the *Customize View* dialog box.
7. Note the *Title* for the two files and the *Project* for the Word document, as shown in Figure 5–80.

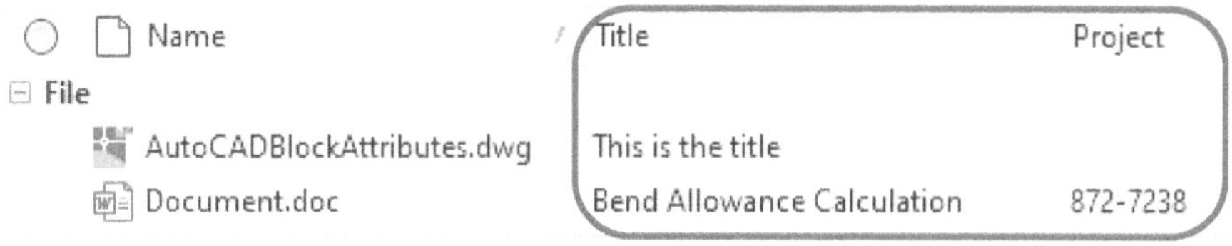

Figure 5–80

8. Close Autodesk Vault and the ADMS Console.

End of practice

5.4 Backing Up and Restoring Vaults

You must back up Vault files and databases on a regular basis so that you can restore them if they are accidentally corrupted or deleted. In this section, you will learn how to back up and restore vaults and their associated files.

Backing Up a Vault

You should back up the Vault file store and databases regularly in case files in the vault are accidentally corrupted or lost. The backup tool backs up all attached vaults and libraries including the master database, vault databases, and vault file stores.

To guarantee that a vault can be restored without problem, the file store and databases must be backed up at the same time while ensuring that no database transactions take place during the backup procedure. The backup tool is preferred over other backup strategies because it automatically stops the Vault service and groups all required files into one folder, guaranteeing that the vault files can be successfully restored.

In Figure 5–81, the vaults are being backed up to a local drive, *C:\VaultBackups*.

Figure 5–81

Excluding Vaults or Libraries from a Backup

If you have vaults or libraries that do not contain important data, you can exclude them from a backup to reduce the size of the backup. For example, a practice vault might not need to be backed up.

You can exclude individual vaults and libraries by detaching them before running the backup tool. When the backup tool is finished, you must reattach them. As an option, you can exclude all of the standard Content Center libraries during the backup procedure.

How To: Back Up a Vault

The following steps describe how to back up vaults.

1. Log in to the ADMS Console. If you do not want to include individual vaults or libraries in the backup, detach them by right-clicking on the vault name and selecting **Detach**, as shown in Figure 5–82. You do not need to detach the standard Content Center libraries because you can exclude them using the backup tool.

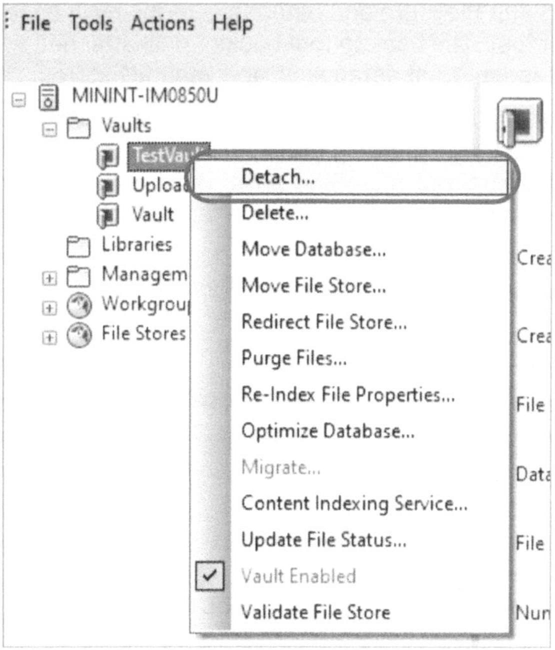

Figure 5–82

2. Select **Tools>Backup**.

3. In the *Backup Vault* dialog box, do the following:
   - Specify a location for the backup files.
   - Select the **Validate the backup files** checkbox to validate the backup files.
   - Select the **Backup Standard Content Center Libraries** checkbox (shown in Figure 5–83) if you want to include them in the backup. Typically, you can leave standard Content Center libraries out of the backup because you can restore them from the installation disks if they are lost or corrupted.

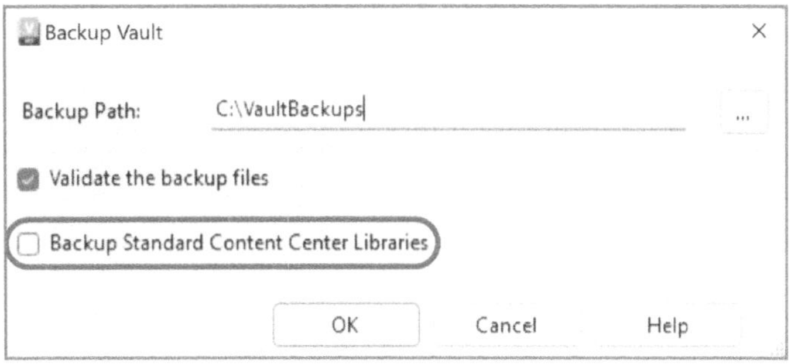

Figure 5–83

4. The Vault databases and file stores are backed up to the location that you specified, as shown in Figure 5–84.

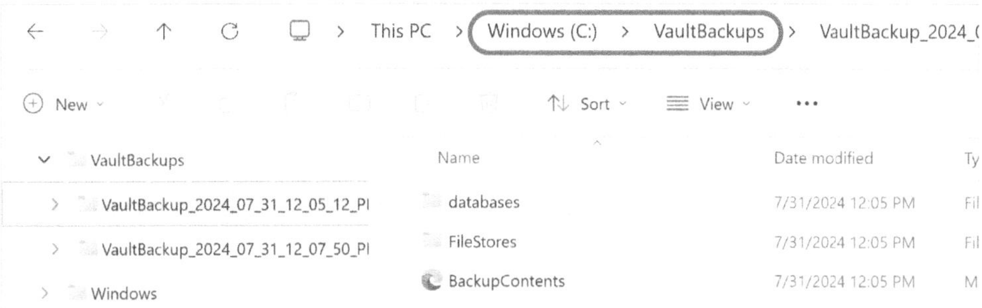

Figure 5–84

5. Check the Console Log if you want to confirm the status of the backup operation, as shown in Figure 5–85.

Figure 5–85

6. If you manually detached any vaults or libraries before you ran the backup tool, reattach them using **Actions>Attach**. The *Attach Vault* dialog box is shown in Figure 5–86.

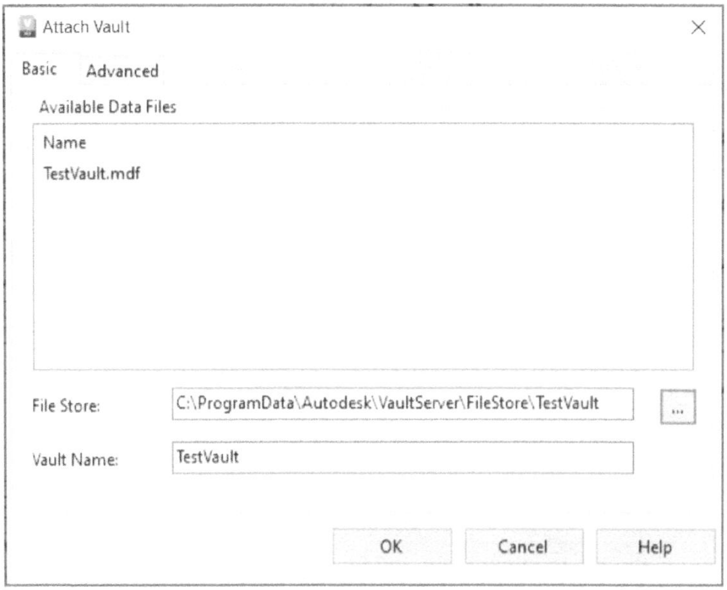

Figure 5–86

Automating Backup Using Batch Files

To schedule vault backups at regular intervals, you can run the command line version of the ADMS Console from a batch file. You can create a batch file that performs all of the operations required to back up your vaults, and then schedule the batch file to run at regular intervals using a task scheduler, such as Microsoft Windows Task Scheduler.

The command line version of the Vault Manager is named **Connectivity.ADMSConsole.exe** and is located in the ADMS installation folder.

The following is a sample command line call:

Connectivity.ADMSConsole.exe -Obackup -BC:\Backup -DBSC -VUadministrator -VPadmin -S -VAL -LC:

\Backup\BackupLog.txt

The command line arguments are described in the following table.

Argument	Description
C:\...\Connectivity.ADMSConsole.exe	Specifies the location and name of the executable file.
-O<operation>	Specifies the operation as a backup.
-B<folder>	Specifies the backup directory.
-VU<username>	The Vault administrator account user name (required).
-VP<password>	The Vault administrator account password (required unless password is blank).
-WA	Use Windows Authentication instead of -VU and -VP.
-DBSC	Excludes the standard Content Center libraries from the backup. The libraries are detached before the backup procedure, the vaults are backed up, and then the libraries are reattached.
-L<backup log name and location>	Specifies the name and location of the log file. If the log file exists, the log data is appended to the file.
-VAL	Validate the backup. Errors are recorded in the log file.
-S	Runs the command in silent mode so that dialog boxes are not displayed.

Restoring a Vault

If a problem arises with your vaults, you might need to restore them from a backup. When you run the restore procedure, all of the attached vaults and libraries are deleted and are replaced by those from the backup. If you excluded vaults or libraries from the backup, you can detach those files before restoring the vault and then reattach them after the restore operation is finished.

If the vault databases in the backup are from a previous version of Vault, the databases are automatically migrated to the current version when you use the **Restore** tool from the ADMS Console.

Restore Options

The *Restore Vault* dialog box and its options are displayed in Figure 5–87.

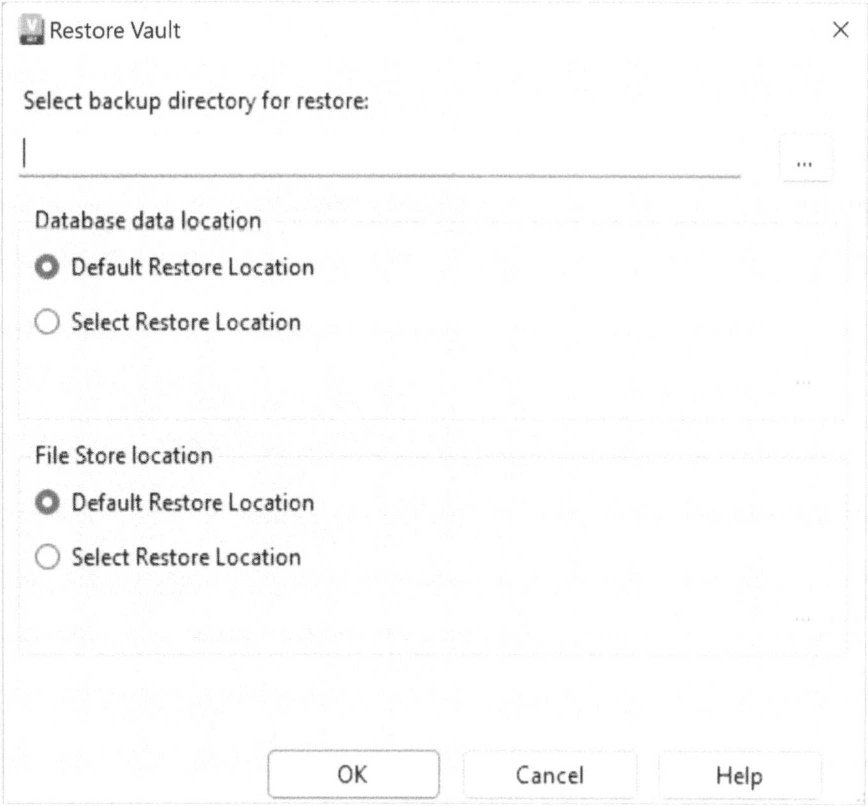

Figure 5–87

Backup directory	The directory where you saved the backup.
Database data location	By default, when you restore a vault, the Vault databases are restored to their default locations on the server, which might not be the locations from which they were backed up. If you have moved the databases from their default location, you must specify the locations rather than using the default location. When you restore the vaults, the databases are deleted from their current location and the files from the backup are restored to the specified location.
File Store location	By default, when you restore a vault, the Vault file stores are restored to their default locations on the server, which might not be the locations from which they were backed up. If you have moved the file stores from their default location, you must specify their locations rather than using the default location. When you restore the vaults, the file stores are deleted from their current location and the files from the backup are restored to the specified location.

Practice 5d
Back Up and Restore a Vault

Practice Objectives

- Back up a vault.
- Restore the vault.

In this practice, you will back up a vault, examine the vault backup folder, and restore the vault. The completed practice is shown in Figure 5–88.

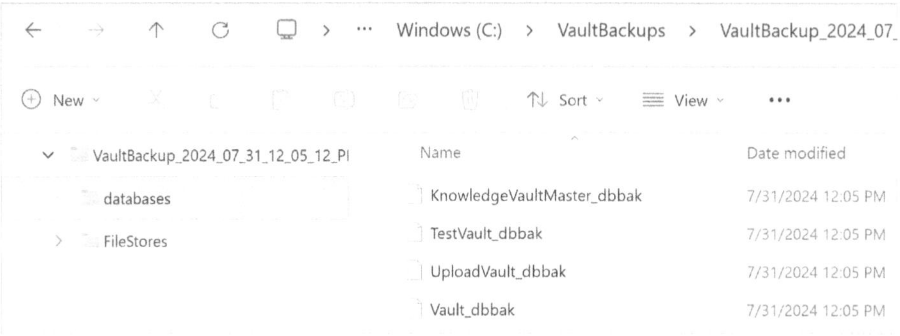

Figure 5–88

1. Start the ADMS Console. Log in as **Administrator** and leave the password blank.
2. Review the total size of the vaults, libraries, file stores, and the number of days since the vault was backed up.
3. Select **Tools>Backup**.
4. In the *Backup Vault* dialog box, for *Backup Path*, create and select the folder *C:\VaultBackups*. Select the **Validate the backup files** checkbox to toggle on validation. Clear the **Backup Standard Content Center Libraries** checkbox.
5. Click **OK**. The *Backup Progress* dialog box is displayed.
6. When the backup operation is complete, click **Close**, then click **OK**.

7. In Windows File Explorer, navigate to the *VaultBackups* folder. Do the following:
   - Confirm that the folder name contains the current date and time.
   - Open the folder that contains the backup and confirm that the backup includes all of the Vault databases and file stores, as shown in Figure 5–89. The databases for the standard Content Center libraries should not be included.

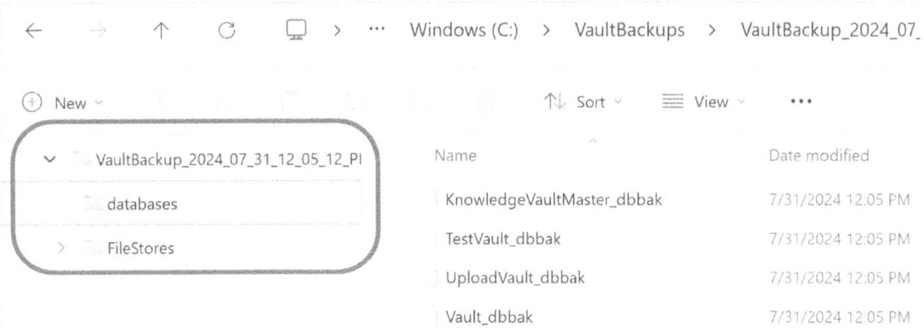

Figure 5–89

8. In the ADMS Console, select **Tools>Restore**.
9. Click **Yes** to restore now and to delete the current datasets. Select the vault backup folder that was created during the backup operation.
10. Click **OK**.
11. When the restore operation is complete, click **OK**.
12. Review the Console Log entry for **Today**, as shown in Figure 5–90. Confirm that the restore operation succeeded.

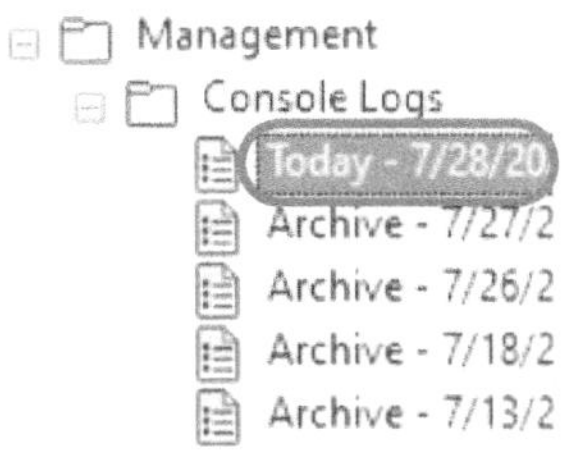

Figure 5–90

13. In the ADMS Console, examine the vaults and file stores.
14. Close the ADMS Console.

End of practice

5.5 Maintaining Vault

As the Vault administrator, you need to perform routine maintenance on vaults and file stores. In this section, you will learn how to get statistics about a vault and how to perform various maintenance tasks.

The statistics for a vault are shown in Figure 5–91.

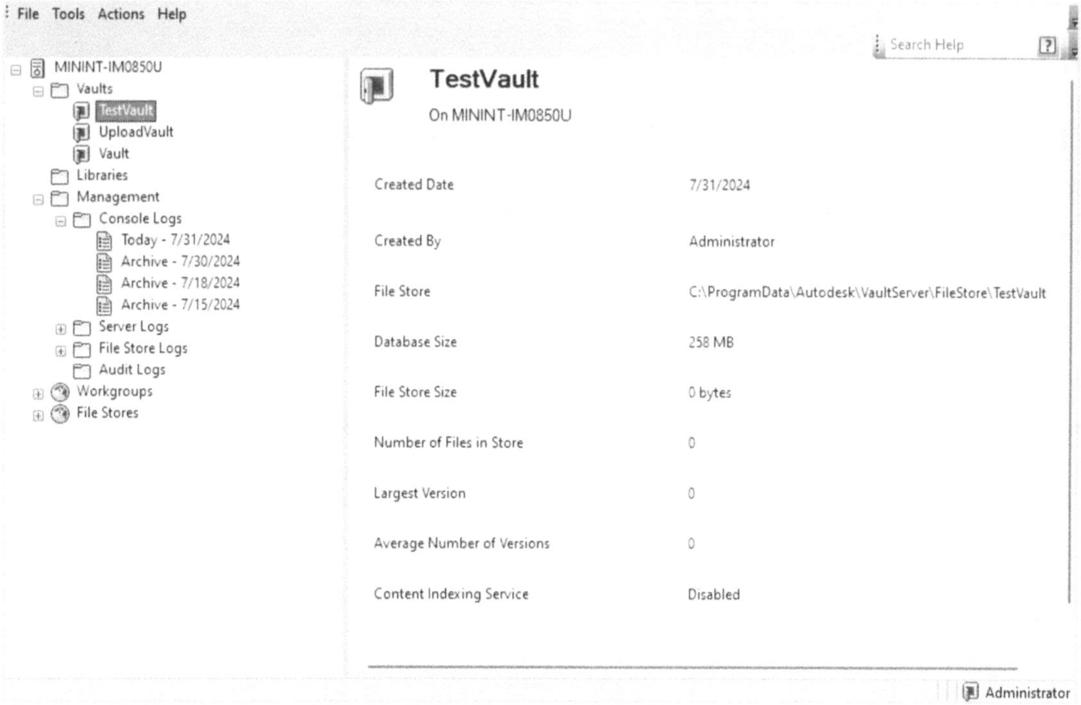

Figure 5–91

Viewing Vault Statistics

The status of vault databases and the size of the databases and file stores must be monitored to determine whether the vault is performing optimally and if maintenance is required.

The statistics for an individual vault are shown in Figure 5–92.

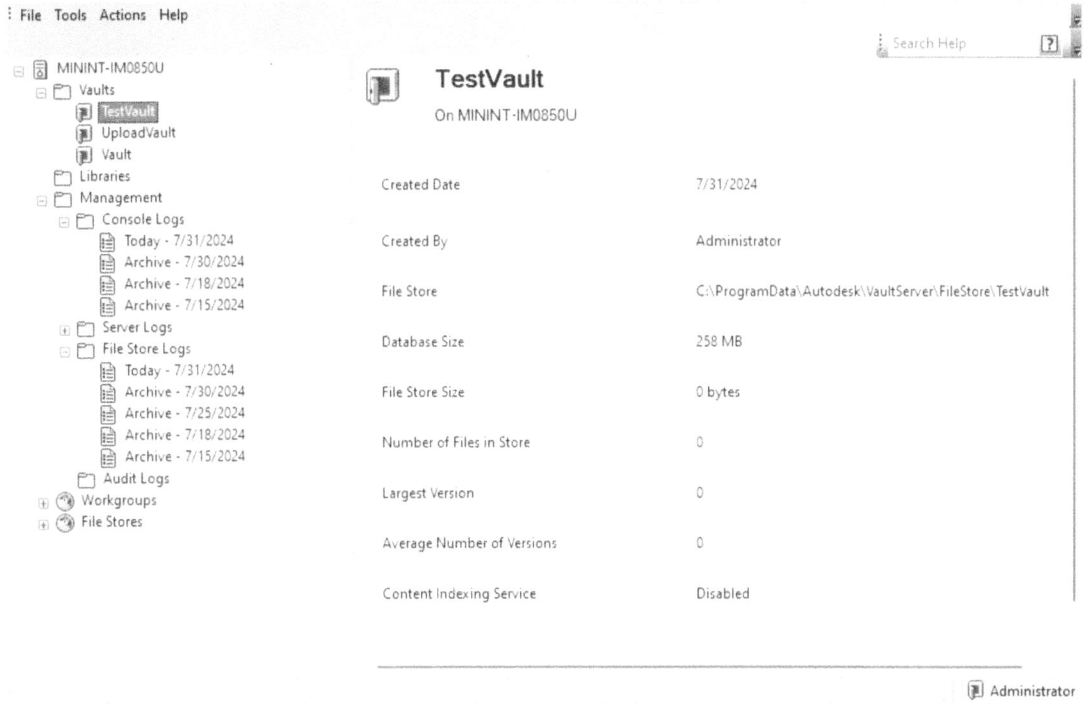

Figure 5–92

Vault Properties

The properties that are displayed for all vaults and libraries are shown in Figure 5–93.

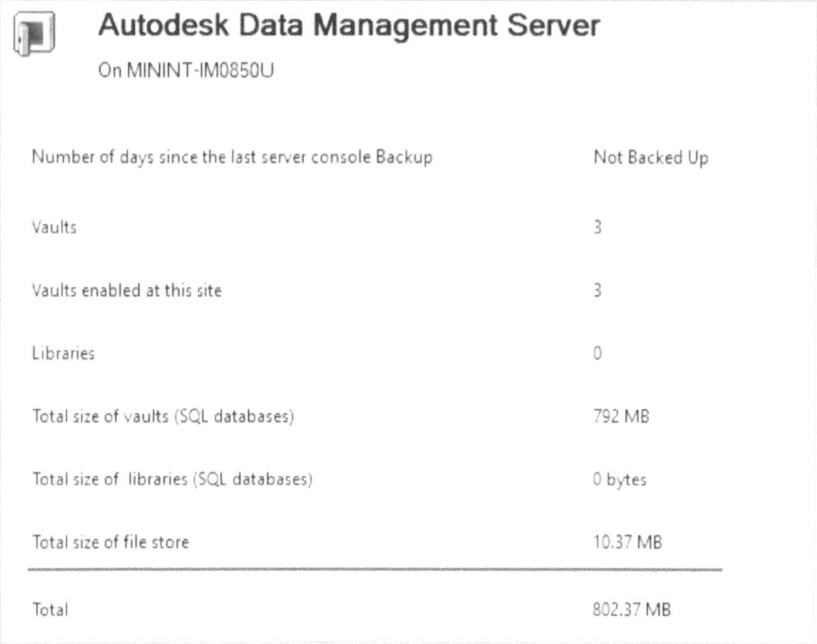

Figure 5–93

- **Number of days since the last backup:** Helps you to determine whether the vaults should be backed up.
- **Number of vaults and libraries:** Indicates the total number of vaults and libraries.
- **Total size of vaults:** Displays the total size of the vault databases. Use the total vault size to determine whether the total size for all databases is approaching the limit for your database server. Note that this is only true in a one Vault site. The database limit relates to individual vault sizes not to the total vault size, which could be more than one vault. If the size approaches the limit, you can reduce the size of the vault databases by removing unused properties and purging unnecessary versions.
- **Total size of libraries:** Displays the size of the libraries that are managed by the server.
- **Total size of file store:** Displays the total size on disk for all files in all file stores. You can use this to determine whether you should move the file stores to another partition, drive, or computer, or if you should purge files to reduce the number of files in the file stores.

The properties that are displayed for an individual vault are shown in Figure 5–94.

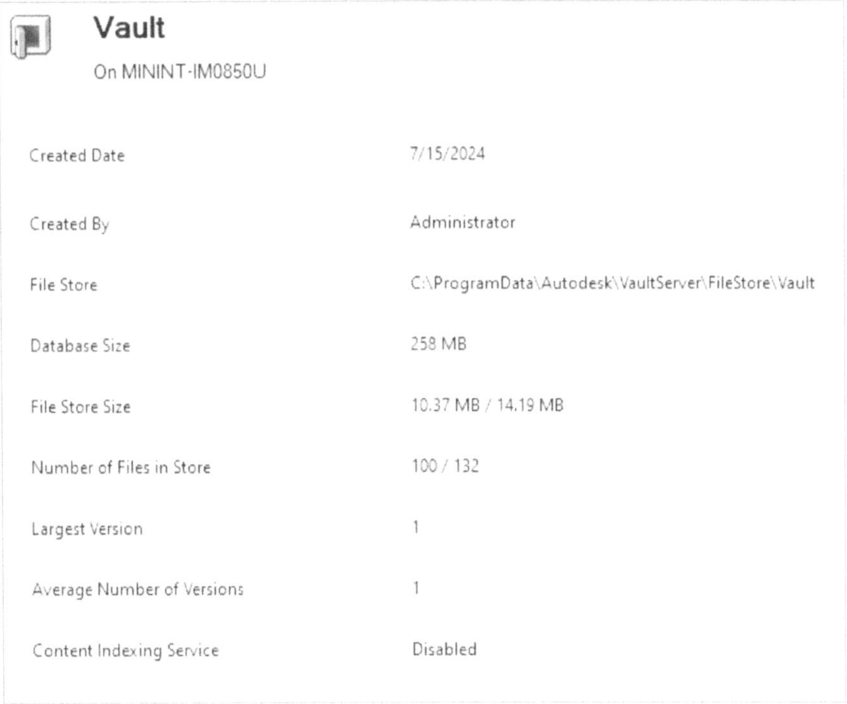

Figure 5–94

- **File Store:** The location of the file store. Helps you to locate the file store and confirm its location.
- **Database Size:** The total size of the MDF and LDF file for the selected vault. Use this information to help you determine whether you should reduce the database size or update the SQL server.
- **File Store Size:** The total size on disk for all files in the file store. You can use this to determine whether you should move the file store to another partition, drive, or computer, or if you should purge files to reduce the number of files in the file store.
- **Number of Files in Store:** The total number of files in the file store including all versions.
- **Largest Version** and **Average Number of Versions:** The largest and average version number of the files in the vault.
- **Content Indexing Service:** The search capability. When you enable the content indexing service, users can search for text in files when they use the **Advanced Find** command in Autodesk Vault.
- **Database Fragmentation:** The databases can become fragmented as files and properties are deleted, resulting in reduced performance. If defragmentation is recommended, run the **Defragment** tool.

How To: View Vault Statistics

The following steps describe how to view information for all vaults and for specific vaults.

1. Log in to the ADMS Console as an administrator.
2. Click the top-level folder to view information about all of the vaults and libraries, as shown in Figure 5–95.

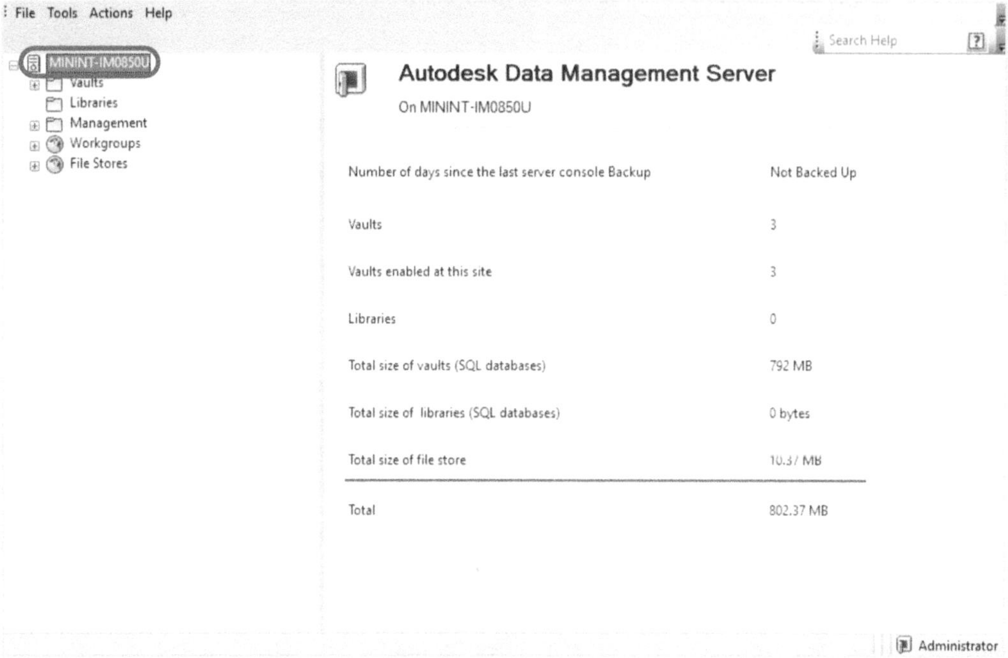

Figure 5–95

3. Select an individual vault to view information about it, as shown in Figure 5–96.

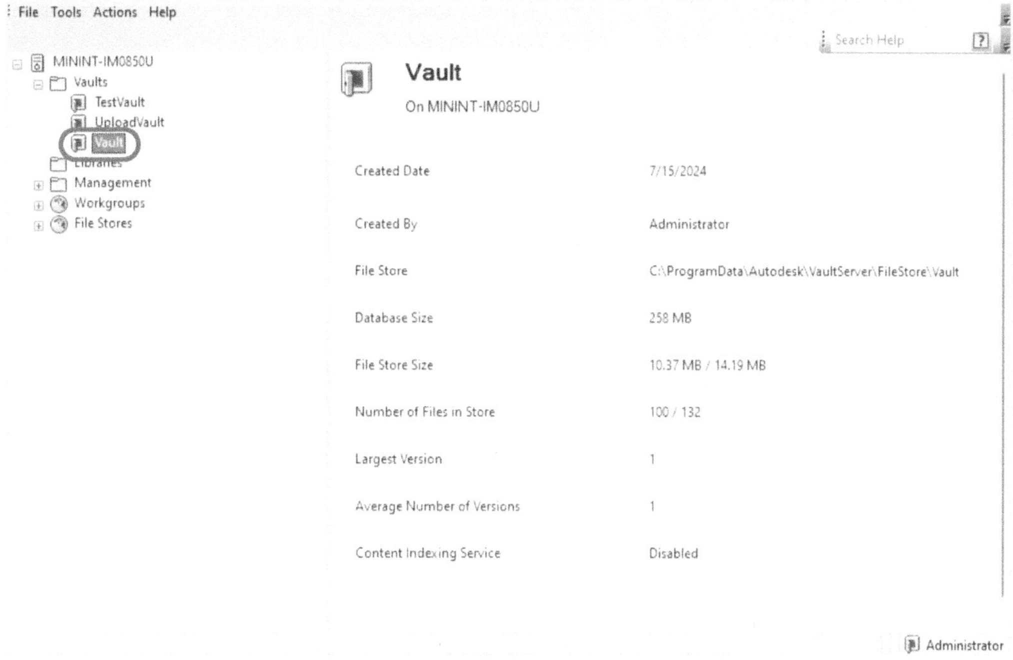

Figure 5–96

Purging Versions

Each version of a file takes up disk space in the file store and databases. You can remove versions periodically from the vault to reduce disk space and increase performance.

When you purge files, the files are removed from the file store and their properties are removed from the vault database, thereby reducing the size of both the file store and database. Files are purged based on the criteria you specify.

Accessing the Purge Command

You can purge files both from the ADMS Console and from Autodesk Vault. In the ADMS Console, the **Purge** command operates on all files in the selected vault. When you run the **Purge** command from Autodesk Vault, you can specify which files to purge.

Purge Criteria

The purge criteria are shown in Figure 5–97. The criteria are the same whether you run the **Purge** tool from the ADMS Console or from Autodesk Vault.

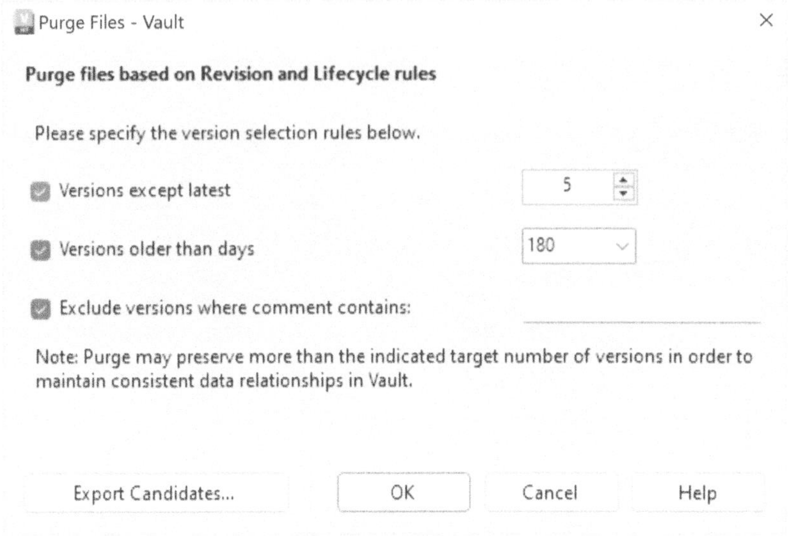

Figure 5–97

The following are the purge criteria:

- **Versions except latest:** Specify how many file versions to leave in the vault.
- **Versions older than days:** Specify how old the files to purge should be.
- **Exclude versions where comment contains:** Any files with comments that contain this string are excluded from the purge process.

Purge Rules (Including Vault Workgroup and Vault Professional)

In addition to the version selection criteria that you specify, the following rules also apply:

- The latest version in a revision cannot be purged (the revision is never removed). To remove a file and all of its versions from a vault, use **Delete**.
- The leading version of a revision cannot be purged.
- File versions linked to items in Vault Professional cannot be purged. To remove a version linked to an item, the item must first be deleted from the item master.
- File versions that are labeled cannot be purged.
- File versions marked as Controlled by the life cycle definition cannot be purged.
- Only the first, last, or first and last versions in a released state can be purged.

- Older versions of files that are currently checked out can be purged.
- Children with a dependent parent version cannot be purged until the parent version has been purged.
- The Administrator role can override purge restrictions and force the removal of versions, except for versions that are linked to items.
- For Autodesk Vault Professional, files are purged based on revision and lifecycle rules unless version selection rules are defined during purge setup.

How To: Purge Files

The following steps describe how to purge files from a vault.

1. Log in to the ADMS Console as an administrator.

   Note: *The Purge command can also be accessed from Autodesk Vault. The command is similar except that in Autodesk Vault, you can select individual files to purge.*

2. Back up the vault. If you accidentally purge required files, you can restore the vault to recover the files.
3. In the list of vaults, select a vault. Select **Actions>Purge Files**.
4. In the *Vault Version Purge* dialog box, specify the criteria for purging. The vault must be locked so that users cannot access it during the purge operation. Before the Purge tool runs, you are prompted to lock the vault.
5. To review the results, select **Tools>View Server Tasks**. In the *Server Tasks* dialog box, from the *Server Task* list, select **File Purge** and click **Details**, as shown in Figure 5–98.

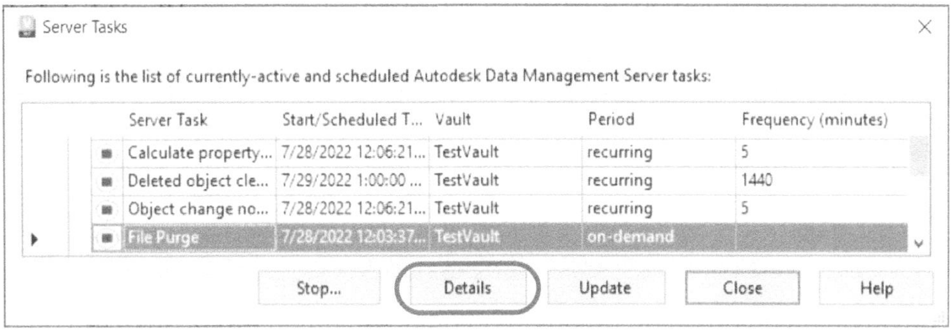

Figure 5–98

Note: *If using Vault Professional, you can also purge items from the ADMS Console or Autodesk Vault client using Actions>Purge Items. Item versions are purged based on their lifecycle control settings. When a lifecycle state is created, the administrator must identify which item and file versions in that state are retained during a purge. For example, a lifecycle state can be defined so that all items in the Review State are purged except for the latest version when the Purge command is invoked.*

Tracking File Status

A parent file in a model might not always reference the latest versions of its children. For example, several users might work on parts or subassemblies of a larger assembly. If the main assembly or drawings are never checked out and updated, they will reference previous versions of their children. In Vault, you can track file status to quickly identify parent files that do not reference the latest children.

The *Status* property indicates if a parent file in the vault references the latest versions of its children. You can display the *Status* property in Vault, as shown in Figure 5–99.

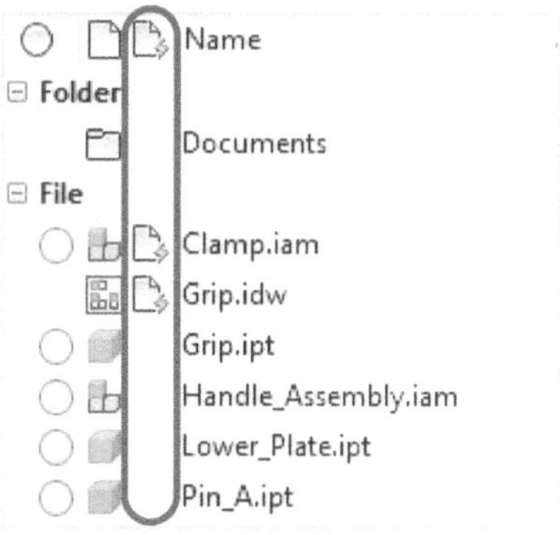

Figure 5–99

About File Status

You can customize the view in Autodesk Vault to display the *Status* property. The following table describes the three file statuses.

Icon	Status	Description
	**Unknown**	The file status needs to be updated. Run the **Update File Status** command from the ADMS Console.
	**Needs Updating**	The file uses a version of a child that is older than the latest version.
	Up to Date	When no icon is displayed, the file is up to date because it references the latest versions of all children.

How To: Track File Status

The following steps describe how to track the status of files in the vault.

1. In Autodesk Vault, select **Tools>Administration>Vault Settings**. In the *Vault Settings* dialog box, select the *Files* tab. Select **Track File Status**, as shown in Figure 5–100. Click **Close**.

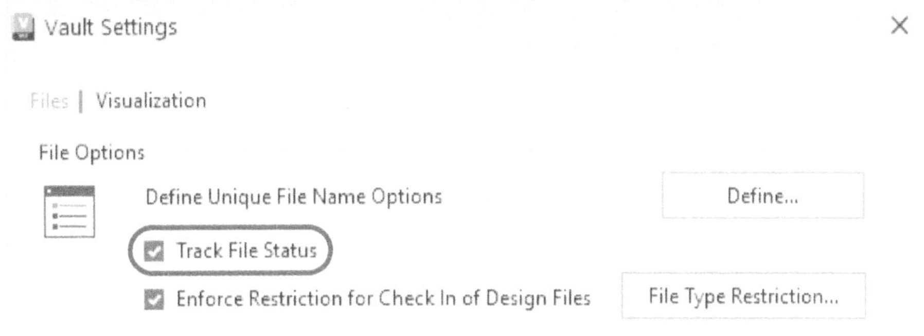

Figure 5–100

Note: *If you do not toggle on Track File Status from Autodesk Vault, you can toggle it on from the ADMS Console when you run the Update File Status command.*

2. In the ADMS Console, select the vault that you want to check. Select **Actions>Update File Status** or right-click on a vault and select **Update File Status...**, as shown in Figure 5–101.

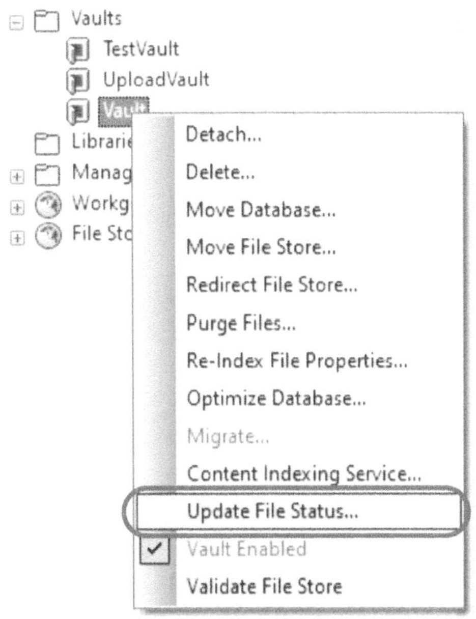

Figure 5–101

3. In Autodesk Vault, customize the view to display the *Status* property.
4. Browse the folders of your designs and view the status. Find the **Needs Updating** icon, as shown in Figure 5–102. To find all files in the vault that need updating, use an Advanced Find with *Status is Needs Updating* as the search criterion.

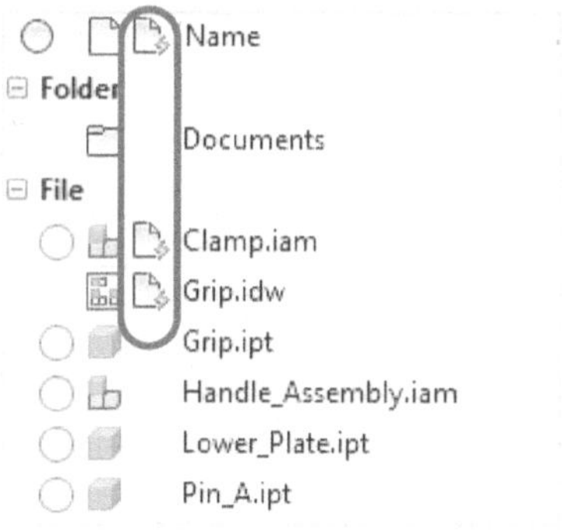

Figure 5–102

Note: *A user with Document Editor (Level 1) or greater permissions can manually override the status property, changing the status to either Needs Updating or Up to Date. When the Update File Status command is run from the ADMS Console, user overrides are removed and the true file status is displayed.*

5. If a file needs updating, press <Ctrl> and click the icon in the *File Status* column. The reason for an update is displayed, as shown in Figure 5–103. The child file(s) that are newer than the files referenced are listed.

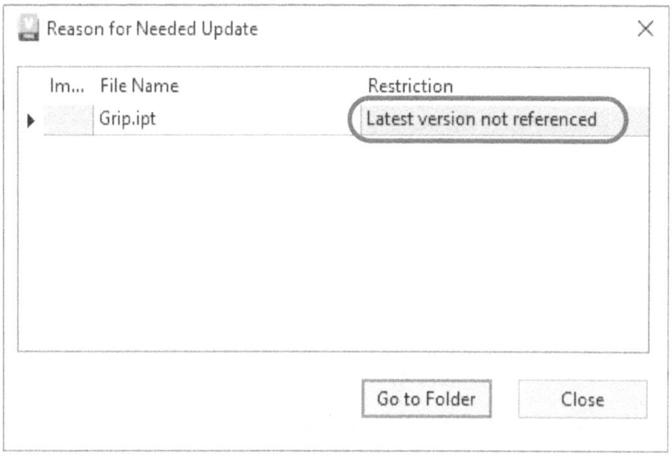

Figure 5–103

6. Click **Go to Folder** to open the folder that contains the child file. Use the *Where Used* tab to determine which versions are referenced.

7. To update the parent file:
   - Get the latest versions of the parent and children.
   - Check out the parent file.
   - Edit the parent file and save it.
   - Check the parent file back in to the vault.

Indexing File Contents

By default, you can search for files in the vault based on file properties. To search for files based on the content of text in files, you must enable content indexing.

When you add a file to the vault, the properties of the file are extracted and added to the vault database. To locate a file in the vault, a user can search for property values. However, important information is often in the contents of documents. If you enable content indexing, users can search for files based on both properties and the contents of files.

The content indexing service requires the appropriate indexing filter (iFilter) to access the properties and contents of a file. By default, iFilters are installed for files whose application has a Vault add-in client. To enable full content searching of other file formats, install additional iFilters on the Vault server. When the indexing service indexes the files, the properties and contents of files supported by the iFilter are added to the index.

How To: Index File Contents

The following steps describe how to toggle the file content indexing on or off.

1. Log in to the ADMS Console as an administrator.
2. Expand the list of vaults. Click a vault and select **Actions>Content Indexing Service**, as shown in Figure 5–104.

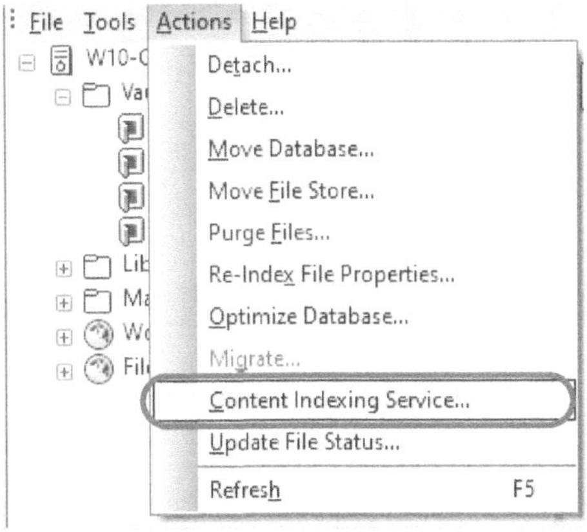

Figure 5–104

3. In the *Content Indexing Service* dialog box, toggle the service on or off as required, as shown in Figure 5–105, and click **OK**.

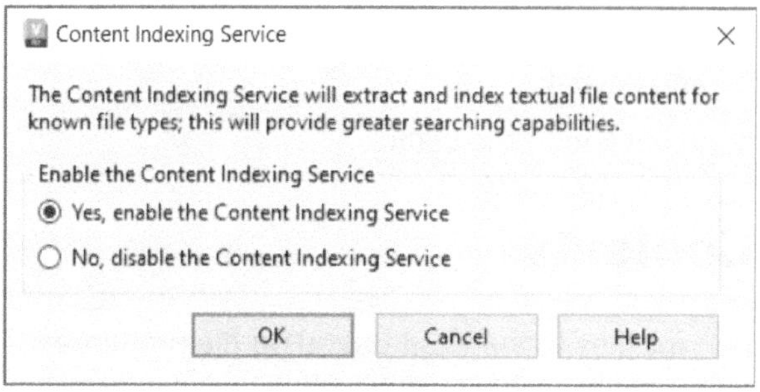

Figure 5–105

4. Confirm that the content indexing service is enabled, as shown in Figure 5–106.

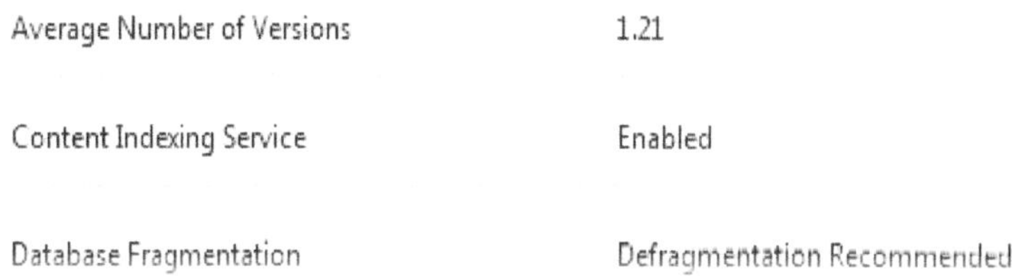

Figure 5–106

5. When you perform a basic search, toggle on **Search File Content** to search for content in files, as shown in Figure 5–107.

Note: *If searching file content is enabled, it will remain so until the user disables it. Searching file content can cause searches to take slightly longer than usual, as it is searching an additional database of information.*

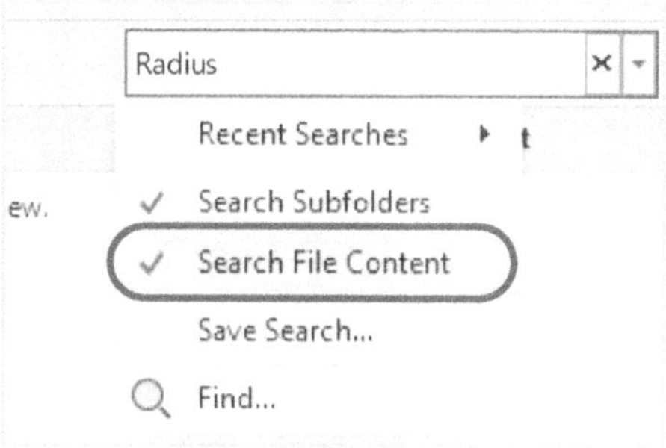

Figure 5–107

Practice 5e
Perform Vault Maintenance

Practice Objectives

- Determine the status of vaults and update file status.
- Index file contents.

In this practice, you will determine the status of vaults, update file status, and index file contents.

Task 1: Enable content indexing.

1. Log in to ADMS. Expand the *Vaults* folder. Click each vault and review its statistics.
2. Select **TestVault**.
3. Select **Actions>Content Indexing Service**. In the *Content Indexing Service* dialog box, select **Yes, Enable Content Indexing Service**. Click **OK**.
4. Click **OK** in the message box that is displayed. On the statistics page for TestVault, confirm that *Content Indexing Service* is **Enabled**, as shown in Figure 5–108.

Figure 5–108

5. Start Autodesk Vault. Log in to TestVault as an administrator. In the search box, type **Radius** and select the drop-down list to enable **Search File Content**. Click the search button.
6. The Word document **Document.doc** that you added in the previous practice should be shown. Open the file and note the word **Radius**, as shown in Figure 5–109.

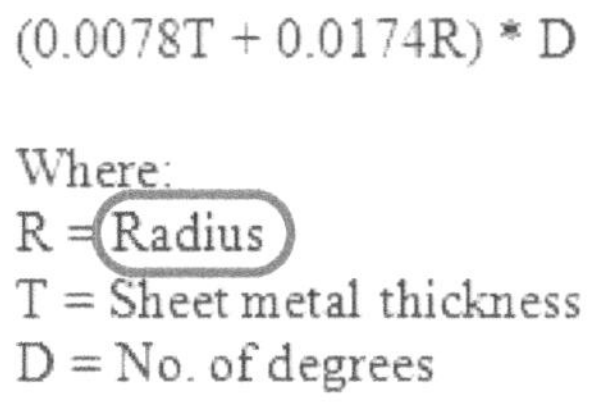

Figure 5–109

Task 2: Track file status.

In this task, you will upload an Autodesk Inventor model to the TestVault vault, enable file status tracking, make a change to a part in Autodesk Inventor, and then review the results.

1. Start Autodesk Vault. Log in to TestVault as an administrator.
2. Select **Tools>Administration>Vault Settings**. In the *Vault Settings* dialog box, click **Define** and clear the **Enforce unique file name** checkbox. Click **OK**. Close the *Vault Settings* dialog box.

   ***Note:** You use Autoloader to load a model into the vault. You cannot use Autoloader if unique file names are enforced.*

3. Start Autodesk Autoloader. Select **Next**.
4. In the *Select Data Source* window, select the folder *C:\Vault Basic Admin Training\Chapter3\Designs\ICU Valve*. The *Select Project* dialog box is displayed.
5. Browse for the project file *C:\Vault Basic Admin Training**ManageVault.ipj***. Click **OK** to dismiss the *Select Project* dialog box.
6. Click **Next**.
7. Scan the files. When the scan is complete, click **OK**. Click **Next**.
8. Log in to TestVault as an administrator.
9. Map the *ICU Valve* folder to the *Designs* folder in the vault. Ensure that the **Direct Mapping** box is checked.
10. Click **Next**.
11. When the Copy and Redirection is complete, click **Next**.
12. Click **Upload**. When the upload is complete, click **Done**.
13. Return to Autodesk Vault.
14. In Vault:
    - Refresh the display.
    - Display the contents of the *Designs* folder.
    - Select **ICULBUTN.ipt**.
    - Click the *Where Used* tab.
    - Note all of the files where ICULBUTN.ipt is used.

15. Select **Tools>Administration>Vault Settings**. In the *Vault Settings* dialog box, on the *Files* tab, select the **Track File Status** checkbox, as shown in Figure 5–110, to toggle on file status tracking. Click **Yes** in the *Warning* dialog box. Click **Close**.

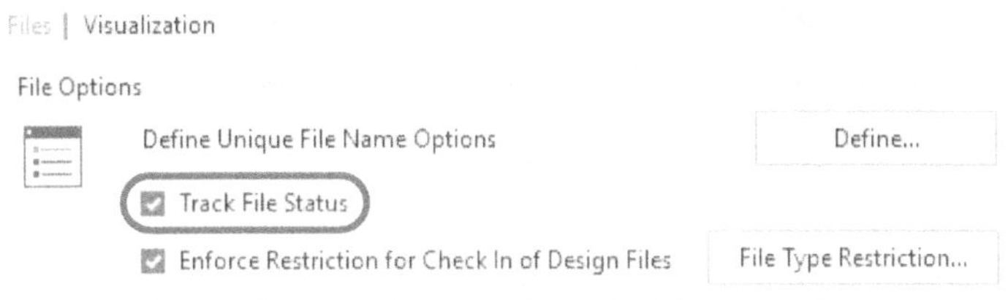

Figure 5–110

16. Right-click on a column header in the main pane and select **Customize View**. Select **Fields** to display the *Customize Fields* dialog box. Select **Any** from the *Select available fields from* drop-down list. Select **Status** from the *Available fields* list and **Add ->** to add it to the *Show these fields in this order* list. Use **Move Up** to move it so it is before **Entity Icon**, as shown in Figure 5–111. Click **OK** to dismiss the *Customize Fields* dialog box and click **Close** to dismiss the *Customize View* dialog box.

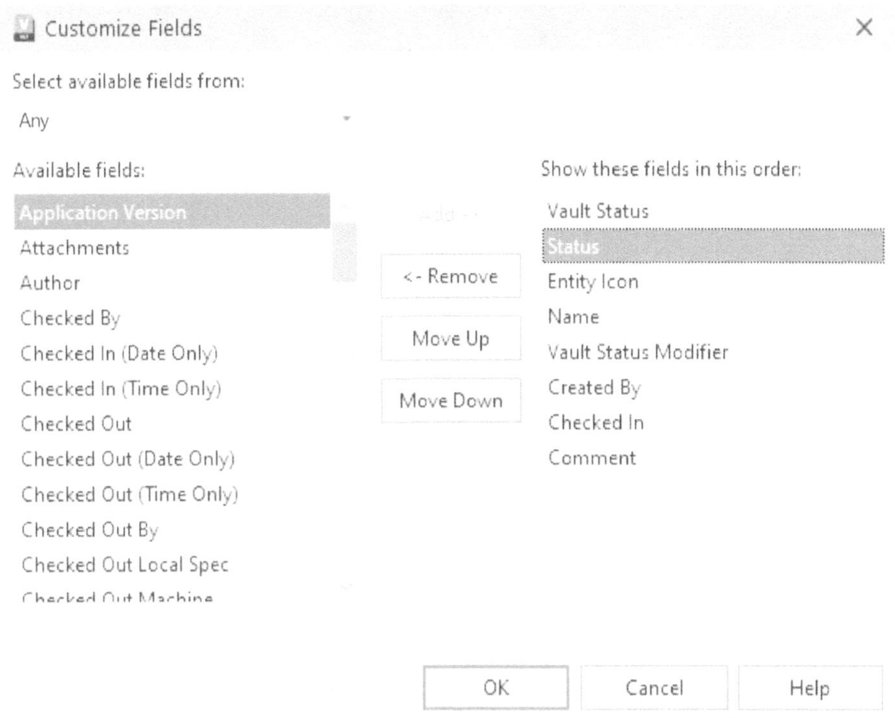

Figure 5–111

17. Hover the cursor over an icon in the *File Status* column to display the tooltip. The status is unknown because it has not been updated from the ADMS Console.

18. Switch to the ADMS Console. Select **TestVault**.
19. Select **Actions>Update File Status**.
20. Click **Yes** to lock the vault. Click **Yes** to confirm that you will lose file status overrides. When the status update is complete, click **OK**.
21. Switch back to Autodesk Vault. Refresh the view. All files are up to date.
22. Select **ICULBUTN.ipt**.
23. Click **Edit>Edit Properties**.
24. In the *Property Edit* dialog box, select **Select Properties** and do the following:
    - In the *Select available fields from* drop-down list, select **All fields**.
    - Find **Title** from the *Available fields* list and use **Add ->** to add it to the *Show these fields in this order* list. Remove any other fields except for **Entity Icon** and **Name**.
    - Click **OK** to dismiss the *Customize Fields* dialog box.
25. In the *Property Edit* dialog box, enter the title **ICU Valve Left Button**, as shown in Figure 5–112.

Figure 5–112

26. Click **OK**.
27. View the results of the Property Edit and then close the *Property Edit Results* dialog box.
28. Refresh the Vault. Note that the version of ICULBUTN.ipt has incremented because you modified the file.
29. Review the icons in the *File Status* column, as shown in Figure 5–113.

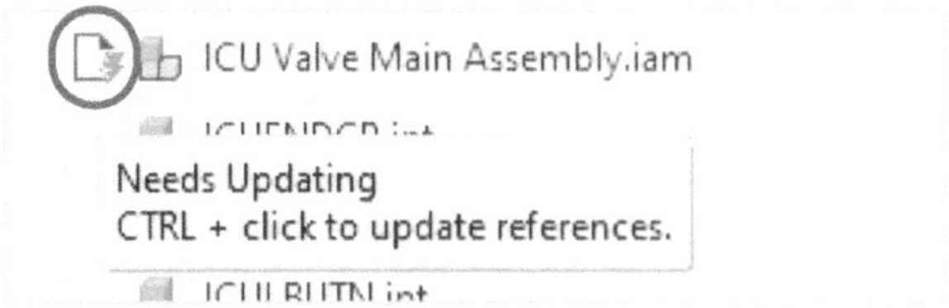

Figure 5–113

30. Press <Ctrl> and click one of the icons in the *File Status* column. Review the reason that the file needs to be updated, as shown in Figure 5–114.

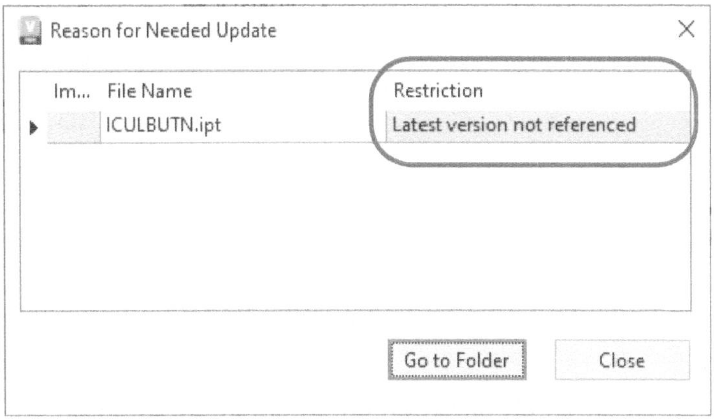

Figure 5–114

- You do not update the parent files in this practice. To update the parent files, get the latest versions of all files, open each parent file in Autodesk Inventor, check it out, save it, and then check it back in to the vault.

31. Close Autodesk Vault and the ADMS Console.

End of practice

Made in United States
Cleveland, OH
04 November 2026

47642858R00101